THE PRACTICAL GUIDE TO STRUCTURED SYSTEMS DESIGN

MEILIR PAGE-JONES

Yourdon Press
1133 Avenue of the Americas
New York, New York 10036

Printed in the United States of America

Library of Congress Catalog Number 79-67259

ISBN: 0-917072-17-0

This book was set in Times Roman by YOURDON Press, 1133 Avenue of the Americas, New York, N.Y., using a PDP-11/45 running under the UNIX† operating system.

---

†UNIX is a registered trademark of Bell Laboratories.

To my father and mother

Acknowledgments

This book would not have been possible without the inspiration, ideas, reviews, and suggestions for improvements of

Bob Asbury	Steve Mellor
Gary Austin*	Ira Morrow*
Michael Bell	John Palmer*
Larry Constantine	Bill Plauger
Tom DeMarco	Roland Racko
Brian Dickinson	Tom Roberts
Sid Dijkstra	Lois Rose*
Pat Duran	David Till
Matt Flavin	Jerry Walker*
Dorothy Kushner	Victor Weinberg
Tim Lister*	Steve Weiss
Steve McMenamin*	Ed Yourdon*
Don McNeil	Carroll Zahn

together with the thousands of analysts and programmers who kept me honest during my Structured Design seminars. Members of my chief technical review team are indicated by an asterisk. Thanks gang!

Special thanks to Suzanne Page-Jones (who also conceived of the cover and put up with many acre-months of paper on our living-room floor) and to Robert Berger of Electronic Precepts, Inc., who allowed me to analyze his order-processing system. (The case study of Appendix E, however, in no way resembles his operation.)

I'd also like to thank Ed and Toni Nash Yourdon for having created a working environment in which I was able to trade "structured" ideas and experiences with so many talented people.

But most importantly I would like to thank the staff of YOURDON Press for their sterling efforts in transforming my fractured, unreadable English into good, legible Americanese. Especially worthy of mention in dispatches is Lorie Mayorga, who, after her experience in deciphering my strange hieroglyphics, has now decided to take up the career of Egyptologist.

Contents

Author's Preface

As you pick up this book, I imagine that you have several questions in your mind. Let me try to anticipate some of them.

The Practical Guide to Structured . . . *what?*

This book is about design: the design of computer programs and computer systems. Although it's directed particularly at the design of systems for commercial and scientific applications, most of the ideas it sets forth apply to the design of any computer system (for example, compilers, operating systems, or process-control systems). Some of the ideas apply even to the design of non-computer systems.

Is this book for me?

It is, so long as you're not a complete novice to data processing. To get the most out of this book, you should be a programmer with at least a year's experience under your belt. (Alternatively, you should be a second- or third-year computer-science student.) You should also be yearning for something bigger and better than mere programming: a view of the structure of systems from well above the statement-level of code.

But isn't this structured stuff only for academics?

Structured Programming, it's true, owes its existence to the farsightedness of several people working in the academic environment. However, Structured Analysis and Structured Design were developed almost exclusively in the real world of commercial and scientific shops. These two techniques have been tried and tested in large systems since the late 1960s by DP professionals for whom deadlines, careers, and finicky users were far more real than any academic considerations.

Why should I be interested in the high-level structure of systems and programs?

The reason is that at this level are the clues to producing maintainable, reliable, and adaptable systems, and, ultimately, to reducing the lifetime costs of systems. Throughout the 1970s, data-processing software costs grew malignantly until users began balking at the high price tags on their systems. Or, as one colleague put it: "Pervasive cynicism about software is the justifiable consequence of the many situations where poor results follow long delays."*

---

*D.H. McNeil, "Adopting a System-Release Discipline," *Datamation,* Vol. 25, No. 1 (January 1979), p. 110.

Our industry has spent the last ten years crawling out on a long limb of expense and poor quality. If, within the next ten years, we don't crawl back again, someone will saw off that limb.

Why shouldn't I read some other book on design?

You should! But there are very few around. A classic in the field is *Structured Design,* written by Ed Yourdon and Larry Constantine.* This is a brilliant — but often difficult and theoretical — work covering almost every conceivable aspect of the structure of a system. Glen Myers has written two excellent books on what he calls Composite Design (*Reliable Software Through Composite Design* and *Composite/Structured Design*).† Both are very readable and informative. Michael Jackson has written *Principles of Program Design,*‡ which, although concentrating on smaller problem sets, adds a splendidly innovative contribution to the area of data structures.

However, all of these books were written before the coming of age of Structured Analysis. A modern book on Structured Design can not ignore this latest and very welcome addition to the "structured family." *Practical Guide to Structured Systems Design* gives a brief outline of the tools of Structured Analysis and shows how these tools are a boon not only to the analyst, but also to the *designer* of a computer system.§

Will this book teach me a language?

No, I assume that you're already familiar with at least one of the following languages: COBOL, FORTRAN, PL/I, Assembler, APL, C, or Pascal.

Will this book teach me better programming techniques?

No, I assume you're already a reasonably competent programmer.

Won't it even teach me about Structured Programming?

No, not even Structured Programming.

Well, what *will* it teach me?

By the time you reach the end of this book, you should know about the fundamental ideas behind Structured Design; how to use the tools of Structured Design; how to interact with a structured analyst and how to read, understand, and use a structured specification; objective criteria for evaluating and improving design quality; strategies for creating a good, maintainable design in a systematic way; the modifications that you must make to a design before you can program from it; the impact of Structured Design on management; and when to use each Structured Design tool in a typical systems development project.

---

*E. Yourdon and L. Constantine, *Structured Design: Fundamentals of a Discipline of Computer Program and Systems Design* (New York: YOURDON Press, 1978).
†G. Myers, *Reliable Software Through Composite Design* (New York: Petrocelli/Charter, 1975), and *Composite/Structured Design* (New York: Van Nostrand Reinhold, 1978).
‡M. Jackson, *Principles of Program Design* (New York: Academic Press, 1975).
§For a detailed study of Structured Analysis, see Tom DeMarco's *Structured Analysis and System Specification* (New York: YOURDON Press, 1978).

Foreword

The field of Structured Design has come a long way since my colleague Larry Constantine initially developed some of the basic concepts ten years ago. The world first began to learn about his ideas in the ground-breaking paper "Structured Design," which appeared in the May 1974 issue of the *IBM Systems Journal*. Then came the books: Glenford Myers, who had been a student of Constantine's at the IBM Systems Research Institute in New York, published *Reliable Software Through Composite Design* in the summer of 1975, and Constantine and I contributed our first edition of *Structured Design* later that fall. Meanwhile, Michael Jackson published his *Principles of Program Design* that same year in England, although it was some time before his work was widely distributed in the United States.

But all of that was five years ago. What has happened since? Well, the most obvious advance is the *refinement* of Structured Design concepts that sounded nice in theory, but needed to be adapted to the real world. That refinement has been taking place on a continual basis here at YOURDON inc., for the simple reason that our technical staff has had the challenging job of presenting lectures and seminars on the subject to some 50,000 EDP professionals around the world. And those 50,000 professionals — together with their colleagues — have been busily adapting the concepts of Structured Design to specific applications, specific operating systems, and specific programming languages. Part of that refinement has already surfaced in Glenford Myers' more recent book *Composite/Structured Design*.

The other major development that has taken place since 1975 is that of *Structured Analysis* — something that the original books by Myers, Jackson, Constantine, and me never mentioned at all. Structured *Design* was concerned with the selection and organization of modules and module interfaces that would provide a "best" solution to a *well-stated problem*. But where did the well-stated problem come from? How could we be sure that the user's requirements had been properly specified? And how should those specifications be documented so as to provide useful input to the designer?

Unfortunately, the last of these questions was somewhat ignored in the first spate of books that appeared on Structured Analysis — notably Tom DeMarco's *Structured Analysis and System Specification,* Chris Gane and Trish Sarson's *Structured Systems Analysis,* and Victor Weinberg's *Structured Analysis.* Thus, the "bridge" between analysis and design has continued to be a source of confusion and trauma for many EDP professionals.

All of which brings us to *The Practical Guide to Structured Systems Design* by Meilir Page-Jones. Meilir's book, in my opinion, represents the best of the Structured Design developments of the past five years: It provides refinement and clarification of some of the original concepts of Structured Design, and it eloquently describes the transition from Structured Analysis into Structured Design.

Meilir's book is the result of nearly three years of teaching and consulting experiences while at YOURDON inc.; the interactions with his students and with the rest of his technical colleagues in the company have contributed, I'm sure, to the clear, easy-going style of writing. And that, by the way, is one of the major advantages of Meilir's book over, say, the *Structured Design* book that we wrote: It's easy to read. Part of that is due to Meilir's command of the English language; an important part is also due to the superb editing skills of Wendy Eakin and Janice Wormington of YOURDON Press; and part of it, I'm convinced, is due to Meilir's unique Welsh sense of humor.

I could go on, but I don't think it's necessary. You'll see for yourself when you read the book that it represents a significant step forward in the field of Structured Design. And if by some chance you've spent the last twenty years maintaining RPG programs on an IBM 1401 and you've never heard of Structured Design or Structured Analysis, my advice is simple: *First* read Meilir's book. *Then* read the other "classics" like DeMarco, Myers, Jackson, Constantine and (blush!) Yourdon.

May 1980   Edward Yourdon
                                                                                                  New York City

SECTION I
INTRODUCTION

The fundamental concepts of Structured Design are drawn from many diverse sources, including engineering, hierarchy theory, Structured Programming, and even human psychology.

Chapter 1, entitled The Ideas Behind Structured Design, introduces the founding theories of Structured Design and explains their evolution into a disciplined design method.

Chapter 2, called The Basics of Design, contrasts the aims of Structured Design with the deficiencies of traditional design techniques. (It was the consistent failure of ad hoc design methods that provided the motivation for the development of Structured Design.) This chapter also defines exactly what the activity of design is by showing how this phase fits into the context of a typical project life cycle.

1

The Ideas Behind
Structured Design

Since the term "design" is usually tossed around with more abandon than precision, I think it's important to define what *I* mean by design before I describe what *Structured* Design is. The *Random House College Dictionary* defines it as

design *n.a.* 9. an outline, sketch, or plan of the form or structure of a work.*

If we apply this definition to the design of a computer system, we have

computer system design *n.* the activity of transforming a statement of *what* is required to be accomplished into a *plan* for implementing that requirement on an electronic automaton.

Notice what the second definition implies: The analysis of the user's requirements must precede design. The definition also indicates that at the end of design we have a *means* of implementing what the user needs, but we haven't yet actually implemented a solution to his problem. Therefore, coding and testing must follow design, for design is simply the bridge between the analysis of a problem and the implementation of the solution to that problem.

Structured Design is a disciplined approach to computer system design, an activity that in the past has been notoriously haphazard and fraught with problems.† Structured Design is a response to the failings

---

Random House College Dictionary (New York: Random House, 1972), p. 360.
†These problems are outlined in Chapter 2.

of the past. It has five aspects:

1. Structured Design allows the form of the problem to guide the form of the solution.

2. Structured Design seeks to conquer the complexity of large systems by means of partitioning the system into "black boxes," and by organizing the black boxes into hierarchies suitable for computer implementation.

3. Structured Design uses tools, especially graphic ones, to render systems readily understandable.

4. Structured Design offers a set of strategies for developing a design solution from a well-defined statement of a problem.

5. Structured Design offers a set of criteria for evaluating the quality of a given design solution with respect to the problem to be solved.

Structured Design produces systems that are easy to understand, reliable, flexible, long-lasting, smoothly developed, and efficient to operate — and that WORK. Structured Design produces, in two words, inexpensive systems! The ultimate objectives of Structured Design are to cure the ills, discussed in the next chapter, that have afflicted classical computer systems. To do that, Structured Design calls for more thought, more discipline, and a better use of tools in the development process than is traditional.

Let me expand each of the five aspects of Structured Design in the following sections.*

1.1 Shaping the solution to the problem

Structured Design is the development of a blueprint of a computer system solution to a problem, having the same components and interrelationships among the components as the original problem has.

What this mouthful is saying is simple: The solution should have the same shape as the problem. It's an old idea. Louis Sullivan, philosopher and architect, said as much in 1896 with the words, "Form ever

---

*In the following sections, I mention terms like "component," "interrelationships," and "shape of the problem" without defining them. But don't worry: Most of the book is devoted to giving meaning to these terms.

follows function," upon which concept the Bauhaus school of design was founded.*

The reason behind this philosophy is that, in computer system design, we have traditionally chosen a preconceived shape to the solution and tried to force the problem to fit that shape. For example, you might choose to use as a model of a computer system a modular technique whereby each subroutine calls exactly three other subroutines — one for input, one for processing, and one for output; or another modular technique whereby one subroutine calls every other subroutine in the system, and those are the only calls allowed. I've seen both these approaches used, with the system designers nobly fighting against reality, trying to pervert the problem to fit their preconceived solution.

Structured Design (and Structured Analysis, which I cover briefly in Chapter 4) resists making decisions on *how* the problem is to be solved until *what* the problem is has been determined. By postponing the how for as long as possible, Structured Design allows the designer to let the what guide his[†] choice of solution. Structured Design, I'll admit, does have *some* prejudices about how the solution should look, but it has had far more success than any previous technique in allowing "form to follow function."

1.2 Simplifying a system

Structured Design seeks to conquer the complexity of large systems in two ways: partitioning and hierarchical organization.

1.2.1 Partitioning the system into black boxes

I first learned of a black box while working in electronic engineering, where the term meant literally a box whose internal electronics were hidden. Therefore, although its actual operation was unknown to me, its function was known, typically because the black box had a label emblazoned on it in large letters. Examples were ANALOG-TO-DIGITAL CONVERTER, SINE-WAVE GENERATOR, PHASE-SHIFTER, and so on. The advantage in using a black box was that I didn't need to know how it worked, for that complexity had already been taken care of by the black box's manufacturer. The burden of having to know how to build a phase-shifter was on someone else's shoulders. So, I was free to shift

---

*L. Sullivan, "The Tall Office Building Artistically Considered," *Lippincott's Magazine,* March 1896.
[†]Throughout this book, "his" is equivalent to "his or her" and "he" is equivalent to "he or she."

all the phases I ever wanted to, blissfully ignorant of whether the phase-shifter contained vacuum tubes, the latest in integrated circuits, or a little demon that chased the waves down the wires.

The characteristics of a black box are

- you know the inputs it expects
- you know the outputs it should give back
- you know its function (what it does to its inputs to produce its outputs)
- you *don't* need to know how it carries out its function in order to use it

The world abounds with black boxes. A stereo system, for instance, contains several of them, and illustrates some advantages in using systems composed of well-defined and independent black boxes.

- *Black-box systems are easily constructed:* It's much easier to build a turntable if no one else cares exactly how you do it so long as it works well. (It also helps if you don't have to worry about making it fit inside the amplifier box.)

- *Such systems are easily tested:* If sound fails to emerge from the right channel of the stereo, you can switch the speakers. If the fault moves with the speaker, then the speaker is kaput; if not, then the problem is in the amplifier, turntable, or the leads connecting them.

- *They are easily corrected:* If the speaker *is* faulty, then it can be sent to the speaker hospital while you continue to listen to your records in glorious, living mono.

- *They can be easily understood:* You can become a turntable expert without knowing anything about loudspeakers.

- *And, they can easily be modified:* If you move to a larger house or apartment, you may want higher quality speakers and a more powerful amplifier to drive them: It's unlikely that you would want a larger turntable.

The stereo example shows not only the characteristics of black boxes but also the advantages of partitioning a system into a number of black boxes. I could just as readily have described the stereo as a single black box, with all four components squeezed inside a compact unit:

Compact units are sold more cheaply in stores than are systems comprised of individual units, but how easily can they be constructed, tested, corrected, understood, and modified? A computer system is no different from a stereo system in that if it is partitioned into black boxes, each of which has a well-defined role, the system is easier to understand, program, test, debug, and modify than a monolithic system is. Chapters 6 through 8 will explain this point more fully.

Thus, the first step in controlling complexity is to partition a system into black boxes so that four goals are met. First, each black box should solve one well-defined piece of the problem. For example, if one requirement of a road freight system is to calculate the efficiency of gasoline usage, then one black box in the system should calculate that efficiency.

Second, the system should be partitioned so that the function of each black box is easy to understand. For example, in a weapons guidance system, there might be a black box to compute the point of impact of a missile. Although it may be a tough black box to implement, its *function* is very easy to understand, because it can be stated simply as "compute point of impact of missile."

Third, partitioning should be done so that any connection between black boxes is introduced only because of a connection between pieces of the problem. For example, in a payroll system there will be one black box to compute the gross pay of an employee and another to compute his net pay. There must be a connection between these black boxes, for gross pay is needed in order to compute net pay.

As the fourth goal, partitioning should assure that the connections between black boxes are made as simple as possible, so that the black boxes are as independent as possible. For example, a programmer writing a black box to compute net pay shouldn't have to find the absolute machine location in which the gross pay is stored. A much better and simpler way to communicate that information would be to pass the gross pay as a parameter to the black box that calculates the net pay.

Partitioning according to these four principles will ensure that problem-related black boxes will be kept together in the system while problem-unrelated black boxes will be kept apart.

1.2.2 Organizing the black boxes into hierarchies

The idea of partitioning an otherwise insoluble problem to achieve results goes back thousands of years. For example, Julius Caesar suspected that Rome was not strong enough to overrun Europe by the "up-lads-and-at-'em" approach later made popular by Ghengis Khan and DP managers. Instead, he exploited the fact that Europe was composed of a large number of squabbling, independent tribes. By treating each tribe as a black box and by cutting off its communications with other tribes, Caesar applied the divide-and-conquer strategy to become Master of Europe one bite at a time.

The idea of hierarchy is even older than the idea of partitioning: It's as old as Mother Nature herself. All of the complex systems in the universe are organized into hierarchies of stable units. Each stable unit is made up of a stable group of smaller stable units. For example, the hierarchy of matter ranges from super-galaxies through galaxies, stellar systems, planets, crystals, molecules, atoms, down to subatomic particles. We human beings have found that the only way to manage the large organizations that we have created is to mimic nature: Business corporations have presidents, vice-presidents, upper management, middle management, lower management, and, finally, peons.

Let's investigate one such corporation, called Meddle, Inc. Here is a part of its organizational chart:

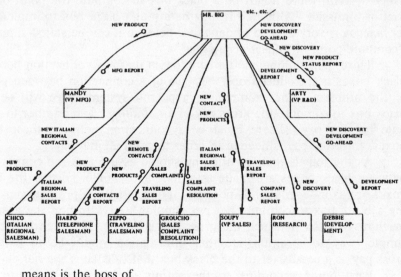

KEY

→   means is the boss of

o→   means a memo
(traveling in the direction
in which it points)

Figure 1.1

If you were called into Meddle, Inc., as a management consultant, I'm sure you'd have plenty of questions to ask about the way it's organized — for instance:

- Why is Mr. Big directly concerned in the day-to-day machinations of Groucho as he resolves sales complaints? Why does Mr. Big actually hand down the individual complaints to Groucho?

- If Arty is really the Vice-President of Research and Development, why does he have no apparent control over Ron in Research, and Debbie in Development? Why do all of Arty's communications with Ron and Debbie have to go via Mr. Big?

- Why is everyone in Meddle, Inc. — regardless of the importance of the job — directly subordinate to Mr. Big? Why is there no middle management?

If you were a medical consultant, you would probably say that Mr. Big is heading for a heart attack. He seems to be a neurotic kind of person who cannot bear to relinquish any authority or delegate any work. Mr. Big has to deal with too many memos, too many subordinates, and too many problems, and he has to make too many decisions for his own good. He's likely to be distracted into making ridiculous errors through sheer confusion.

Perhaps we should reorganize Meddle, Inc., like this:

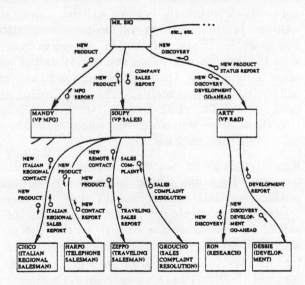

Figure 1.2

Now that Mr. Big has learned to delegate, many of the management difficulties of Meddle, Inc., have disappeared.

"People systems," like Meddle, Inc., give us several general guidelines that can be applied to the organization of computer systems.

- A manager shouldn't have more than about seven immediate subordinates reporting directly to him.*

- <u>Work and management should be separated: Work should be done by subordinates with no managerial duties, and managers should be restricted to coordinating the work of their subordinates.</u>

- Every department in a company should have a well-defined function. Most companies, however, do have a department called "General Services," which encompasses every miscellaneous job that won't fit into any other department. A General Services department is difficult to manage because each of its jobs creates its own special problems for the manager, who soon becomes a likely candidate for an ulcer.

- Every job should be allocated to the proper department. A large volume of memos and phone calls between departments causes chaos, and usually signifies faulty allocation of people to departments. For example, if you put half of the programmers on your project into one office and the other half into an office a mile away, then the chances are their phones will be continually ringing. Obviously, being on the same part of the same project, they'll have plenty to talk about, and, therefore, the whole team should be put together in the same area.

- Reports should be readable, meaningful, and clearly laid out. They don't have to be glossy, multicolored productions; but neither should they be someone's cigarette-pack scribblings. The information in them should be comprehensive enough so that the manager who receives them can make the necessary decisions for his level of the organization. However, the manager shouldn't have to wade through irrelevant details about every single action of each of his subordinates.

---

*See Chapter 8 for the derivation of this number.

- A manager should have a secretary who can type reports neatly, put them into envelopes, and mail them.

- A manager should give only as much information to a subordinate as that person needs in order to do his job. This is a contentious point, because an employee likes to be able to see a larger corporate view than is provided by the horizons of his own job. However, for security reasons, military organizations operate on this need-to-know basis; and even an ordinary manufacturing company would not pass down the minutes of every board meeting to its factory-floor workers.

Analogies are rarely completely precise and are sometimes downright misleading. However, as you read about hierarchies of computer system components throughout this book, you may find what I say about them to be clearer if you pretend that the systems I describe are being executed by people and not by computers.

1.3 Using graphic tools

Structured Design uses tools, especially graphic ones, to render systems more understandable.

If Structured Analysis precedes Structured Design, then the analyst will present the designer with a structured specification, which is the output from analysis and the input to design. It is expressed by means of the tools of Structured Analysis: data flow diagrams, data dictionary, structured English, decision trees, decision tables, and data access diagrams. (In Chapter 4, we look in detail at each of these tools.) Structured Design uses two additional tools: pseudocode and structure charts. I describe each below.

1.3.1 Pseudocode

Pseudocode is an informal and very flexible programming language that is not intended to be executed on a machine, but is used to organize a programmer's thoughts prior to coding. Although pseudocode is a tool of Structured Programming, it can also be used in Structured Design to clarify the detailed internal procedure of some of the black boxes on the structure chart. An example of pseudocode for PROD CUSTOMERS FOR UNPAID BILLS, one of the modules of the structure chart shown in Fig. 1.3, is as follows:

```
module prod customer for unpaid bills
        /* scans the unpaid bills file and issues notices to
           customers who are slow in forking out their payments */
        open unpaid bill file, customer details file
        get today's date
        repeat
            call get next unpaid bill
                    getting unpaid bill, end of unpaid bill file
        until end of unpaid bill file
            set days overdue to today's date − bill date
            if days overdue > 90
            then call generate legal threat using unpaid bill
            elseif days overdue > 60
            then call generate stern warning using unpaid bill
            elseif days overdue > 30
            then call generate gentle reminder using unpaid bill
            endif
        endrepeat
        close unpaid bill file, customer details file
endmodule
```

In Chapter 5, I cover other uses of pseudocode.

1.3.2 Structure chart

The structure chart illustrates the partitioning of a system into modules — its black boxes — showing their hierarchy, organization, and communication. Here's an example of a piece of a structure chart:

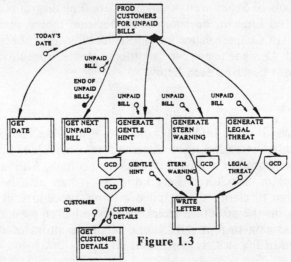

Figure 1.3

This structure chart depicts a small system intended to scan a file of un-paid bills and to generate letters to debtors. Three kinds of letters are generated, depending on how overdue the payment for a bill is: a gen-tle reminder, a stern warning, and a legal threat. Each box on the structure chart represents a module (for example, a PARAGRAPH or a PROCEDURE), each large arrow represents an invocation (for example, a PERFORM or a CALL), and each small arrow represents communications between modules. These symbols are explained in detail in Chapter 3.

The advantages of using a structure chart, which is the chief Structured Design tool, are that it is

- graphic
- partitionable
- rigorous, but flexible
- useful input to Structured Implementation
- documentation of the system
- an aid to maintenance and to modification

In this paragraph and the ones that follow, I will address each of these advantages in detail. First, let us consider the graphic nature of the structure chart: The structure chart is a picture that conveys a great amount of information very quickly. Any information that the struc-ture chart does not portray can be supplied by pseudocode or by some other description of the structure chart modules.

Before I explain why a graphic representation is so valuable, let me present this picture:

Figure 1.4

In Fig. 1.4, a man and a woman are skating on a frozen lake. They are holding hands: right hand in right hand, left hand in left hand. They are wearing hats, gloves, thick sweaters, and . . . but I don't have to tell you all this. You already absorbed at a glance all of the above description.

However, I could have added further details that you couldn't have gleaned from the picture. For example, the man is named Wilhelm; he is 29 years old. The woman is named Ingrid; she is 25. The lake is a tiny Swiss lake known locally as Lac Jacques, and the mountains are the Alps.

But the point is that a picture is worth a thousand words. The reason is that the part of the brain that assimilates pictorial information is much faster, and much older in evolutionary terms, than the part that interprets verbal information. In the primeval blob-eat-blob world, the dubious gift of survival was awarded to the organism that could most efficiently and accurately assess the scenario in which it found itself. If you were a primitive creature, speed and precision were valuable to you in order to recognize and capture dinner, and they were *essential* to you for recognizing and avoiding a beastie whose intentions were to dine at your expense.

Consequently, the brain evolved into a spectacularly sophisticated parallel-processing and pattern-recognition mechanism. When "reading" pictures, the brain is much more at home than it is when reading words, and so it tires less quickly. An additional advantage of pictures is that they are two-dimensional, whereas text is linear — that is, one-dimensional. The patterns within a system, and its overall shape, are at least two-dimensional. Therefore, a graphic tool is more "readable" than a verbal one, can be more accurately interpreted by the brain, and is a more realistic description of a system. Parents admonish their children, "Don't just look at the pictures." Structured Design encourages designers, "*Do* look at the pictures!"

Why is the structure chart any better than that other graphic tool — the well-known program flowchart? The problem with the flowchart is that it shows only the details of the system and offers little clue about how those details are organized. To gain an overall understanding of a computer system, you need a concise bird's-eye view of it. Trying to understand it from its code or from a detailed program flowchart alone is about as easy as trying to draw a map of the United States when you're standing in a forest in Idaho. But, on the other hand, if you're actually interested in a specific forest in Idaho, then a map of the whole country is not of much use. For an individual tree, branch, or leaf, the map is totally useless.

The top level of the structure chart paints a picture of a system in broad, bold strokes. It shows the major functions of the system and their interfaces. But the top of the structure chart provides few clues to the system's finer details (such as the functions making up the validation of a customer input record). You would find such minutiae at the bottom of the structure chart. Thus, you have your choice: Because the structure chart is partitionable, you can look at the overview of the system, or you can look at any part of it in as much detail as you desire.

And since the structure chart is partitionable, you can share it with a friend. Not only can two people read it at once, but — more usefully — two people can develop different parts of it at the same time and thus speed the design process.

The third characteristic of a structure chart is that it is rigorous but flexible. I say rigorous *but* flexible because these are usually conflicting aims. Codifiers of laws, for example, have a two-fold problem. They have to make sure that there are no loopholes in their laws, but they also have to make them flexible enough to keep pace with the ever-changing mores of society.

Structured Design balances on this tightrope by partitioning (separating different functions), and by avoiding redundancy (wherever possible depicting each function in one place only). Modifications to the structure chart are consequently localized. Also, since the structure chart remains aloof from the system's detailed code, it will not need to be changed so frequently as the code itself. Rigor is achieved by precise descriptions of the functions shown as black boxes in the structure chart. But, although precise, these descriptions also remain elevated above the level of procedural code. Thus, they, too, are subject to comparatively few modifications.

The usefulness of the structure chart doesn't end with the design phase. Just as the plan of a bridge aids its designers and also serves to direct its eventual construction, the structure chart acts not only as the design blueprint of a system but also as a guide to its implementation. The structure chart guides the coding of the system's pieces, the order in which its pieces will be constructed and tested, the assignment of programmers to each part of the system, the packaging of the system into programs, and the possible optimization of the system for speed or response time.

Documentation has traditionally been the bugbear of every analyst, designer, and programmer who has ever put together a computer system. Typically, people have to be coerced into developing documentation *after* the system has been produced. As a result, documentation usually is (1) as welcome as tidying up after a party; (2) "not my job" (Everyone tries to slink out of doing documentation with such an excuse as, "You surely don't pay me N thousand dollars a year to be a technical writer."); (3) done skimpily (The poor soul who's stuck with the job gets it done as quickly as he can, so that he can get on with the glamorous work of analyzing the next system.); or (4) old before it's new. Often, when (and if) system documentation finally lumbers out into the light, it's acclaimed with a tumultuous yawn. People such as the system's maintainers, who *have* to know about the system, will already have worked out what they need to know. Chances are that the system will have been changed anyway by the time its documentation appears.

The structure chart is a documentation tool that actually helps the designers during the design effort, rather than hindering them after design is over. It is also flexible enough to remain current with modifications made to the system during its lifetime.

In any kind of complex system, the location of a bug is rarely where its symptoms manifest themselves. Computer systems — as you doubtless know by bitter experience — are no exception. If you were attempting to repair a TV, you would be crazy not to have a diagram of its circuits in front of you. Without one, you could fumble and mumble for days and still get nowhere.

In the same way, the Sherlock Holmes in the maintenance department needs all the help he can get to maintain systems. Although, as we shall see, one of the objectives of Structured Design is to set up road blocks to restrict bugs to a small region, one or two may still slip through. The structure chart then serves as a map, which the maintainers can use to decide where to look in order to quickly apprehend the villainous bug in its lair.

The structure chart is also a useful tool for implementing user changes. It can show, first of all, the extent of the system to be modified. And — perhaps most important of all — it helps to avoid bugs that are created by an ill-thought-out change by identifying subtle relationships within a system that were hitherto missed for want of a graphic system description.

1.4 Elaborating a design solution

Structured Design offers a set of strategies for developing a design solution from a well-defined statement of a problem.

If a problem is stated by means of a set of data flow diagrams such as those produced by Structured Analysis (see Chapter 4), Structured Design offers two major strategies for smoothly developing a good design: The strategies are called transform analysis and transaction analysis (covered in Chapters 9 and 10, respectively). A very simple example of what they might accomplish is shown in Fig. 1.5:

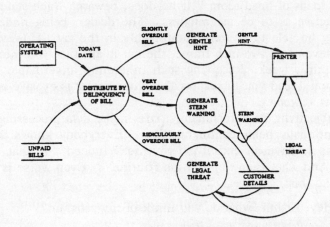

Figure 1.5

This data flow diagram would be transformed into the structure chart in Fig. 1.6:

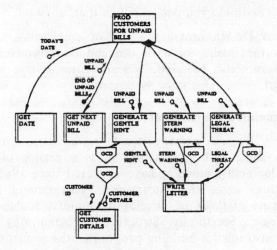

Figure 1.6

1.5 Evaluating a design solution

Structured Design offers a set of criteria for evaluating the quality of a given design solution with respect to the problem to be solved.

When you visit your neighborhood car dealer to buy a new car, he might tell you: "This is a great car. It goes fast, doesn't use much gas, and has loads of head room." If he does, beware! Such statements are so subjective as to be meaningless. The dealer, being under six feet tall, may be able to sit very comfortably in the car. However, if you have a seven-foot two-inch frame, the car might turn you into a hunch-back within a week. Receiving such inherently unverifiable "information" should lead you to suspect that your dealer is evasive at best and dishonest at worst.

Subjectivity is, unfortunately, rife in the data processing industry. One continually hears comments like, "Everybody knows that a program has to have an end-of-job routine." Indeed? Is that *every* program? And what *is* an "end-of-job routine"? Even worse is a conversation like this:

"Hey, Arthur, what do you think of my program?"

"I wouldn't have done it that way."

"Why not?"

"It stinks."

"What do you mean, it —"

"Why on earth did you design it like that, anyway?"

Structured Design provides a set of empirically tested criteria against which the quality of a design can be objectively measured. These criteria can also be used, whenever necessary, to improve a deficient design.

1.6 What Structured Design is not

Structured Design is not Structured Programming. Structured Programming, as some authors describe it, is a catalog of every great software development method to have appeared since 1965. But, more moderate authors agree that Structured Programming is concerned chiefly with sane methods of developing understandable and reliable source-code logic. Specifically, Structured Programming offers but a small set of constructs for building programs: the sequence of instructions; the choice between one group of instructions and another group of instructions (e.g., by an IF test); and the repetition of a group of instructions (e.g., by a PERFORM UNTIL loop). Additionally, Structured Programming offers a strategy called top-down or stepwise refinement to help the programmer identify which constructs he needs where.

However, Structured Programming does not work well by itself for large systems. It has no strategy that really helps you to tackle a great deal of complexity and produce a thoroughly maintainable computer system. Structured Design, you might say, takes up where Structured Programming leaves off: at medium- to large-size systems. You can use Structured Design and Structured Programming independently. However, if you use Structured Design to develop the overall form of a system, then you will find it very natural to use Structured Programming to develop its more detailed logic.

Structured Design is not a means to a good problem specification. Structured Design takes as its input a statement of what the system is supposed to accomplish. Without such a statement, the designers of the system will just spin their wheels. The best they can hope for, using Structured Design (or any other technique), is a brilliantly maintainable solution — but to the wrong problem!

Structured Design is not modular programming or top-down design. Structured Design *does* work almost exclusively with modules and it *is* deeply committed to the ideas of top-down organization. However, modular programming and top-down design have become trademarks for very specific development methods that were popular around the late 1960s and early 1970s. Structured Design has not merely taken these methods down from the shelf and given them a brand-new title. Instead, Structured Design is a logical and major extension of both modular programming and top-down design; but nothing in Structured Design contradicts anything said by modular programming and top-down design.

Structured Design is not automated design (not yet, anyway). There is no set of Structured Design formulae into which you can plug a problem specification and — presto! — get a perfectly designed system. However, Structured Design does have a set of guidelines by which you can fairly readily derive a good design; and another set of guidelines by which you can turn that good design into a better one. Structured Design, if you like, is more of an engineering discipline than a science.

Structured Design is not a one-way ticket to Utopia. I cannot promise if you adopt Structured Design principles that design will become a rose garden. There will still be difficulties, pitfalls, and false starts in store for you. But Structured Design will enable you to recognize difficulties, pitfalls, and false starts for what they are and will offer you a set of tools and guidelines that you can use to correct design problems.

The discipline of Structured Design does not stifle creativity any more than paragraphs stifle novelists or bar lines stifle musicians. Indeed, truly creative designers make use of Structured Design's discipline to *further* their creativity, rather than to smother it. Standardization of discipline, language, and tools stimulates interaction among designers. It allows one designer to build upon the work of others, instead of having to start afresh on each design he attempts. It also allows a designer to offer his perhaps unique insights to others. Another way to say this is that now there are bad designers and good designers; in the future, there should be good designers and better designers. And their specific relative talents should also be apparent.

In the past, the training of a new designer often consisted of making the trainee an apprentice to a sorcerer who effortlessly — but mysteriously — designed good systems time after time. The hope was that the trainee would absorb some of the elder designer's magic by osmosis, since the experienced person could rarely explain it in words. Henceforth, rather than saying, "Now watch what I do and see if you can copy it," master craftsmen should be able to communicate their skills to their apprentices using the tools of Structured Design.

Exercise

In this chapter, I have extolled the virtues of partitioning. If partitioning is so terrific, why not continue to partition a system indefinitely?

Answer

Unfortunately, like most good things, partitioning must end somewhere. The price of partitioning is the interfaces between the black boxes that partitioning creates. The more black boxes one produces, the more interfaces one has to understand. Eventually, the increasing complexity of the many interfaces outweighs the decreasing complexity of the smaller black boxes. Structured Design seeks to attain the balance point at which both the function of modules and the interfaces between them are as easy to understand as possible.

2

The Basics of Design

2.1 The context of design

In Chapter 1, I said that design is the bridge between analysis and implementation. Let's look at design in the wider context of the whole project. Then we can look at some of the specific ills of traditional project development. Figure 2.1 on the next page is a rough diagram of the early phases of an average classical project showing the documents that are passed from one phase to the next.*

Broadly, the "Seven Ages" of a classical computer system are

- problem recognition
- feasibility study
- analysis
- design
- implementation
- testing
- maintenance

The sections that follow provide a closer look at these traditional phases.

---

*In Appendix D, there is a diagram depicting how a project might be organized to include Structured Analysis and Structured Design. Appendix D also shows the individual activities of Structured Design.

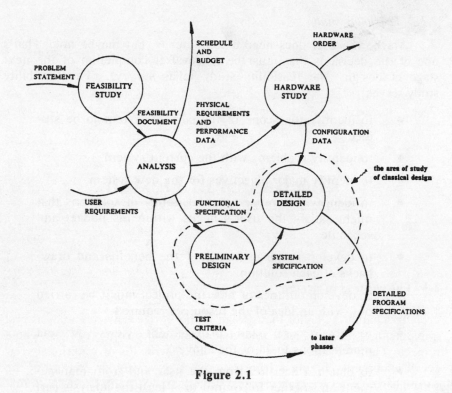

Figure 2.1

2.1.1 Problem recognition

The idea of developing a new system occurs to the user when he recognizes that he has a problem with the means by which he currently carries out his business. This awareness marks the beginning of the problem-recognition phase, as almost all computer systems replace an existing (either manual or automated) system.

Typically, the user is concerned less about the *way* in which he's doing his business than about the physical deficiencies of the system that he uses to do it. For example, his recognition of a problem might culminate in this assessment: "Here at Albert Ross Marine Insurance, we've increased our staff by 43 percent in the past two years. We've also doubled our policy range and have increased our business by more than 100 percent. The cost for all of the extra clerks and policy supervisors we've taken on is becoming exorbitant. I think we need a computer. . . ." With this statement, the user now is ready to start the second phase.

2.1.2 Feasibility study

Maybe the user does need a computer — but maybe not. That's one of the decisions that must be made after completion of the next stage of design: the feasibility study (alias survey). The feasibility study serves

- to identify the scope of the current system to be studied
- to identify problems with the current system
- to identify major objectives for the new system
- to identify a number (possibly zero!) of solutions that might satisfy the user's needs within his budget and schedule
- to develop rough estimates of the benefits and drawbacks of each solution
- to develop outlines of how the project might be carried out, with an idea of the resources required
- to obtain user and management views on and modifications to all of the above
- to obtain a decision from the user and from management on whether to commit to at least the analysis part of the project

The first six of the above functions must be approached very tentatively. Otherwise, the feasibility study will defeat its purpose of avoiding the expense of a full analysis on a hopeless project. For most projects, the feasibility study will take less than a month.

2.1.3 Analysis

The information gathered during the feasibility study, although probably not very detailed — or even accurate — will be the jumping-off point for a full analysis. Analysis (alias external design, business systems analysis, or specification phase) consists of grilling the user about what his current system does, what extra features he wants in his new system, and what constraints (such as response time) his new system must satisfy. The output from analysis should include

- a cost/benefits/schedule report for each suitable system
- data-base requirements

- physical requirements (e.g., new hardware, new software, new personnel)
- conversion requirements

But, most importantly, analysis must produce a functional specification. This document states the requirements for the new system. In the past, the functional specification has been a weighty document composed by several analysts whose writing styles have in common only the ability to combine excruciating detail with a lack of clarity. The user is supposed to read it, digest it, and sign it as being a correct statement of what he wants.

2.1.4 Design

The design phase (alias internal design, computer systems analysis, and program design) takes the hefty tome produced during classical analysis and determines how to organize what it describes in a way suitable for computer execution. Conventionally, this involves writing systems flowcharts, job steps, program narratives, and so on, which is known as preliminary design. Preliminary design is followed by detailed design, during which time program flowcharts, file layouts, data descriptions — everything but code — are developed. Structured Design consolidates preliminary and detailed design into a single design phase comprising a well-defined set of design activities.

2.1.5 Implementation

In this phase (alias programming or coding), what was produced during design is turned into code.

2.1.6 Testing

The testing phase is sometimes interleaved with implementation, and traditionally involves the testing, first of separate parts of the system and then finally of the system as a whole. The whole system is then turned over for acceptance testing (alias quality assurance). Acceptance testing is carried out by the user, the user's representative, the analysts, the standards group, external systems auditors, or any combination thereof.

2.1.7 Maintenance

Once the system has been coaxed into passing the acceptance test, it is ready for delivery (alias cutover, production inception, parallel operation, and so on). Anything that happens to the system from then on is called maintenance.

A few years after the delivery of a traditional system, its changes during maintenance become extremely tedious, error-prone, and expensive. Ideally, management recognizes the problem and does a feasibility study on replacing the old system with a new one. Thus, the cycle begins anew. . . .

2.2 Who does design?

Who does design? Why, the designer, of course! But, who *is* a designer? I'm sure you've met users, analysts, programmers, and even programmer/analysts, but have you ever met anyone with the job title "designer"? Probably not, for although the *role* of designer is well-defined, few people actually are assigned the job title of designer. Instead, the task of designing systems typically is given either to the analyst or to the programmer. Consequently, design becomes confused with either analysis or programming. If design becomes the domain of the analyst, then the user finds himself treated to a confusing pageant of flowcharts, file layouts, and so on. If design falls into the programmer's jurisdiction, then the overall plan of the system somehow "just emerges" from the code — if it emerges at all. In any case, a plan for coding is a little out of date after the coding's been done!

Then who should do design if there isn't a specialist designer? A senior programmer is probably the person best fitted to the role — but with the strict understanding that he *must* do design before he begins programming. Alternatively, a junior analyst may do design — with the understanding that he keep all DP jargon away from the user.

2.3 How design is done

How is design done? Too often, not at all! As I have just pointed out, a design that emerges from the code is no use whatsoever — but surprisingly often that's exactly what happens. System flowcharts and the like are a little better than nothing, but even they yield only a superficial, low-quality design.*

The disease of poor design is endemic in almost all conventional systems; its symptoms are that a system becomes

- unmanageable

---

*System flowcharts are valuable only in the right context. That context will be explained in Chapter 11.

- unsatisfactory and unproductive
- unreliable
- inflexible and unmaintainable
- inefficient
- a combination of the above

2.3.1 Unmanageable systems

Many computer systems have been developed by what I call the "Instant Karma" approach. Memos and rumors vaguely describing the purpose of the system are passed around a large group of analysts and programmers. This unruly mob is then unleashed upon the development of the system. Analysts and programmers have one salient talent in common: the ability to generate reams of paper bearing verbiage in every known language from broken English to COBOL.

Managers somehow think that out of this chaos will come order. While code is being churned out, everything must be all right, they assume, for the cosmic destiny of the project is manifestly to arrive at a working system within schedule and below budget. What such a manager usually fails to do is to put the necessary guardian angel on his payroll.

Planning and monitoring progress by this "weigh-the-code-and-assume-it's-OK" approach is like measuring progress in aircraft construction by the weight of the parts assembled. Instead of letting things happen and hoping that they will all mystically fall into place, managers need definite guidelines by which they can work.

Managers who do organize the project before work begins usually split the project into phases, the ends of which are marked by "milestones." Although there is nothing wrong, in theory, with phases and milestones, there are practical problems when it comes to actually using them to measure the progress of a project.

First, a mile is a large gap between stones. If a manager has to wait until the end of a whole phase before he can tell how the project is going, then he may well waste valuable time before he can correct something that is awry.

Second, it is often hard to say for sure when a milestone has been passed. Each milestone is certainly marked with a list of deliverables, so, on the face of it, all you have to do is to check the list of what you've got against the list of what you should have. However, there has to be some method of checking the quality — and not just the quantity — of the deliverables; otherwise, we're back to a variation of the weighing-code approach. For example, at the end of analysis you might have a very large, ostensibly complete specification. But if it is so unreadable that the users won't touch it with a ten-foot pole, then you have no way to tell whether it's right, almost right, or absolutely wrong. In other words, you don't know if you've passed the analysis milestone yet.

Third, since it's difficult to tell when a phase really is complete, the project manager tends to declare it complete when the calendar says it's complete. So, the phases of the moon become the arbiters of the phases of the project. For example, if the original project plan predicts that analysis will be done by March 23, then on March 24 the whole project will drift into design, regardless of the true state of analysis. Any extra analysis work that has not been completed will have to be done during design (or during programming or testing!). Doing analysis during a later phase is very expensive, since that phase is staffed by the wrong people, uses the wrong tools, and has no time allocated for unfinished analysis activities.

2.3.2 Unsatisfying and unproductive systems

System development can be not only managerially but also technically haphazard. Most engineering professions have strong disciplines by which they develop their products. Software "engineering," however, has little discipline. Far too many DP systems are developed by a sulfurous mixture of mythology, witchcraft, and bad habits and hardly offer true creative satisfaction to a professional developer.

Development of a traditional system — especially in the coding and testing phases — often seems like moving three steps forward and two steps back or occasionally two steps forward and three steps back. Figure 2.2,* which shows the amount of work devoted to each stage of system development, clearly illustrates this lack of productivity. The pie chart in Fig. 2.2 shows that, for a typical system, about 45 percent of development time is devoted to testing and debugging. Now, there's nothing wrong with testing a system or debugging it.[†] But since most of the effort of testing actually goes into debugging — at the expense of real testing — it looks as if traditionally we spend about half our time making mistakes and the other half of our time fixing them. And that *is* wrong.

---

*M.V. Zelkowitz, "Perspectives on Software Engineering," *ACM Computing Surveys,* Vol. 10, No. 2 (June 1978), p. 198. Copyright 1978, Association for Computing Machinery, Inc., reprinted by permission.
[†]The difference between the two terms is that *testing* is the relentless search for bugs, and *debugging* is the relentless extermination of them.

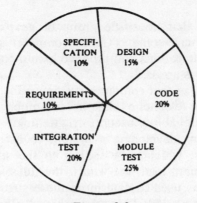

Figure 2.2

As Myers* puts it:

> We try to solve the problem by rushing through the design process so that enough time is left at the end of the project to uncover the errors that were made because we rushed through the design process.

2.3.3 Unreliable systems

The system may have been completely developed and tested. The exterminators may have removed every last bug from it. The users may have shown up in force to ensure that what is being unloaded on them is of the highest quality. The developers may have given due thanks, sprinkled holy water over the system, and pushed it through the door. But when the system reaches production, it inexplicably crashes every night.

There are too many systems that are pronounced sound, because they scrape through some tests that are (consciously or unconsciously) stacked in their favor. Few developers can sincerely have more than blind faith in what they've produced, especially if their product has been hastily patched at the last moment with string and tape. So long as the system *seems* to work, developers too often consider that to be enough.

The worst aspect of this faith-hope-and-parity attitude is that many system developers unwittingly become Frankensteins, begetting monster systems that escape the control of their creators. There are thousands of these systems in production at this moment. Such a sys-

*G. Myers, *Composite/Structured Design* (New York: Van Nostrand Reinhold, 1978), p. 2.

tem is so complex that no single group of people can understand it completely. Every day, some of these computer systems execute extremely involved calculations and produce *almost* correct results without a hint that anything is amiss.

When you realize that computer systems affect our lives in respect to everything from telephone bills to automobile design, the ramifications of their unreliability become frightening. For example, I was once part of a team developing a system to ascertain the safety of ocean-based oil rigs, which were subject to the stresses of their own weight, their equipment load, the winds, the tides, and so on. The engineering calculations used to determine these stresses were so complicated that — to use a 1950s "electronic brain" illustration — it would have taken one hundred engineers five years to check the system's results using desk calculators. So not one of our team could say for sure that our system was producing the correct results. All we could say was that the results *looked* reasonable. But we knew in our hearts that although we had tested the system exhaustively (that is, until we were exhausted), there could still be some bugs.

Fortunately for all concerned, those bugs never wreaked havoc, so the trust that the oil-riggers had to have in their watery perch was justified. But it *could* have been different.

2.3.4 Inflexible and unmaintainable systems

The overriding consideration of system developers is to deliver a system by the deadline and within the budget. Judging from the times I've seen system testing hastily drawn to a premature close because of the impending due date, I would say that delivering a *working* system is a secondary consideration. Well down on the list — and seldom even considered — is delivering a flexible system. If the system works at all, that's often regarded as a miracle. Future changes are scarcely given a thought.

However, barely is the system in production when an unexpected avalanche of changes will rumble down from the user on to the poor development team, who are still patting themselves on the back over the "success" of this latest system. Usually the system, only just hanging together in the first place, cannot absorb these changes gracefully. Many systems lose their dubious stability early in their lifetime: After a few months, they never again function completely correctly.

Trying to incorporate quite reasonable user changes after development is even more frustrating and costly than it is during the development effort. I know of one very large system that is currently occupying the full-time attention of more than one hundred maintenance programmers. These lost souls are organized into six-person chain gangs (their term, not mine). Each chain gang is responsible for one set of features, aspects, or functions of the system. Whenever a problem arises in a particular part of the system, the appropriate chain gang shuffles off to eliminate the offending bugs. Unfortunately, this approach, while good in theory, doesn't work well in practice. Too often, when one gang makes a change to its part of the system, a part belonging to a very different gang stops working correctly. So that gang shuffles over to make *its* corrections. This fix-and-shuffle routine is almost non-stop. The system wobbles along, barely working at all and never working completely.

The pie chart for the whole system's lifetime, which is shown in Fig. 2.3,* dramatically depicts the ratio of expense incurred after delivery of a system to total systems cost.

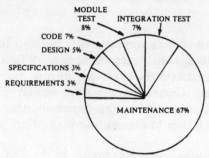

Figure 2.3

Sixty-seven percent of the whole lifetime cost of the system — twice as much as was spent on development — is spent on maintenance. Testing and debugging account for a further 15 percent of the total cost; so 82 percent of the money spent on a system is consumed by putting it right and keeping it right. Only 15 percent is spent on constructing it in the first place. Boehm[†] points out with cynical realism that the maintenance costs are only as *low* as they are because many systems become so unmaintainable early in their lifetime that they have to be scrapped. Consequently, they drain away no more cash. (On the other hand, I have seen many a system that became unmaintainable early in its lifetime go on to live a long and unhealthy life simply because no one had the sense to commit euthanasia.)

---

*M.V. Zelkowitz, op. cit., p. 202. Copyright 1978, Association for Computing Machinery, Inc., reprinted by permission.

[†]B. Boehm, "Software Engineering," *IEEE Transactions on Computers,* Vol. C-25, No. 12 (December 1976), pp. 1226-41. [Reprinted in E.N. Yourdon, ed., *Classics in Software Engineering* (New York: YOURDON Press, 1979), pp. 325-61.]

Why is maintenance so expensive? Because none of the six steps that comprise maintenance is easy. The steps involved in changing a system include

1. understanding how the current system works (or why it doesn't work)
2. figuring out the required modification
3. assessing the impact of the modification on the rest of the system
4. making the modification
5. testing the modified system
6. managing, organizing, controlling, and documenting the above

Steps 1, 2, and 3 are usually unnecessarily difficult in conventional systems because of the system's lack of design. When the true impact of the lack of design becomes apparent, during maintenance, it's too late to make amends. Correcting the poor design of a system in production is an order of magnitude more expensive than correcting it during design. (Imagine trying to change the plan of an office building *after* it's been built.)

Another major problem making Steps 1, 2, and 3 extremely difficult is the typical lack of high-level documentation for a system. Trying to understand a system from its code alone has been compared to investigating an elephant from a distance of two inches: All you can tell is that it's gray!

Steps 5 and 6 are always tedious and dull. Therefore, in practice, Step 4 is the only one that will definitely be carried out. But, without the other steps, a quick succession of Step 4's will soon beat the system into an unmaintainable pulp. (That's especially true if the modifications are carried out over many years by many generations of maintenance programmers. Their diverse prejudices, talents, and levels of experience result in systems with immensely confusing and inconsistent programming styles. Such systems have been called Baskin-Robbins systems — 31 flavors of code!)

This amounts to saying that with classical systems the six steps of maintenance are far too time-consuming and costly if you do them. And, they're even more time-consuming and costly if you don't!

2.3.5 *Inefficient systems*

Oddly enough, I'm going to accuse traditional computer systems of being inefficient. I say "oddly enough" because one of the taunts of traditionalists is that systems that have been developed by Structured Design and Structured Programming are inefficient. But it all depends on what you mean by "efficiency." In the production costs of a system, there are factors other than speed to be considered:

- memory requirements
- normal running time
- abnormal running time
- lifetime deterioration
- running costs

Memory requirements are becoming less and less of a problem. As the cost of fast memory drops — almost exponentially at times — the amount of real memory available in most machines increases. With the development of virtual-memory management systems, few applications-system designers have to worry about the cost or availability of storage. (Structured Design adds about 10–15 percent to the size of the executable part of a normal system. However, modular systems are more amenable to being reorganized for virtual-memory environments.)

Normal running time (or normal response time for an on-line system) will always be a factor in systems development. Although it is true that modern machines are fast and getting faster, someone will always come up with an application for which the fastest machine isn't fast enough. But such an application is the exception. Most applications systems do not need to be at the frontier of speed. As long as a daily run doesn't take more than twenty-four hours, that's often enough. (Structured Design imposes a run-time overhead of up to about 15 percent over a reasonably fast traditional system, but can actually produce a system more than twice as fast as a mediocre traditional system with many job steps. However, if speed is a genuine concern, Structured Design offers techniques by which that 15 percent — and more — can be recovered with minimal modification to the system's design.)

Abnormal running time is the amount of time a system spends on its way to a crash or in producing the wrong results. In many systems — especially those in which user changes are tested in production — such abnormal running time is large. (Structured Design will not completely eliminate crashes and wrong results. However, it will reduce their numbers considerably, typically by up to an order of magnitude.)

Code may be written with the objective of saving every microsecond of CPU time; or code may be written to be flexible. It is seldom possible to write a piece of code with both qualities. Historically, many systems were written with tight, well-tuned code. But when they were modified, their speed usually had to be sacrificed to accommodate the changes. One of the goals of Structured Design is flexible systems; a structured system has little or no tight, tricky code. Even if a structured system doesn't start life fantastically fast, it tends to retain the speed it has much better over the years than its unstructured sibling does. The race is not always to the swiftest!

But, how many of us even need to care about slight differences in speed? For a system to be truly efficient, it has to make efficient use of people. In the early 1960s, hardware accounted for 80 percent of a system's cost, whereas "peopleware" accounted for less than 20 percent. But, in these days of salary inflation, we've already passed the 50-percent point. And, as hardware costs drop still further, we are reaching the point at which hardware amounts to 20 percent of the total, and peopleware, 80 percent (see Fig. 2.4).*

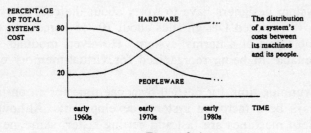

Figure 2.4

So now, as machines become fantastically large and powerful, it makes not only moral sense but also economical sense for the machine to be the slave of the people. Anything we can do to use the time of our human staff more efficiently will invariably be worthwhile — even if it means that the machine has to work a little harder.

---

*T.R. Lister and E. Yourdon, *Learning to Program in Structured COBOL, Part 2* (New York: YOURDON Press, 1978), p. 170.

Exercise

The poor quality of systems and the low productivity of programmers (about ten lines of debugged source code per person-day is often quoted) has traditionally been blamed on the incompetence of the programmers themselves. Is this fair, or can you think of mitigating circumstances that might force programmers to develop poor products?

Answer

Programmers' tools, such as the program flowchart, and inadequate programmer training are no doubt partly to blame for poor programs. However, it's seldom realized that inadequate analysis and design more than any other factor deny programmers the chance to perform well. Programming without a precise statement of requirements or a plan for achieving those requirements has been compared to trying to reach an unknown destination in the dark without a map.

SECTION II
THE TOOLS OF STRUCTURED DESIGN

Like all engineering disciplines, computer systems development requires the use of tools. But successful systems design requires choosing the appropriate tool for a specific purpose. In the next three chapters, we explore various Structured Design tools and their suitability for particular systems development tasks.

Chapter 3 describes the central tool of Structured Design, the structure chart, which can be used for design either at the program level or at the system level.

In *Chapter 4,* we learn that the tools of Structured Analysis are invaluable for *system* design. Together, they form the major output of Structured Analysis, called the structured specification.

Some of the same analysis tools are also used for module specification, the subject of *Chapter 5.* With these tools, a designer can define a design sufficiently for a programmer to code from it.

3

The Structure Chart

In the 1940s and 1950s, computer applications were necessarily small owing to the limitations of the machines on which they ran. As machines grew in both capacity and power, so did users' computer requirements. And because the users' requirements became more sophisticated, the tools for analyzing and implementing systems had to become more sophisticated.

One of the earliest programming tools was the flowchart, which many programmers found to be useful for organizing their thoughts prior to programming — especially whenever the logic or procedure of a program was particularly tricky. Other programmers refused to use it, regarding it as a stumbling block in the way of the real activity of coding. Only if their managers or standards people threatened to throw them into a pit of starving rats would they produce flowcharts — and then only after they had coded the system and decided that they'd eliminated that famous last bug.

Flowcharts didn't survive the 1960s unscathed. As systems grew, the difficulties with flowcharts became apparent: They provided no organizational insight for anything larger than small-to-medium sized systems.

Structured Programming was the first technique to address the complexity of modern systems. First, it proposed a very small set of programming constructs for developing code. Second — and more important — Structured Programming recognized that in order to attack the details of a problem, it is very important to have a firm grasp of the overall problem first. The technique that Structured Programming suggested for making a steady progression from overview to detail became known as top-down design (or stepwise refinement). Top-down design is an informal design strategy for breaking problems into smaller problems. Unfortunately, it presents few guidelines for achieving this partitioning. Structured Design, as we shall see in later chapters, sets forth the guidelines that top-down design lacks.

Following is an informal example of the use of top-down design to devise a program that calculates the final result of a Grand Prix even before the cars reach the starting grid. The whole problem can be stated as

> Predict order of finish of Grand Prix

The above line of "code" is perfectly correct, but unfortunately cannot be implemented directly on any known computer. So we must break it into simpler pieces:

1. Get track details
2. Get other race details
3. For each entrant
   3.1 Get driver history
   3.2 Get car history
   3.3 Get other details of entrant
   3.4 Calculate expected time of finish
4. Order the entrants by time of finish
5. List entrants by time of finish

At this stage, although we haven't arrived at the final details of the program, we should ask whether steps 1-5 are sufficient to establish the winner of a Grand Prix. If we are satisfied, then we can continue to refine each step to a more detailed set of steps until we reach steps that are simple enough to be expressed directly in COBOL or Fortran, for example. The power of this top-down technique is that we can develop and review the solution to a larger problem in manageable pieces and can avoid the instant chaos of confronting all of the details at once.

Structured Programming produced systems that were more smoothly developed and more reliable than systems ever had been before. Of course, cynics pointed out that the top-down approach made the success of a whole system depend on the feasibility of implementing all of its functions at its bottom, most detailed level. In the Grand Prix example, the success of the whole system depends on my naive assumption that I can eventually write code for "calculate expected time of finish."

Perhaps the point can be made clearer through the following top-down elephant joke:

> Q: How do you get seven elephants into a Volkswagen?
> A: Three in the front and four in the back.

The point of the joke is that all top-down design has achieved in this case is converting one large insoluble problem into two smaller insoluble problems!

But, cynicism aside, Structured Programming greatly improved the quality of systems delivered to the user. However, it had only partially tackled the problem of maintainability. Although systems developed by means of Structured Programming had fewer bugs in them than traditional systems had, it was still almost as difficult as ever to install user changes or enhancements to a system. The reason was that Structured Programming had failed to take into account the large-scale structure of systems, which is where a large part of maintainability lies. (I explain this important concept in Chapters 6, 7, and 8.) For instance, although the major guideline of top-down design is to split the problem into subproblems, there are no further rules to explain where to make the cuts.

About the time that Structured Programming was first gaining acceptance, Stevens, Myers, Constantine, and Yourdon, among others, were crystallizing the ideas of Structured Design.* All the concepts of top-down design remained valid in Structured Design, but many other principles were added so that a grander view of systems — especially large ones — could be obtained. For the first time, Structured Design escaped from the tyranny of the statement-level of computer code; even Structured Programming had never fully managed to do that.

The major tool used in Structured Design to depict the structure of a system is the structure chart. Figure 3.1 on the next page is an example of a small one.

As we see in this diagram, there are eight well-defined hunks of code (modules) in the part of the system shown. Some modules call other modules, as indicated by the arrow →, and communicate data with one another, as indicated by the ○→ . Certain details, on the other hand, we have few clues about. We don't know how many lines of code are in CALCULATE GROSS PAY FOR HOURLY WORKER, for example, or what particular algorithm this module uses. All we can say is that it is called with the information PAY RATE and HOURS WORKED and returns to its caller the information GROSS HOURLY PAY.

---

*W. Stevens, G. Myers, and L. Constantine, "Structured Design," *IBM Systems Journal,* Vol. 13, No. 2 (May 1974), pp. 115-39. [Reprinted in E.N. Yourdon, ed., *Classics in Software Engineering* (New York: YOURDON Press, 1979), pp. 207-32.] See also E. Yourdon and L. Constantine, *Structured Design: Fundamentals of a Discipline of Computer Program and Systems Design* (New York: YOURDON Press, 1978).

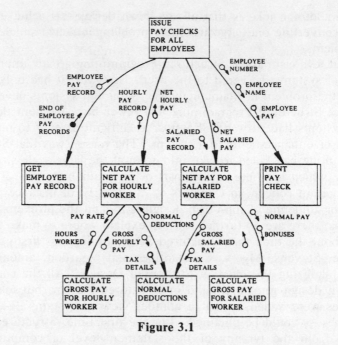

Figure 3.1

We'll return to this piece of structure chart later in this chapter; but first of all, let's look closely at each of the components on it: modules, connections between modules, and communication between modules.

3.1 The module

Earlier, I spoke glibly of a "module." Well, what is a module? Perhaps, you're thinking that a module is a number of statements that do some activity, or a subroutine, or perhaps up to fifty lines of code. All these ideas are valid, although not very precise. Let me give you some examples from various languages of what may be considered a module in Structured Design:

> in PL/I or ALGOL: PROCEDURE
> in COBOL: PROGRAM, SECTION, or PARAGRAPH
> in FORTRAN: SUBROUTINE, FUNCTION
> in APL: FUNCTION

Some of these examples meet the definition of a module more obviously than others, for the definition of a module is almost identical to that of a black box. A *module* is defined as a collection of program statements with four basic attributes: input and output, function, mechanics, and internal data.

1. input   (what it gets from its invoker)
   output   (what it returns to its invoker)
2. function   (what it does to its input
                    to produce its output)
3. mechanics   (the procedural code or logic
                    by which it carries out its function)
4. internal data   (its own private workspace,
                    data to which it alone refers)

Input and output are, respectively, the information that a module requires and provides. The function of a module is what it does to its inputs to produce its outputs. Inputs, outputs, and function comprise the outside view of the module. Mechanics are the procedural code or logic by which a module carries out its function; internal data is the module's private workspace — data to which it alone refers. Mechanics and internal data comprise the inside view of the module.

A module also has other attributes: It has a name, by which it can be referenced as a whole unit. It can use or be used by other modules — for example, by a CALL. A module usually occupies one place on a listing and (depending on the compiler and the operating system) occupies one area of memory.

In Structured Design, we are concerned almost entirely with the outside view of a module — *what* a module does, rather than *how* it does it. We'll also rely on the fact that a module has a name and that each module can invoke another. But we won't be concerned with the particular internal coding or logic details of modules. So long as a module can accomplish its stated function, we'll be content to leave the best implementation of its insides to a programming technique such as Structured Programming (or even flowcharting!).

But so that you can get a feel for what a module might be, here are a couple of examples of modules showing their outsides *and* their insides. The first example is a module to calculate the interest for a month on a customer's balance. Given his BALANCE RECORD, the module returns his INTEREST. It is written in a language resembling PL/I. As you can see on the next page, the lines of code comprising the module are bounded by a beginning and an end: specifically, the lines COMPUTE MONTHLY INTEREST and END COMPUTE MONTHLY INTEREST. COMPUTE MONTHLY INTEREST is also the name of the module; when we refer to COMPUTE MONTHLY INTEREST, we're referring not just to the first line of the module but to the whole module. And since the name of a module should say what the module does, COMPUTE MONTHLY INTEREST is also a statement of the module's function. BALANCE RECORD is the input to the module; it contains the information that you must provide the module when you call it. INTEREST is the output from the module; it contains the result of the module's computations. Inside the module are the lines of code and data declarations by which the module carries out its function.

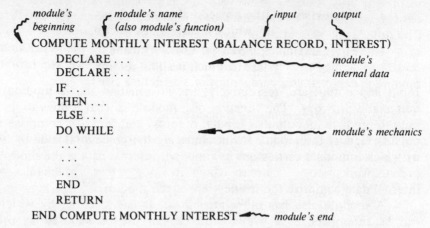

```
module's          module's name                    input        output
beginning         (also module's function)
     COMPUTE MONTHLY INTEREST (BALANCE RECORD, INTEREST)
          DECLARE ...                                    module's
          DECLARE ...                                    internal data
          IF ...
          THEN ...
          ELSE ...
          DO WHILE                                       module's mechanics
          ...
          ...
          ...
          END
          RETURN
     END COMPUTE MONTHLY INTEREST     module's end
```

The example that follows shows the same module expressed in a language like COBOL. Although this module has a different format, it possesses the same modular characteristics as the previous example.

COBOL Example

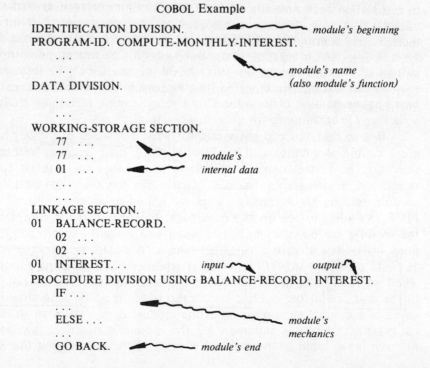

```
IDENTIFICATION DIVISION.                    module's beginning
PROGRAM-ID.  COMPUTE-MONTHLY-INTEREST.
     ...
     ...                                    module's name
DATA DIVISION.                              (also module's function)
     ...
     ...
WORKING-STORAGE SECTION.
     77 ...
     77 ...                  module's
     01 ...                  internal data
     ...
     ...
LINKAGE SECTION.
01   BALANCE-RECORD.
     02 ...
     02 ...
01   INTEREST...            input              output
PROCEDURE DIVISION USING BALANCE-RECORD, INTEREST.
     IF ...
     ...
     ELSE ...                                  module's
     ...                                       mechanics
     GO BACK.              module's end
```

If you use COBOL, the best way to think of a module is as a separately compilable program. I emphasize "think of" because I don't mean that all modules will be implemented as CALLed subprograms: Many will wind up as SECTIONS or PARAGRAPHS. (In Chapter 11, I explain why this is true.) However, the subprogram is conceptually the closest in COBOL to the black-box module; so whenever I refer to "module," you should think "callable program."

These two examples illustrate what is meant by the *inside* or the *outside* of a module. In the subsections that follow, we see how the module is depicted as a component of a structure chart.

3.1.1 *Graphic representation of a module*

In a structure chart, the module is shown as a rectangular box with its name inside, as shown below:

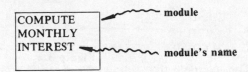

The module's name is a statement of its function, that is, what it does to completion each time it's called. I didn't call it CONTROL ROUTINE or PROCESS ROUTINE, because these provide vague statements about its logic, rather than indicate its function.

A pre-defined module is shown graphically by adding lines inside and parallel to the vertical lines. This is a module (or little subsystem) that you won't have to write because it already exists in a systems or applications library.

Most shops use the same symbol for modules in the operating system, for example:

3.1.2 *Connections between modules*

Modules are not hermits. A system is not an anarchy of sullen boxes, but a set of modules organized into a hierarchy, cooperating and communicating to get the job done. You've already seen in Fig. 3.1 the symbol that joins modules: It's the arrow showing "boss-hood" or, more precisely, a module call.

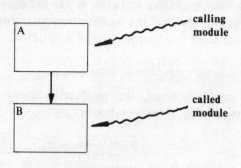

Figure 3.2

Figure 3.2 means that

> A calls (invokes, performs) B
> B does its function
> B returns (goes back) to A immediately after the point at which A called B

In other words, the arrow shows a normal subroutine call, with the direction of the arrow showing which module calls which.

What does this diagram tell us about the code in A or in B? Practically nothing! We know that A contains a CALL B statement. But that CALL B may be inside an IF statement or inside much more complicated code. There may be 10, 27, or even 37 CALL B statements within A. The arrow doesn't tell us anything about the code within A (or B either). It doesn't even tell us how many times A calls B or whether on a given run A will call B at all. All it tells us is that A is *capable* of calling B: B is *subordinate* to A.

Don't be worried by this lack of detail. It's deliberate. After all, what we're striving for in Structured Design is a tool that can give us the structure of a system without miring us in its gory details.

3.1.3 Communication between modules

Notice that in Fig. 3.2 above, A is calling B without saying anything to B. I'm sure that whenever you call someone on the phone, you speak to that person — unless perhaps you're into heavy breathing. Modules are like you and me. They talk, and Fig. 3.3 below illustrates how we show their communication. In the figure, GET CUSTOMER DETAILS calls FIND CUSTOMER NAME in the way we've already seen, but this time we can see that the modules also communicate information to each other:

- GET CUSTOMER DETAILS sends *data* (CUSTOMER ACCOUNT NUMBER) to FIND CUSTOMER NAME
- FIND CUSTOMER NAME (having done its function) returns *data* (CUSTOMER NAME) to GET CUSTOMER DETAILS
- FIND CUSTOMER NAME also returns a *flag* (ACCOUNT NUMBER IS OK) to GET CUSTOMER DETAILS. (This is used to tell the caller that everything went well, because sometimes GET CUSTOMER DETAILS may inadvertently send an account number for a nonexistent customer.)

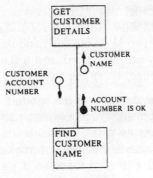

Figure 3.3

Let's look at an actual line of code in GET CUSTOMER DETAILS, which would implement its interface to FIND CUSTOMER NAME. In COBOL, it would be

```
CALL 'FIND-CUSTOMER-NAME'
    USING CUSTOMER-ACCOUNT-NUMBER,
        CUSTOMER-NAME, ACCOUNT-NUMBER-IS-OK.
```

In a language similar to FORTRAN or PL/I, the code would be

    CALL FIND CUSTOMER NAME
        (CUSTOMER ACCOUNT NUMBER, CUSTOMER NAME,
        ACCOUNT NUMBER IS OK)

CUSTOMER ACCOUNT NUMBER (which is the input to FIND CUSTO-
MER NAME) must be given a value by GET CUSTOMER DETAILS before it
calls FIND CUSTOMER NAME. (Whatever garbage is in the other two
parameters is irrelevant.) FIND CUSTOMER NAME has to keep its side of
the bargain, by not tampering with its input (CUSTOMER ACCOUNT
NUMBER). Before going back to its caller, it must assign values to its
output: ACCOUNT NUMBER IS OK and, if all *is* okay, CUSTOMER NAME as
well.

I'm sure you've guessed by now what the symbols for the communication between modules mean:

    ⟰ is called a data couple   ⟰ is called a flag

The direction of the arrow shows which module sends information to
another, that is

    ○————————▶

    SENDER   RECEIVER

If the sender is the caller, then the receiver is the called module. If the
sender is the called module, then the receiver is the caller.

Why are there two symbols for module communication, and what
is the difference between data (○→) and a flag (●→)? Rather than there
being a single difference, there are two:*

- Data is processed. (That's what data processing is all
  about, after all!) A flag is not really processed. A field
  may be left-justified, or a sales-tax rate may be multi-
  plied by sales price. But it makes little sense to left-
  justify a flag, to add three to it, or even to write it out.
  A flag typically is set and tested. (I'm not denying that
  data may be tested. But that's not its primary purpose.)

- Data relates to the problem itself. For example, pieces
  of data may be AGE OF APPLICANT (for an insurance
  policy) or VOLUME OF CARGO SPACE SOLD (in a space
  shuttle). Both of these have a strong relevance to the

---

*The differences between data and flags are further elaborated in Chapter 6.

outside world. But a flag tends to be one step removed from the world of the problem, for it communicates information about a piece of data. For example, ZIP CODE IS VALID describes ZIP CODE; END OF PENDING ORDERS describes the state of the PENDING ORDERS FILE.

3.2 The structure chart revisited

Let's return to the structure chart shown in Fig. 3.1 and reproduced below. Now that I've defined the symbols on it, what additional pieces of information can we learn from it?

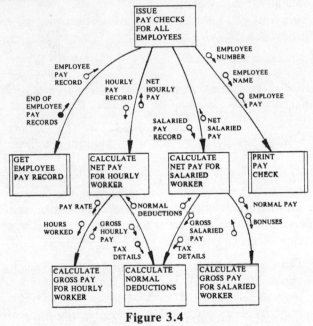

Figure 3.4

- CALCULATE NORMAL DEDUCTIONS appears only *once* in the chart although it has *two* bosses. By convention, we don't show it twice because the chart is harder to draw and to update if the same module appears more than once. Moreover, if CALCULATE NORMAL DEDUCTIONS had subordinates, we would have to show a great many modules in two places. Showing the module only once with "fan-in" (that is, receiving calls from more than one boss) also makes it easier to check that each of its bosses calls it with parameters of the same number and type (interface consistency).

- In a left-to-right sense, we don't necessarily know in what sequence modules are called. For instance, does CALCULATE NET PAY FOR HOURLY WORKER call CALCU-LATE GROSS PAY FOR HOURLY WORKER before or after it calls CALCULATE NORMAL DEDUCTIONS? We can infer from the application that the answer is before, but we couldn't tell that from the structure chart. (If you think the left-to-right sequence does give it away, take a look at the subordinates of CALCULATE NET PAY FOR SALARIED WORKER.)

  What I'm saying is that these structure charts in Fig. 3.5 all are equivalent:

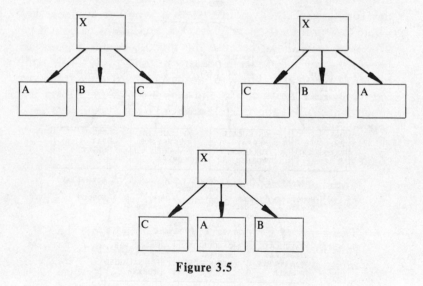

Figure 3.5

  But if you know that module X will contain the lines

```
CALL A
CALL B
CALL C
```

  in that order, you might as well be kind to the reader and depict the chart as in the first example, since most people read from left to right.

- What do you call a piece of data when the calling module knows it by one name and the called module knows it by another? This is allowed in most languages; for example, in a calling module, you could say

CALL FRED USING A, B

while FRED itself, in its LINKAGE SECTION, calls the interface data X and Y, respectively.

The convention is that the boss pulls rank: The data is given the name by which the boss knows it. Look at CALCULATE NORMAL DEDUCTIONS in Fig. 3.4. One of its bosses uses GROSS HOURLY PAY; the other uses GROSS SALARIED PAY. Inside CALCULATE NORMAL DEDUCTIONS, this input parameter may well be known by a quite different name, such as GROSS PAY.

• The name of a module sums up its function, that is, *what* it does for its boss. (The top module of the system must state the function of the whole system.) Whether it does the whole function by itself or "hires" subordinates to help it is irrelevant to its boss, because the module is still *responsible* for getting the job done. Look at CALCULATE NET PAY FOR HOURLY WORKER in Fig. 3.4. It has perhaps only three or four lines of code within it and gets a lot of help from its subordinates. But the module still does the function of calculating the net pay for an hourly worker just as much as if all the code were within it and it had no subordinates. I could rephrase this important rule as

> The name of a module should sum up the names of its immediate subordinates.

or

> The name of a module must sum up not only the function of its own code but also the functions of *all* its subordinates' code.

This is analogous to having the name of a department sum up all the activities performed by that department or making the boss of a department take responsibility for the action of all his subordinates.

3.3 Summary of the structure chart

A structure chart shows

• the partitioning of a system into modules
• the hierarchy and organization of modules

- communication (input and output) interfaces between modules
- names — and therefore functions — of modules

A structure chart does *not* show

- the internal procedure of modules (for example, the sequence of calls to other modules, loops, or IF-statements)
- the internal data of modules

Because of what a structure chart does not show, you may be distraught at the prospect of having a programmer program from such a chart. The chart has a few good clues for programming, such as the names of the modules and of the data on their interfaces, but those obviously don't take you very far. How, for instance, could you implement a module called CALCULATE BASIC CUSTOMER ELECTRICITY CHARGE without knowing anything about the utility company's charging policy?

So, accompanying the structure chart must be a description of everything — each module and each piece of data — appearing on it. In Chapter 5, I show how — and how not — to specify modules to the programmer. In Chapter 4 on Structured Analysis, I show how to specify data, too. In Chapter 6, we see the first use of the structure chart as a tool to evaluate the quality of a design.

Exercises

1. What is the difference between a flowchart and a structure chart? Illustrate your answer by pretending to be a machine executing each of the following:

    (a) flowchart   (b) structure chart

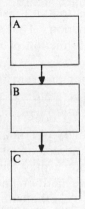 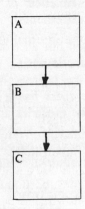

    What is the sequence of events in each case?

2. What are the three things wrong with the following structure chart?

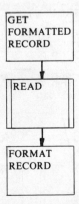

3. When might crossing lines be unavoidable on a structure chart? Suggest two ways of coping with them.

4. How would you ensure continuity if your structure chart spanned several pages (as most do)?

Answers

1. A flowchart shows flow of control, that is, the sequence of steps to be executed. In (a), the sequence would be A, B, and C. A structure chart shows hierarchy, that is, which functions are subfunctions of which. In (b), if we assume each call is executed exactly once, the sequence would be A begins, A calls B, B begins, B calls C, C begins, C does its function, C returns to B, B finishes its function, B returns to A, and A finishes its function. That sounds complicated but all it amounts to is B is a subfunction of A, and C is a subfunction of B.

2. (a) No data and flags have been shown.
   (b) The name of a module must sum up all of the activities beneath it. GET FORMATTED RECORD does that, but READ doesn't. (How can READ be a summary of FORMAT?)
   (c) Subordinates of a pre-defined module are never shown in a structure chart. (A pre-defined module may have hundreds of subordinates but by definition we neither know nor care how it has been implemented.) READ is the culprit again.

Errors (b) and (c) betray some flowchart-thinking on the designer's part. If we assume a sequential file, this is how the piece of structure chart should look:

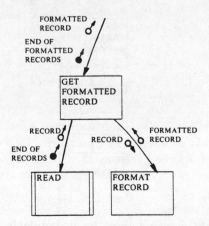

Check that this has corrected all three faults.

3. Crossing lines may be unavoidable in certain cases when a module has fan-in (more than one boss). There are two popular remedies:

    (a)

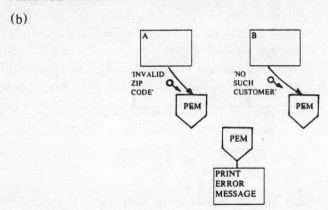

    Alternative (b) is a connector, only to be used when solution (a) would create spaghetti. A notorious "villain" is a PRINT ERROR MESSAGE module.

    (b)

4. There are several solutions to ensure continuity. The one most widely used is to show a module at the foot of one page and then repeat it on another page with a page reference, along with its subordinates, as shown in the example on the following page.

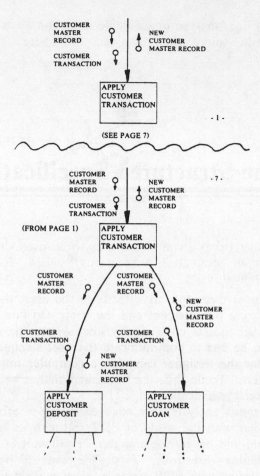

Showing the module and its interface on both pages is redundant but well worth it for the sake of continuity. The alternative to having connectors from one page to another does not afford the reader such continuity.

For a complete summary of all symbols used on a structure chart, see Appendix C.

4

The Structured Specification

4.1 Introduction

The designer does not talk directly to the user; the analyst is the go-between linking the designer and the user. On one side, he has to converse with the user to elicit exactly what system the user needs. On the other side, he has to communicate the user's requirements to the designer so that the designer can plan a computer implementation of the user's system. To do this, the traditional analyst writes a document called a functional specification.

Many systems analysts were once designers or programmers, and are more familiar with the world of EDP and with its jargon than with the user's world and his business jargon. The result of this has all too often been doubly disastrous: First, the user is bewildered by a specification buzzing with EDP terms — such as disk drives, job steps, and HIDAM — whose meaning he can only guess at. Yet the user is expected to peruse, correct, and finally accept this specification as being a true representation of his needs.

Second, the designer, whose job it is to decide the best implementation for the user's business system, is pre-empted by the analyst in his decisions. The analyst may frustrate the designer by imposing premature and often arbitrary constraints upon him. Indeed, in many a shop where I have worked or consulted, the user community and the design/programming community are two peoples separated by a common document — the functional specification.

Structured Analysis is a response to the fact that a specification that improperly records the user's needs, more than any other single factor, is likely to jeopardize a project's success. Therefore Structured Analysis replaces the old-style functional specification with a *structured* specification, with the qualities of being

- graphic and concise
- top-down partitioned
- non-redundant
- logical, not physical*

These same characteristics, as you will recall from Chapter 3, also describe the designer's main tool, the structure chart — a similarity that derives from a shared structured philosophy. Below I briefly explain each of these qualities; in the remainder of the chapter, I elaborate on them more fully.

Graphic and concise: The structured specification contains pictures of the system, rather than screeds of turgid verbiage. Users are more likely to look at pictures than they are to read a document that is longer than *War and Peace* but less interesting than a telephone directory. For the same reason, designers are likely to read it and understand it, and are less likely to throw it away and start all over because of its length and baffling inconsistencies.

Top-down partitioned: Because the system is broken into pieces that are as independent as possible, the user can review the system in small, digestible segments. The partitioning is done in a top-down fashion to show broad, general views of the system, followed by narrow, detailed views of a "local" area. The advantage for the designer is that the top-down partitioned specification helps him not only to understand the proposed system, but also to design it in a top-down partitioned fashion.

Non-redundant: In the structured specification, a piece of information is recorded once and only once. This non-redundant aspect ensures consistency and easy updating — but it doesn't ensure correctness! In fact, the author of a structured specification must pay great attention to correctness because, as the adage goes, "if you say something only once, you'd better say it right." The user does not get bogged down in repetitious detail. The designer can readily identify system components and then translate these into areas to be designed.

Logical, not physical: Finally, the structured specification concentrates on what the system will do for the user (the logical), and not on how the system will be implemented by any particular machine (the physical). Since physical decisions are deferred, the designer, at the proper time, can make whatever computer-oriented decisions are deemed best to implement the user's system.

---

*"Physical," as used in Structured Analysis, means having the characteristics of a particular implementation. "Logical" means showing the essential features without regard to any specific implementation.

Using a structured specification, the user gains a clear understanding of the system being specified, and the designer can create a Structured Design more quickly and accurately than he could from an old-fashioned functional specification (as we will see in greater detail in Chapter 9).

4.2 Components of the structured specification

The tools of Structured Analysis are

- data flow diagram (DFD)
- data dictionary
- tools to describe policy: structured English, decision tree, decision table
- data access diagram

These tools not only provide an analyst with the means to carry out a disciplined, accurate analysis, but they also comprise the end-product of analysis — the structured specification. Therefore, as a designer, you must be conversant with each tool, even though you may not be directly concerned with analysis yourself. I describe each of the tools below and give you a brief résumé of how a structured specification is created, so that you can talk to the analyst on his own terms. However, this chapter will not make you a structured analyst. So, if you intend to use the tools of Structured Analysis to talk to users or to do any analysis yourself, then I implore you *please, please* to first read at least one book on modern analysis.*

4.2.1 The data flow diagram

The data flow diagram is used to partition a system, and (with the data dictionary) is the principal tool of Structured Analysis and the principal component of the structured specification. It is chiefly to this tool that the structured specification owes its desirable qualities of being graphic, concise, partitioned, and non-redundant. A DFD is a network representation of a system, and shows the active components of the system and the data interfaces between them. It is also known informally

---

*Among the best sources are: T. DeMarco's *Structured Analysis and System Specification* (New York: YOURDON Press, 1978); C. Gane and T. Sarson's *Structured Systems Analysis: Tools and Techniques* (New York: Improved System Technologies, Inc., 1977); V. Weinberg's *Structured Analysis* (New York: YOURDON Press, 1978); and *IEEE Transactions on Software Engineering,* Vol. SE-3, No. 1 (January 1977), issue devoted to Structured Analysis.

as a **Bubble Chart**, since it consists of little circles resembling bubbles.

The DFD has been around for a long time. Its origins are lost in the mists of history, but it seems to have been invented independently by a number of people at several different times. The earliest usage of the DFD recorded in folklore was in France in the 1920s. There, it was used to reorganize an office full of clerks in a large quill-and-inkpot bureaucracy. The consultant tackling the reorganization drew one circle for each clerk and one arrow for each document passing between clerks. Using this diagram, he devised a scheme by which two clerks passing many documents to and fro would sit close together, and clerks with little interaction would sit far apart. Thus was born the first document flow diagram, the forerunner of the DFD.

4.2.1.1 Components of the DFD

The DFD comprises four graphic elements: the data flow, the process, the data store, and the source/sink, shown in Fig. 4.1 and described in the following paragraphs.

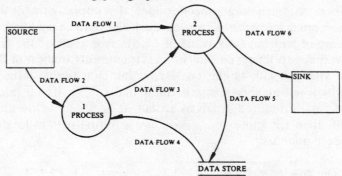

Figure 4.1

The *data flow* is an extremely important DFD element. (It must be: It gives its name to the whole tool.) You might think of it as a conveyor belt in a factory, and picture the part orders on the conveyor belt moving along one after another through the factory.* The name of a typical piece of data is written alongside the data flow, and must be as precise as possible; the direction of the arrow shows which way the data is flowing. For example,

PART ORDER

---

*An alternative way to visualize a data flow is as being a pipeline, carrying not water or oil but pieces of data.

If a data flow is like a conveyor belt in a factory, then a *process* is like a worker in that factory. A process can transform data in either of two ways.

1. It can transform the structure of data, for example, by reformatting it.

2. It can transform the information contained in data (or generate new information), for example, by changing a regular price to a trade-discount price.

In Fig. 4.2, the bubble shows the process with its name (PRICE EGG ORDER, in this case) written inside. The name of the process should be a meaningful statement of its function — the same convention we had for naming modules on the structure chart. Within the bubble is a reference number which is used, as we'll see in Section 4.2.1.2, to find the details of the bubble on another diagram.

This particular "worker," PRICE EGG ORDER, is at the end of EGG ORDER conveyor belt and at the beginning of PRICED EGG ORDER conveyor belt. It takes each order for eggs as it comes along, adds the appropriate price by referring to the PRICE OF EGGS FILE, and puts each priced egg order onto the PRICED EGG ORDER conveyor belt.

In order to "earn its salary," a process must transform data. Very clearly, PRICE EGG ORDER has done some transformation. But what about the situation shown in Fig. 4.3?

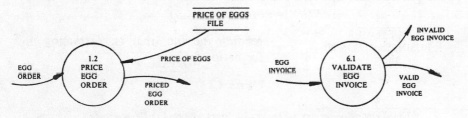

Figure 4.2   Figure 4.3

VALIDATE EGG INVOICE checks each EGG INVOICE. If the invoice is correct, the data is sent along the VALID EGG INVOICE conveyor belt; otherwise, it goes onto the INVALID EGG INVOICE conveyor belt. But the data still looks *exactly the same!* How can we say that VALIDATE EGG IN- VOICE has transformed data, because any particular VALID EGG INVOICE looks no different than it did as it came in as an EGG INVOICE? The process VALIDATE EGG INVOICE has transformed data because there is more information in a VALID EGG INVOICE than there is in a raw EGG IN-VOICE; we can guarantee that each VALID EGG INVOICE is valid. Any process that separates sheep from goats, good records from bad ones, wheat from chaff, or goods received transactions from customer billing transactions is performing a real job.

The clue to whether the data has been transformed is if the name of the data flowing out from a process is different from the name of the data flowing in.

So far, the data that we've seen has been riding through the DFD on data flows. But there are areas within the DFD in which data can find havens of rest from their otherwise hectic lives. Those places are *data stores.*

A data store is a time-delayed repository of data. It's not a place to buy discount data, but rather, it's another term for a file — so long as you keep in mind that a data store is not necessarily a computer disk file or a tape file. It could be one of those, but it could also be a wallet or purse in which you keep credit card vouchers, a 19th century slate on which a shopkeeper maintains a list of all customers owing money to the shop, an area of working storage, a circular card index, a futuristic read-only chromosomic memory, a diary of appointments, or anything else that can hold information.

A data store on a DFD is drawn as a pair of parallel lines. To find the name of the file, you have to read between the lines. The operations you can perform on a file are shown below:

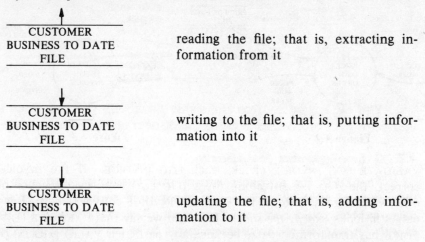

CUSTOMER BUSINESS TO DATE FILE — reading the file; that is, extracting information from it

CUSTOMER BUSINESS TO DATE FILE — writing to the file; that is, putting information into it

CUSTOMER BUSINESS TO DATE FILE — updating the file; that is, adding information to it

You might think that an update would be shown as a read and a write. However, if a file is read only to enable a subsequent write, then the read is customarily omitted. For example, in order to write the new business to-date to a file, you'd first have to read the old business to-date and add this month's business to it. Not showing the read makes it easier to spot mistakes, such as a write-only file (which would have inward data flows without any outward flows). If, however, you were using the information from the read for a purpose additional to the update — for example, to generate a report — then you'd certainly include the read on the DFD.

Most files need to be accessed by means of a key, the piece of information that identifies a unique record in a file. Why haven't I shown any keys? The reason is that the key is an access mechanism, not a flow of information, and therefore has no place on a DFD. An additional reason for not showing a key on a DFD is that we don't want to commit ourselves to any particular access method.

When is it necessary to show a file on a DFD? There are two main purposes for a file: The first is to be able to access a piece of information more than once, and the second is to use information in a different order from that in which it entered the system. Clearly, in each case data flows alone will not do the job: Data will have to be held in a data store for some length of time.

The *source and sink* show, respectively, where the data required by the system comes from and where the data produced by the system goes. A source is a provider of data flows for the system, and a sink is a receiver of data flows from the system. A single box could be a source and a sink. For instance,

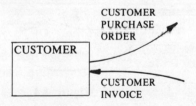

You can regard sources and sinks, along with the data flows that they provide or receive, as defining the domain of study for a system.

4.2.1.2 Leveling a data flow diagram

The DFD for a sizable system may consist of thousands and thousands of bubbles. A piece of paper large enough to hold all of these bubbles could cover the floor of an office and probably the walls as well. A way out of this problem might be to cut the large sheet into, say, one hundred smaller sheets, and to mark each data flow that appears at the edge of a sheet with a connector to show how the sheets fit together. Such a DFD would be photocopiable and more portable, but would have all the readability of a disassembled jigsaw puzzle.

A better solution to the problem is to partition the DFD in a top-down way. A reasonable partitioning to choose is one that reflects the way in which the user perceives his business as well as how the analyst carried out his analysis.* For example, an analyst studying the operations of a company would be likely to look first at how the company was organized into departments before he looked at how Peggy Blatz dealt with pink form GXRQ 93 B-1.

An analyst called in to data flow World-on-a-Chip, Inc., the microprocessor company owned by Bert Ramcode, might come up with a DFD like the one in Fig. 4.4:

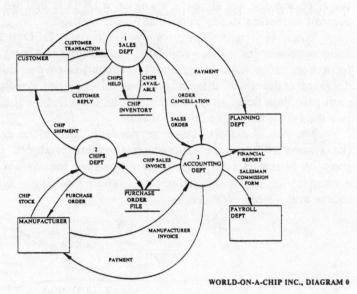

WORLD-ON-A-CHIP INC., DIAGRAM 0

Figure 4.4

Notice that the analyst's assignment was not to analyze the whole company: The Research and Development department, for example, is not shown at all. The Payroll department is shown only because of its interaction with the Accounting department; however, its business is outside the domain of the analysis.

If we want more detail, we can look, in turn, inside the Sales, Chips, and Accounting departments, by examining the information represented by a particular bubble in the DFD. Let's choose the Sales

---

*Later in analysis, the analyst should change his partitioning to reflect the fundamental nature of the business, rather than the way in which the user happens to carry it out. This second — logical — partitioning will be of more use to the designer.

department bubble, Bubble 1, and treat it as a whole little system in it-self (see Fig. 4.5).

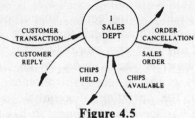

Figure 4.5

When we look inside Bubble 1, we see that it comprises further bubbles ("workers within the department," if you like), as shown in Fig. 4.6:

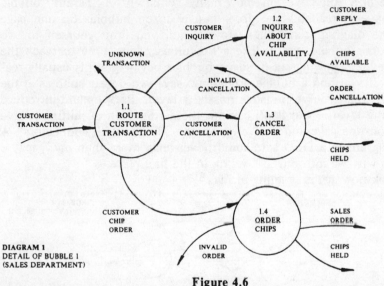

Figure 4.6

Notice that the inputs to and the outputs from Bubble 1 correspond to the inputs and outputs of Diagram 1: CUSTOMER TRANS-ACTION, CHIPS AVAILABLE, CUSTOMER REPLY, ORDER CANCELLATION, SALES ORDER, and CHIPS HELD are present in both. That correspon-dence of inputs and outputs should come as no surprise, because Di-agram 1 is just a detailed version of Bubble 1. But there is one excep-tion: Rejects — for example, unknown transactions or invalid orders — do not correspond to outputs from Bubble 1. This convention prevents a DFD from turning into a mass of spaghetti. In a typical DFD, errors, or rejects, are detected by many different bubbles. There's usually little that can be done about these errors except to report them. To obscure the DFD with crossed lines and to double its size in order to list errors is pointless. *Detect* errors, certainly, but leave them as reject stubs.

Concentrate first on the normal flow of data, rather than on the abnormal flow.

How detailed should leveling get? The purpose of leveling is to partition a large system without sacrificing one's sanity. Diagram 1 hasn't really *specified* anything any more than did the higher-level diagram. That specification will be provided by an English-like description of the procedures of the bottom-level bubbles. So, when you get to the point at which the operation of a bubble can be described in about a page, leveling has served its purpose. It has partitioned the system into manageable units, and further partitioning is pointless, unproductive, and often very difficult.

The only rule governing how many "children" a "parent" bubble should have is readability. More than a dozen bubbles on one page makes the diagram confusing. However, if you limit yourself to two offspring per bubble, you'll take a ridiculously long time to reach the bottom level. Drawing six or seven bubbles per diagram is usually reasonable. If you find a bubble producing, say, two dozen bubbles at the next level, then you've probably missed a level. Back up and introduce the missing level — but don't commit the cardinal sin of putting twelve bubbles on one page and twelve on another, linked with connectors. A single diagram in a DFD set should never span more than one page — for that's why we introduced leveling in the first place.

Look now at the leveling in Fig. 4.7:

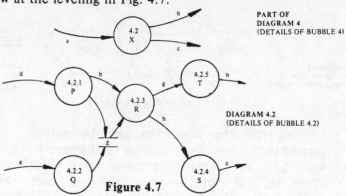

PART OF
DIAGRAM 4
(DETAILS OF BUBBLE 4)

DIAGRAM 4.2
(DETAILS OF BUBBLE 4.2)

Figure 4.7

On first examination, there appear to be two errors. First, in Diagram 4.2, there's a file called z, which wasn't in Diagram 4. That's not an error. The reason we didn't see it before is the same reason we didn't see data flow g before: It's a detail of the inside of Bubble 4.2, and of no concern to us at the Diagram-4 level. The convention for files follows: Show a file at the highest level at which it's used by more than one bubble; at that level, show all references to the file; at lower levels, you may show the file again to enhance the readability of the DFD.

The second possible error in Diagram 4.2 is that inputs d and e don't balance with input a to Bubble 4.2. This may be an error, but it's also possible that d and e together comprise input a. For example, PART CODE NUMBER and PART QUANTITY ORDERED might comprise PART ORDER LINE. If you encounter this situation, you should rush to the data dictionary and verify that an a really consists of a d and an e. If so, this is a legitimate case of data leveling; otherwise, it's a mistake.

I'm sure that by now you've guessed the numbering convention used in leveling DFDs. The children of Bubble 1, for example, are numbered Bubbles 1.1, 1.2, . . . , 1.5. Conversely, the parent of Bubbles 1.1, 1.2, . . . , 1.5 is Bubble 1. You find the parent of a bubble by striking the last digit of its number; the parent of Bubbles 1, 2 and 3 is by convention numbered Bubble 0.

Bubble 0 is the granddaddy of them all, representing the whole of the system under analysis. It appears in the very top diagram of the DFD set, the diagram that is called the *context diagram*. This diagram is designed to show the system in perspective to the rest of the world.

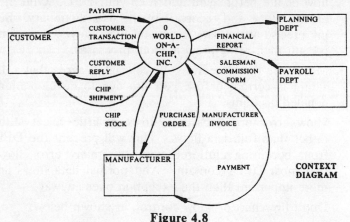

Figure 4.8

The context diagram looks trivial: just one bubble for the whole system with the inputs and their sources, and the outputs and their sinks. But it's an essential diagram, because it delineates the scope of the analysis and defines the system in terms of its inputs and outputs. For example, the system depicted in Fig. 4.8 isn't really World-on-a-Chip, Inc. — it represents only a part of that august company.

I've described the context diagram in terms of its use to the analyst and user. It does, however, serve a useful purpose for the designer as well. It enables the designer to identify the major transactions of a system in terms of their inputs and outputs. The act of identifying transactions forms the cornerstone of the design strategy called transaction analysis, which is covered in Chapter 10.

4.2.1.3 Drawing a data flow diagram

As a designer, you will have less call to create DFDs than an analyst will, but you should have a working knowledge of how to set about drawing one. The essential steps are set forth below:

- Start at the outside of a particular diagram. Draw all the inputs and outputs.

- Work from the outside in, or from the middle out, or from the input to the output, or from the output to the input. Build your DFD as you would a jigsaw puzzle, staying with one strategy until you get stuck. Then you switch to another one. Often you'll find that this new strategy allows you to break your previous logjam. So it is with DFDs. If you get stuck with one strategy, don't give up. Work some place else on the diagram.

- Make sure you know the composition of a new data flow or file before you add it to your DFD. Give it a precise name and record it in the data dictionary. Being precise about data flows and files is even more important than being precise about processes.

- Make sure that you and your colleagues agree that a diagram is correct before you proceed to develop more detailed diagrams.

- Show error or reject data flows as little reject stubs rather than full data flows. This will prevent the DFD from becoming cluttered with the many error flows that most DFDs contain. And normal data flows are more important than the exception ones anyway.

- Don't flowchart or show control, as shown below:

WRONG, WRONG, WRONG

There's no need for a loop back to get another data item, as there is in a flowchart. Remember our image of the data flow as a conveyor belt or pipeline.

- Ignore problems of initialization (opening files) and of termination (closing files), for on a DFD we can pretend that the system has been running forever and always will (there's nothing like optimism!). If we look at the system in its steady state, then we needn't be concerned about dealing with the first or last of anything.

- Be prepared to use and throw away a lot of paper while developing DFDs. Very few of us achieve perfection at the first attempt. So, take advantage of the fact that the human brain is very good at spotting flaws: Draw *something* and then concentrate on improving it.

There are some telltale symptoms of likely errors in a DFD: One sign is bubbles that magically create output from data they don't have; for example, a bubble that calculates net salary without having gross salary as an input. Other symptoms are write-only files and dead-end data flows, which enter a system but never get used. All these symptoms derive from a faulty analysis.

Symptoms of bad partitioning are unnameable data flows, unnameable processes, and overly complicated interfaces. A pair of bubbles with ten different data flows between them is likely to occur in a high-level DFD. But in more detailed DFDs, this number of data flows between bubbles represents an analysis that has probably not uncovered the fundamental functions or data flows of the system. The aim of the analyst should be to attain minimal interfaces between bubbles. The way in which the analyst achieves this aim is through leveled DFDs, discussed in the previous section.

4.2.1.4 Differences between DFDs and flowcharts

A data flow diagram is sometimes confused with that traditional development tool, the program flowchart. However, the two tools are very different. Below I sum up the characteristics of a DFD and contrast it with the flowchart.

A DFD partitions a system into pieces small enough to be specified concisely, and shows the data flow interfaces between the pieces. The contents of data flows (and data stores) are specified precisely in the data dictionary. (See Section 4.2.2.) A leveled set of DFDs shows both the broad organization of a system and the specific details of each portion of the system.

DFDs don't show control or procedural sequences as a flowchart does: A flowchart is a view of the world from a mythical CPU. It's a log of "first you do this, then this . . . and finally this" — exactly one thing at a time in some defined order. The real world just doesn't work like that — if you attempt to draw a flowchart for a user's office, you'll see what I mean. (Furthermore, if you ask a user where his program counter is, he'll have you committed for life.)

The real world of factories, small offices, and giant corporations is one of cooperating processes, all working at once and all communicating data with one another. The DFD portrays exactly that. But should you ever find yourself analyzing the Random Dormouse Corporation (in which one person works on a document while everyone else sleeps and then that person wakes up another person, hands over the document, and goes to sleep), you have my full permission to use a flowchart.

4.2.1.5 Physical and logical data flow diagrams

A fundamental tenet of Structured Analysis is that DFDs should be used to sweep aside as many irrelevancies as possible in how a user currently *happens* to do his business, and to uncover the logical functions essential to the way in which he *has* to do his business.

The way in which the user *happens* to do his business is depicted on a *physical,* or *implementation-dependent, DFD.* For example,

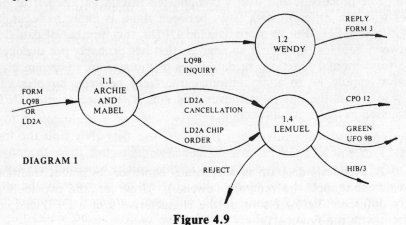

DIAGRAM 1

Figure 4.9

Figure 4.9 is utterly implementation-dependent. The names of actual people are shown, together with the code numbers of the user's specific forms. The DFD below (which we've already seen as Fig. 4.6) is the logical equivalent of Fig. 4.9. Figure 4.10 depicts the functions *essential* to the user's business and is called a *logical DFD.*

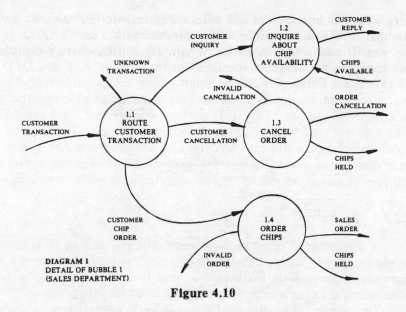

Figure 4.10

The physical DFD is a useful document with which the analyst obtains a good initial feel for how the user's shop is run. It's also useful for communicating with the user, who can relate to such bubbles as Lemuel or Wendy and to such data flows as the Green UFO 9B. But it's not a very useful document from which to develop a computer system (or any other equivalent system, for that matter). To have a function simulating Lemuel would be futile, since Lemuel may have 101 distinct and unrelated activities in World-on-a-Chip, Inc.

The physical DFD should serve only as a springboard toward deriving a logical equivalent. However, the user may find the logical DFD of his business a little harder to understand than the physical DFD: VALIDATE CUSTOMER TRANSACTION might be rather less tangible to him than Archie and Mabel. But, there's no reason why the analyst shouldn't annotate a logical DFD with some physical information (either graphically, in a different color, or orally, as he walks the user through it). This extra information will help the user to relate his logical functions to the way in which he happens to implement them in his shop.

Since I said that Structured Analysis shies away from the physical, you might think it strange that on the DFD for Bert Ramcode's World-on-a-Chip, I showed the actual goods — the chips — flowing as if they were data. When the user's primary business deals with the flow of materials, the analyst almost always has to include them in his DFD in order to reach a common ground of understanding with the user. However, if the domain of study had been simply employees' payroll, then I certainly *would* look askance at seeing product names on the DFD.

Let us take a look at another example: Sid Cardome's Odds and Sods Corporation, shown in the DFD below. Figure 4.11 is a DFD of one part of Sid Cardome's corporation.*

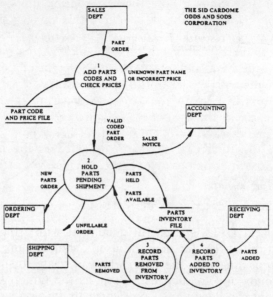

Figure 4.11

Sid is in the unusual business of selling spare parts for vacuum cleaners and jet-aircraft engines, and describes his operation as follows:

> "Orders from customers are received typically (but not necessarily) by phone in the Sales department. Someone in the Sales department enters the order on the standard green parts-order form, which he then hands to Artie Choake. Artie checks it against his card file, and enters the code number of the part alongside the part name. Sometimes, however, the order is for a part that Artie doesn't know or that has been mispriced by the Sales department. In each of those cases, he marks the order invalid and puts it aside.

---

*For the purposes of this DFD, I'll consider only a very small part of Sid Cardome's operation. I'm not concerned with his payroll, the taxes he pays to the government, how he collects payment from his customers, or even how the Accounting department interacts with, say, the Shipping department.

"Valid orders, which Artie has coded, he hands to Attila O'Rafferty in the Holding Area. Attila first checks the Parts Inventory Book to see whether enough parts are in stock to fill the order. If stock is insufficient, Attila rejects the order and sends a note to the Ordering department to buy more. (I'm thinking of changing this cavalier policy of rejecting too-large orders, because I'm losing my best customers.) If there are enough parts in stock, Attila marks the quantity ordered to be held pending shipment of this order, and he sends a pink sales notice to Accounting.

"Doris Onedin in the Shipping department ships the ordered parts to the customer, and marks on the Parts Inventory File that the parts are no longer being held. Cray Z. Leggs in the Receiving department increases the parts inventory count when a shipment is received from the manufacturer."

Sid Cardome's description of his business contains many details that are not apparent from the DFD in Fig. 4.11. For example, we cannot deduce from the DFD that part codes and prices are kept on a card file. However, there are several points on which it, as a classical English description rather than a specification, can be criticized. Using what I've said about specifications and DFDs in this chapter, let us look more closely at that description:

- We're told that the Sales department receives orders from customers typically by phone, but should the Sales department be considered as part of our domain of study or not?

- We don't care what color the standard "green" parts-order form is — but we would like to know what information it bears.

- We don't care who checks the parts-order form, nor do we care that Artie's file is on cards. But, we do care what the name of the file is and what it holds.

- Is the Parts Inventory Book used by Attila the same as the Parts Inventory File used by Doris? In fact, it is. (Inconsistencies in terminology in large specifications have contributed to several large projects' demise.)

- The whole description is rampantly physical. (But mercifully at least we're not talking about disks and tapes and job steps yet.) There's little likelihood that a verbose specification, with its inconsistencies, redundancies and plain old errors, could ever be successfully translated into its logical equivalent for a typical project. The task would be just too gargantuan.

In the DFD in Fig. 4.11, Sid Cardome's Accounting department is shown as a sink; that is, it is just outside the boundary of our study.

To put it graphically,

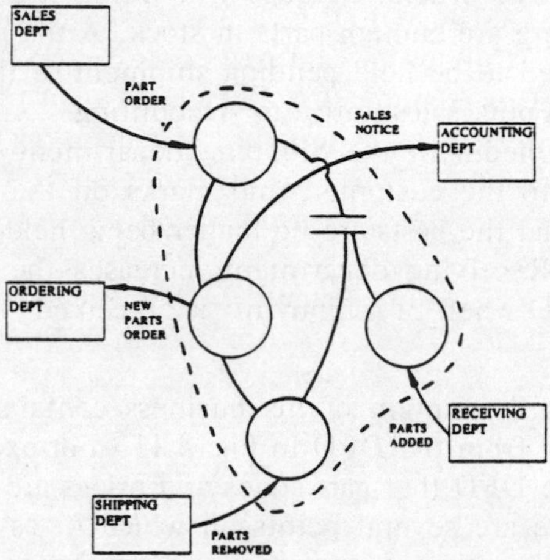

Figure 4.12

The dotted lines in Fig. 4.12 mark the boundary of the system to be studied. Whatever is within them *is* the system and is subject to analysis; whatever is outside isn't our concern and is worthy only of cursory scrutiny. How the sources obtain their data and what the sinks do with it is their affair and cannot affect us. (The domain of the analysis should be defined so that this will be true.)

Had the study been enlarged to include the Accounting department, that department would have appeared as a process (or a group of processes) interacting with the rest of the system and, no doubt, having new sources and sinks.

So far, we've explored the use of the DFD to partition a complex system into manageable pieces. However, we have yet to specify the components of the DFD — the data and the processes. In the next section, I describe the data dictionary, the chief tool for specifying data. (In Section 4.2.3, I describe tools for specifying processes.)

4.2.2 The data dictionary

The *data dictionary,* as it is used in Structured Analysis, *is not* one of those packages developed in the 1960s to enable the generation of the PIC × (23)s for a COBOL DATA DIVISION. The Structured Analysis data dictionary is an analysis tool that primarily records the information content of data, and includes physical format details of data only as an addendum. More precisely, the data dictionary contains the definitions of all data mentioned in the DFD, in a process specification, or in the data dictionary itself. Composite data (data that can be further divided) is defined in terms of its components; elementary data (data that cannot be further divided) is defined in terms of the meaning of each of the values that it can assume. Thus, the data dictionary is composed of definitions of data flows, files, data used within processes, and elementary parts of the above.

Later in analysis, or in design, further secondary information about data may be added. This extra information may include details of frequency and volume, peaks and valleys, size, response time, data capture devices and protocol (for data flows), data storage devices and data access methods (for files), affected users, security, priority, implementation schedules, and so on. I shall not mention these physical characteristics of data again. Henceforth, we shall be concerned only with keeping track of the *logical* information content of data in the data dictionary.

4.2.2.1 Data dictionary definition of composite data

Composite data is data that is made up of smaller items of data. There are three fundamental ways in which composite data can be constructed: by sequencing data items, by repeating a single data item a number of times, and by selecting one from several items of data. In the data dictionary, these means of construction are shown like this:

sequence:	data item A	IS	data item P
		AND	data item Q
		AND	data item R
repetition:	data item B	IS	ITERATIONS OF
			data item S
selection:	data item C	IS	EITHER
			data item T
		OR	data item U
		OR	data item V

Below is a concrete example of the use of each of the three relationships:

mailing address	IS	name
	AND	street address
	AND	city name
	AND	state
	AND	zip code
customer payment file	IS	ITERATIONS OF
		customer payment record
customer transaction	IS	EITHER
		customer deposit
	OR	customer withdrawal

Surprisingly, *any* piece of data can be defined by various combinations of these relationships. For example,

invoice	IS	mailing address
	AND	invoice number
	AND	ITERATIONS OF invoice line
	AND	invoice total

where I've used both the sequence and repetition relationships in one definition.

Now, the operators (such as ITERATIONS OF and EITHER) used in these definitions are very verbose. There is a short form for each of the operators, which most analysts use for their entries in the data dictionary. There is also a graphic notation (adapted from Michael Jackson*) that can be a useful tool, but suffers from not being so easily machine-updateable. These three notations are different ways of saying exactly the same thing:

Long form

sequence:	telephone number	IS area code AND office code AND number
repetition:	passenger list	IS ITERATIONS OF passenger name
selection:	customer order	IS EITHER vacuum cleaner order OR jet engine order

Short form

sequence:	telephone number	= area code + office code + number
repetition:	passenger list	= {passenger name}
selection:	customer order	= [vacuum cleaner order	jet engine order]

---

*M.A. Jackson, *Principles of Program Design* (New York: Academic Press, 1975).

Graphic form

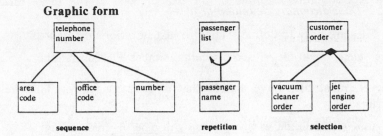

sequence   repetition   selection

In general, there are many different ways to define a piece of data in the data dictionary. But some definitions are easier to understand than others. For example, let's say that the following two definitions are true:

invoice = invoice number + mailing address + {invoice line} + invoice total
invoice line = quantity ordered + item number + unit price + item subtotal

Read these definitions to yourself. Visualize how an invoice would look before you proceed. Why couldn't I have defined invoice as

invoice = invoice number + mailing address +
{quantity ordered + item number + unit price +
item subtotal} + invoice total

which amounts to the same definition as the preceding one? I could have defined invoice in the second way, just as I could have leveled a DFD straight from the context diagram to the very bottom-level bubbles in one pass. But the second definition of invoice omits a well-defined level of the data. To leave out the invoice line — a good, problem-related piece of data — would certainly confuse the user. The data dictionary should have top-down characteristics similar to those of the leveled DFDs.

Some additional data dictionary symbols are shown below:

* everything between asterisks is a comment *

$^5_1$ {invoice line} means "between 1 and 5 invoice lines"

(area code) means "area code may or may not be present," that is, that it's optional[†]

[†]Some analysts also use parentheses in data flow names on a DFD — for example, (VALID) EGG ORDER. In this case, the parentheses mean: Look for the definition of the data flow in the data dictionary under EGG and not under VALID.

4.2.2.2 Data dictionary definition of files

Files are easy to define: They're just iterations of records.

customer credit file = {social security number + credit rating}

However, most files have a field that is used as a key. That field is underlined:

customer credit file = {<u>social security number</u> + credit rating}

Sometimes, it is worthwhile to add a comment giving the organization of the file, for example,

* organization is sequential by social security number *

For more complex files and interrelated groups of files, another tool, the data access diagram, is needed to depict file organization. (See Section 4.2.4.) This diagram is also included in the structured specification.

4.2.2.3 Data dictionary definition of data elements

A *data element* is a piece of data that we cannot (or choose not to) partition further. Sooner or later, as you continue to partition a composite piece of data, you'll reach the data elements at the bottom (in the same way that you reach the primitive bubbles at the bottom level of a DFD). Often a data element is self-defining, such as customer name or zip code; there's little point in elaborating on those. However, other data elements might not be so obvious. These must be defined in terms of the values (either discrete or continuous) that they can take on.

Here is an example of a data element entry:

DATA ELEMENT NAME:	credit rating	
ALIASES:	none	
VALUES/MEANINGS	AA	great
	A	good
	B	acceptable
	C	poor
	D	deadbeat
	DD	criminally deadbeat

4.2.3 Tools to express policy

A set of leveled DFDs doesn't specify anything. Rather, it partitions the system so that each part can be specified concisely and independently of the other parts, and it declares the interfaces between the parts. The smallest parts of the system are the bubbles at the lowest level (usually called *functional primitives*). Only these bubbles need to be specified, for together they comprise the whole system. It would be pointless to specify bubbles at a higher level, since they are nothing more than collections of lower-level bubbles.

Having gotten this far in partitioning, we wouldn't get into too much trouble if we wrote our specifications for bottom-level processes (mini-specs) in plain English, as we used to write our functional specifications. But we already saw some problems with plain English in the prose description of Sid Cardome's operation: Plain English isn't always so plain! In particular, an English specification can be confusing, ambiguous, inconsistent, verbose, and incomplete to its readers, although its author will defend it to the death as being clear, definite, consistent, terse, and complete. And such subjectivity is always compounded when the prose has been written by a herd of analysts. In order to avoid the pitfalls of the old-style specification, we need some goals for our specification tools:

- There must be one mini-spec for each functional primitive in the DFD set.

- The mini-spec must state the way in which the data flows entering the functional primitive are transformed into the data flows leaving it.

- The mini-spec must state the policy that governs the transformation, not the method for implementing that policy. That is, it should say *what* is to be done but should be inscrutable about *how* it is to be done.

- The mini-spec should seek to control redundancy. In particular, it should not restate something already stated in the DFD or in the data dictionary. (However, a little redundancy *is* permissible if it improves the readability of the mini-spec.)

- The set of constructs used to build the mini-spec should be small and simple. In addition, they should oblige us to express ourselves in a standard way.

Structured Analysis offers three tools for expressing policy: structured English, the decision tree, and the decision table. Structured English is the most generally applicable of these tools; however, though the decision tree and decision table are more specialized, they are superior to structured English when the policy to be specified concerns combinations of many independent conditions. In the next three sections I describe the form and application of each of these specification tools.

4.2.3.1 Structured English

Structured English is a specification tool that provides a pruned-down version of English embedded in the simple constructs of Structured Programming. Its vocabulary comprises

- imperative English verbs (adjectives and adverbs are frowned upon because they're subjective and liable to be misinterpreted)
- terms from the data dictionary
- reserved words to denote policy logic

Its syntax comprises

- simple sentences
- closed-end decisions
- closed-end repetitions
- combinations of the above three

An example of a mini-spec written in structured English follows. The number 6.4.7 relates the mini-spec to the bubble whose policy it describes.

6.4.7 PRODUCE CUSTOMER INVOICE

For each customer order form, do the following:
1 Enter the customer name and address on the invoice.
2 If the customer category is "SPECIAL"
   2.1 Get the discount from the discount file
      using special indicator
   2.2 Otherwise (ordinary customer)
      Set discount to 0%.

3 For each sales item on the customer order form, do the following:
   3.1 Copy stock number and quantity order to the invoice.
   3.2 Get unit price from the price file
      using stock number.
   3.3 Set item subtotal to unit price $\times$ quantity ordered $\times$ $(100 - \text{discount})$.

4 Set invoice total to sum of item subtotals.
5 Set amount due to invoice total $-$ amount paid.

I stress that there is no *one* structured English dialect. The analyst has to compromise between making structured English tight and precise on the one hand, and making it palatable to the user on the other. He mustn't get too fussy about its exact form, especially if he's likely to scare the user with austerity and rigor.

We have already seen use of the constructs of structured English in the above example. Below is a table showing the representation of each structured English construct in flowchart form, with some examples of how each construct might be written:

CONSTRUCT	FLOWCHART EXAMPLE	STRUCTURED ENGLISH EXAMPLE
sequence of simple sentences	A	Copy . . . Get . . . Set . . . . . .
repetition	B	For each . . . do the following:
selection	C	If . . . Otherwise

The first remarkable characteristic of these three constructs is that they each have one flow of control in at the top and one flow of control out at the bottom. That means that they're guaranteed to fit one inside the other. For example, the flowchart A could fit inside the box of B. Or the flowchart C could fit into any of the boxes of A. This "nesting" could be carried to any depth — although, in practice, we seldom need to nest more than three deep.

The second remarkable thing about the constructs is that they are all you need to describe any policy. It has been proved that other constructs (such as the GOTO) are superfluous.*

The third remarkable quality is that we used exactly the same constructs — sequence, repetition, selection, and combinations thereof — to build data in the data dictionary.

---

*C. Böhm and G. Jacopini, "Flow Diagrams, Turing Machines and Languages with Only Two Formation Rules," *Communications of the ACM*, Vol. 9, No. 5 (May 1966), pp. 366-71. [Reprinted in E.N. Yourdon, ed., *Classics in Software Engineering* (New York: YOURDON Press, 1979), pp. 13-25.]

One advantage of using these building blocks for structured English, and of forbidding constructs like the GOTO, is that a policy can be read in a straight line. This is exactly the same advantage that Structured Programming gains with code. The human brain hates to jump about when it's reading: If it must, it very quickly goes off track. Further advantages are an enforced clarity and a consistency of style among different authors. If an analyst wishes to indulge in poetic license, he should do so somewhere other than in a system specification.

4.2.3.2 Decision trees

Structured English is not appropriate for some types of user policy. For example, if the user's action depends on several variables that together can take on a large number of different combinations, then a structured English description would be confusing and probably too deeply nested. In this case, use a *decision tree,* which is a graphic tool that separates out the independent conditions and shows the action(s) resulting from each possible combination. To "read" a decision tree, start on the left and trace a path to the right, using the value of each condition to direct you along the appropriate branch of the tree.

To show how simple a decision tree is to use, I give an example of a company-assisted savings policy, described first of all in the CUE language (Confusing Unstructured English) and then as a decision tree in Fig. 4.13:

"Here at H.H. Purvis Manufacturing, Inc., we believe in encouraging our employees to save. So we add a contribution of our own to whatever they put into our Savings Plan. In addition to the standard interest, participating employees receive from our Munificence Department our contribution of fifty percent of what they invest — provided they keep the sum in the plan for two years or more.

"However, we do limit the amount that an employee can save, depending on his salary and his length of service with us. An employee can put away up to five, six, or seven percent of the first $15,000 of his salary if he's been with us one year, two years, or more, respectively. If he's been with us one year, he can put away up to four percent of the next $10,000 and up to three percent of any excess. Two-year workers get five percent of any amount from $15,000 to $30,000 and four percent after that. Long-service people get to save up to seven percent of their first $15,000 — perhaps I already said that — and then six percent and five percent after that."

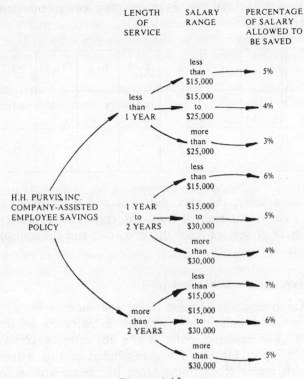

| LENGTH OF SERVICE | SALARY RANGE | PERCENTAGE OF SALARY ALLOWED TO BE SAVED |

Figure 4.13

In the figure, I've assumed that "long-service" means "having worked for H.H. Purvis for more than two years," and that long-service workers have the same $30,000 limit that one- to two-year employees have.

I believe that a decision tree is much clearer than the average narrative English — so clear, in fact, that it is self-explanatory.*

4.2.3.3 Decision tables

A *decision table†* is a tabular form of a decision tree. A decision table is more easily stored in a textual, machine-readable form than is a decision tree. However, I find a decision table to be less immediately understandable and user-acceptable than is a decision tree.

---

*However, if you want to read more about decision trees and their application, consult T. DeMarco, op. cit., pp. 222-25; or V. Weinberg, op. cit., pp. 126-30.
†T.R. Gildersleeve, *Decision Tables and Their Practical Application in Data Processing* (Englewood Cliffs, N.J.: Prentice-Hall, 1970).

The Purvis Savings Plan example produces a reasonably clear decision table:

LENGTH OF SERVICE	1	1	1	1—2	1—2	1—2	>2	>2	>2
SALARY ($000)	<15	15—25	>25	<15	15—30	>30	<15	15—30	>30
PERCENTAGE ALLOWED	5	4	3	6	5	4	7	6	5

In this decision table, the maximum percentage of salary that an employee can save is determined from the third row by selecting the appropriate length of service from the first row, and the appropriate salary from the second row.

4.2.3.4 Other specification techniques

Structured English, decision trees, and decision tables — although extremely valuable tools — by no means exhaust the possible tools for specification. For example, none of the above tools would be suitable to describe a report format. I was reminded of this when I visited a shop in which reams of deathless prose had been written to describe a CRT screen:

1. Put PROPERTY TAX ASSESSMENT as a header on LINE 1, centered
2. Put out 2 blank lines
3. On the left . . .

Yawn! Obviously, to describe a picture (a screen format, a user form, an aircraft terrain display, for instance), one would use a graphic format. Together with the data dictionary, that will be specification enough.

Other specification tools include formulas, extracts from existing user manuals, tables, and so on. The possibilities are endless!

4.2.4 Data access diagrams

A *data access diagram* (also known as a data structure diagram or a data subschema) shows the paths of access through stored data that are required by a particular application. An example is shown below in Fig.

4.14.* (Although I've shown the definitions of each file on the data access diagram for clarity, in practice these definitions of file contents would be kept in the data dictionary.)

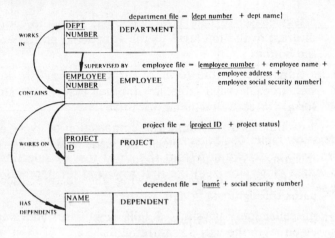

Figure 4.14

This diagram shows that we have four files: DEPARTMENT, EMPLOYEE, PROJECT, and DEPENDENT, whose keys are, respectively, DEPT NUMBER, EMPLOYEE NUMBER, PROJECT ID, and NAME. The diagram indicates that, for instance, if we have a DEPT NUMBER, then we want to find all the EMPLOYEES contained in that department. (The ⟶⟶ means that there's more than one EMPLOYEE contained in each DEPARTMENT.) Also, given an EMPLOYEE NUMBER, we can find the DEPARTMENT in which that EMPLOYEE works. (The ⟶ means that each EMPLOYEE works in exactly one DEPARTMENT.)

However, the data access diagram tells us that given a PROJECT ID, we have no desire to find out the EMPLOYEES engaged on that PROJECT. (There is no arrow from PROJECT to EMPLOYEE.) Also included alongside the data access arrows might be physical information such as the frequency of access, or required response times.

---

*Drawing a valid data access diagram is much harder than reading one, for there are many subtleties that may snare the unwary. If you want to learn about drawing them, I urge you to consult C. Date, *An Introduction to Data Base Systems,* 2nd ed. (Reading, Mass: Addison-Wesley, 1977); J. Martin, *Computer Data-Base Organization,* 2nd ed. (Englewood Cliffs, N.J.: Prentice-Hall, 1977); T. DeMarco, op. cit.; or C. Gane and T. Sarson, op. cit. A rigorous treatment of data access diagrams is beyond the scope of this book.

4.3 The assembled structured specification

In the structured specification, the following information should appear:

- a leveled set of data flow diagrams, from the context diagram at the top level to the functional primitives at the bottom

- a mini-spec (in the form of structured English, decision tree, decision table, or another easily understood form) for each functional primitive

- a data dictionary defining the composition of every data store and composite piece of data, and giving the meaning of every data element

- a data access diagram showing the required access paths through data in data stores

- miscellaneous physical details that are considered essential to the user's requirements

The tools of Structured Analysis are also extremely important to the designer to enable him to create a high-quality design. So we'll return to these analysis tools (especially the DFD) in Chapter 9, where we cover transform analysis, the major strategy for converting a DFD into a structure chart. But before that — in Chapters 6, 7, and 8 — we'll explore just what qualities we desire in a design. In the case study in Appendix E, we shall see all the tools of Structured Analysis and Structured Design used in concert.

Exercises

1. What is wrong with the following DFDs or pieces of DFDs?

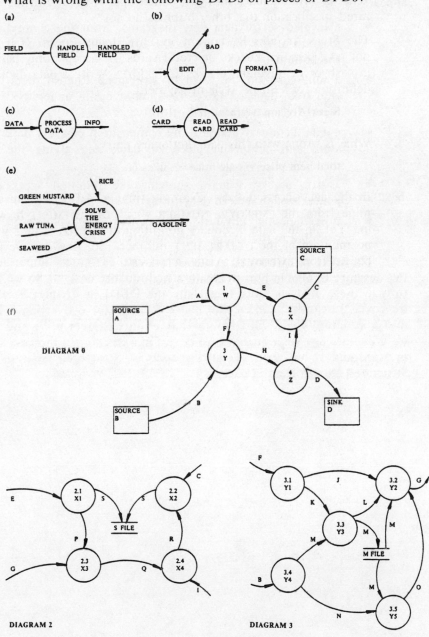

(a)

(b)

(c)

(d)

(e)

(f)

DIAGRAM 0

DIAGRAM 2

DIAGRAM 3

2. Why is the data flow that enters or leaves a file sometimes unnamed?

3. What is a functional primitive? What does it require in the structured specification that other bubbles do not?

4. The Steak-Acclaim Restaurant in East Hocus Pocus, N.J., does not take personal checks or credit cards. It accepts only payment in cash or in traveler's checks (or both). Write a data dictionary definition for a Steak-Acclaim payment.

    Steak-Acclaim payment = ?

5. What is wrong with this data dictionary entry?

    total item price = sale price + sales tax

6. In the data access diagram example (in Fig. 4.14), we can determine from the EMPLOYEE NUMBER which DEPARTMENT he works in. Yet, in the data dictionary definition of EMPLOYEE FILE we see no mention of the DEPARTMENT number. So, how can we possibly get from EMPLOYEE to DEPARTMENT?

Answers

1.   (a)   HANDLE FIELD isn't a process. A verb like HANDLE is much too wishy-washy to qualify as a process name.

    (b)   A data flow without a name does not exist. The guy who drew this piece of DFD evidently didn't have a clue as to what he was supposed to be editing and formatting.

    (c)   Having a data flow called DATA is like having a dog called "Dog." The name tells you nothing more than what you can see. Of course, a data flow carries DATA. Of course, it carries INFO. But what kind of data? The process name PROCESS DATA wins my Vagueness Sweepstakes every time. I defy you to tell me what that bubble does not do.

    (d)   In the old days of DFDs, READ CARD (or READ ANYTHING) was considered a process. Nowadays, it is not considered a process, since the data flow name doesn't change in any meaningful way from one side to the other; so we simply omit it.

    (e)   If you think that this bubble is OK, then I'd be very grateful if you'd send me the mini-spec for it. We believe in the old Structured Analysis adage that states that whatever is output must have been input.

    (f)   *Diagram 0:* The names are lousy. Bubble 2 (called X) is a great black hole, sucking data in and letting nothing out.

          Diagram 2: The names are still lousy. The diagram (with inputs C, E, I, G) doesn't correspond to Bubble 2 in Diagram 0 (with inputs C, E, I). The S FILE is a write-only file.

          Diagram 3: The names haven't improved yet. Diagram 3 (which has an output G) doesn't correspond to Bubble 3 (which has an output H) — unless G and H are aliases. If Bubble 3.3 doesn't use the data flow by putting it in the M FILE, then the partitioning is poor. Bubble 3.4 should put the M into the M FILE itself.

2.   In most cases, no name is the best name you could give to a data flow leaving a file. On the following page, the data flow has been named CUSTOMER RECORD:

which doesn't tell you much. The only time that annotating a reference to a file would tell you anything extra is when the data flow carries only part of a record from the file, for example:

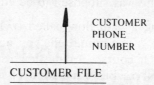

3. A functional primitive is a bubble in a leveled set of DFDs not partitioned into "children" bubbles. (It is *not,* as one of my students once suggested, a post-Impressionist artist.) Each functional primitive requires a mini-spec describing the policy by which it transforms its incoming data flows into its outgoing data flows.

4.
$$\text{Steak-Acclaim payment} = [\text{cash} \mid {}_1\{\text{traveler's check}\} \mid \\ \text{cash} + {}_1\{\text{traveler's check}\}]$$

Alternatively,

$$\text{Steak-Acclaim payment} = [\text{cash} + {}_0\{\text{traveler's check}\} \mid \\ {}_0\{\text{traveler's check}\}]$$

where ${}_0\{\text{traveler's check}\}$ means zero or more traveler's checks. There are a number of other solutions, some of which are almost incomprehensively obscure. In the data dictionary — as elsewhere — simplest is best.

5. The sign + is not a summation operator; it's a concatenation operator. In other words, it's *not* the + of

$$6 = 4 + 2 \quad (\text{NO!})$$

but the + of

$$\text{'}42\text{'} = \text{'}4\text{'} + \text{'}2\text{'} \quad (\text{YES!})$$

6. We don't know how to get from EMPLOYEE to DEPARTMENT. The data access diagram only records a requirement: It doesn't tell us how to implement it. The implementor of the data access diagram may choose to use a pointer, physical adjacency, or any other method. He may even choose to include a DEPT NUMBER in each EMPLOYEE record!

5

Module
Specification Methods

The structure chart, as I emphasized repeatedly in Chapter 3, shows only the overall structure of a system and deliberately suppresses almost all procedural detail. However, the programmer, who will be using the structure chart in order to derive his code, is very interested in procedural detail. How then can this information be provided to the programmer?

The answer is, by specifying each module on the structure chart. Three possible methods that you may use to specify a module are outlined in this chapter: module interface specification, specification by means of a Structured Analysis tool, and specification by pseudocode. These methods progress from the least detailed to the most detailed and illustrate the most commonly used of the many module specification methods available to a designer.

Specifying modules to programmers is a touchy political business. You must give a programmer something more than the structure chart in order to specify exactly what he has to program, but every programmer I've met would bristle and seethe if you told him *how* to do his job. And quite rightly. Deciding the most appropriate way to program what is required is the programmer's job; therein lies the creativity of programming.

5.1 Module interface specification

The best compromise between specifying too much and, even worse, specifying too little is to define what the module should do as an *interface specification* (or *interface contract*). This method allows you to define the function of a module without delving into excessive detail.

You tell the programmer of the module what input you promise to provide when you call his module, what output you expect when his module returns, and the function you expect his module to carry out. The function should be stated in a simple sentence that establishes the relationship between the module's inputs and outputs.

This is rather like what you would do if you were farming out work to a subcontractor: You would tell him what you want done and, so long as he delivered a quality product on time and within budget, you wouldn't care particularly about the details of how he did it. Presumably that was why you subcontracted the work in the first place: to let someone else worry about the details.

Figure 5.1 shows part of a structure chart containing a module called FIND TOTAL WORTH, which computes the total net assets of a group of bank customers.

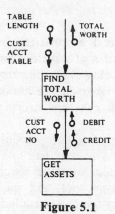

Figure 5.1

Following is an interface specification for the module FIND TOTAL WORTH:

module find total worth
function to find the total assets of a group of bank customers
uses table length PIC 9(3)
            (the number of customers in the group)
        cust acct table PIC 9(6) occurring 999 times
            (the valid account numbers of the customers to be summed)
returns total worth PIC S9(8).99
            (the total net assets, i.e., total credit − total debit of the group)

This interface specification provides a minimal amount of procedural detail to accompany the structure chart. Notice that I've included some physical descriptions (PIC 9(3), for example). In practice, this would not be necessary, because all of the data on the module inter-

faces would already be defined to the element level in the data dictionary by the end of the design process.

Equipped with the interface specification, the programmer is free
to code FIND TOTAL WORTH as he pleases, using a standard method or
some pet algorithm of his own.

Ideally, the contract between FIND TOTAL WORTH and its calling
module will be left in the final code, as documentation for the maintenance programmers that will indicate what that module is supposed to
do. Without a module specification, there is no way to debug a module.
Suppose you're called in to investigate a malfunction in a system written years ago by someone else. After some painstaking sleuthing, you
decide that the bug must be in one area of code — a single module,
say. Your line of thought may continue like this:

"Now, if only I knew what this module is *supposed* to do. There
doesn't seem to be any explanatory documentation anywhere. I guess
I'll just have to figure it out from the code. But wait a minute —
there's a bug in the code!"

This Catch-22 over which many a maintenance programmer has
lost sleep would be avoided if the original programmer had provided a
definition of the module's function. At the very worst, if the code being maintained were a total disaster, the module could be completely
rewritten from its specification.

5.2 Specification using a Structured Analysis tool

If Structured Analysis has preceded Structured Design, then the
process mini-specifications written for the structured specification will
also serve as module specifications. Although there isn't always an exact correspondence between the specification of a bubble and the
specification of a module, the bubble specification is usually sufficiently
descriptive for a programmer to work from.* I won't include a mini-
spec sample for the module FIND TOTAL WORTH since the previous
chapter showed techniques for creating a mini-spec.

---

*Typical differences between bubble specification and module specification include control,
end-of-file indicators, and error reporting (added during design); the accessing of physical
files; and the factoring of one bubble into several modules. These differences are covered
in Chapter 8.

5.3 Specification by pseudocode

Pseudocode is a much more detailed way to describe a module than is an interface specification, and it may well be more detailed than the mini-spec. Essentially, pseudocode strays from "what to do" into the domain of "how to do it." It is an informal language similar to structured English, but with two differences: First, it is not a tool of the user and analyst, but of the designer and programmer. Second, since the user doesn't have to see it, pseudocode can look as much like actual code as necessary.

Since pseudocode is much more detailed than module interface specification, there is less margin for error when the programmer translates it into actual code. Since pseudocode is closer to code than, say, structured English, there is less work for the programmer to do in order to attain the final code: In one shop where I worked as a consultant, there was a stringently enforced standard that called for detailed pseudocode for every module. As I reviewed the systems, I noticed a very odd thing: The final COBOL code typically had about thirty percent fewer lines than the pseudocode from which it was derived. I confronted the designers with this observation and asked them why they didn't just code each module in COBOL in the first place. Their unforgettable reply was, "But *we're* not programmers!"

Following is an example of one person's dialect of pseudocode:

```
module find total worth
        /* finds the total net assets of a group of bank customers
          who are specified by a table of their account numbers */
        uses cust acct table   /* contains the (valid) account numbers
                                   numbers of all the customers to be summed */
             table length      /* the number of customers */

        set total worth to 0
        repeat varying cust no from 1 to table length incl
            set cust acct no to cust acct table (cust no)
            perform get assets using cust acct no
                              receiving debit, credit
            add (credit − debit) to total worth
        endrepeat
        return total worth     /* the total net assets of the group */
endmodule
```

Another person might use the following style of pseudocode:*

---

*Presumably, the target language used by this second person would be Pascal or C.

```
module find total worth (cust acct table, table length : total worth)
      /* finds the total net assets of a group of bank customers who are
         specified by a table of their account numbers */
      /* cust acct table contains the valid account numbers
         of all the customers to be summed */
      /* table length is the number of customers */
      /* total worth is the net assets of all the customers */
         total worth := 0
         cust no    := 1
      repeat until cust no > table length
             cust acct no := cust acct table [cust no]
             call get assets (cust acct no : debit, credit)
             total worth +:= (credit − debit)
             cust no +:= 1
      endrepeat
endmodule
```

As I've just shown, pseudocode can be used for module specification, but it can also be applied to module programming and module maintenance.

In fact, pseudocode is at its best when used as a programming tool. It allows the programmer to try out ideas at any level of detail without the constraints of any particular programming language. Pseudocode can be used as a top-down programming tool and as a Structured Programming tool, especially whenever the target language doesn't readily support the Structured Programming constructs. (An example of this application was shown in Chapter 3 when I attempted to derive a program to predict the winner of a Grand Prix race.)

When pseudocode was first introduced, advocates touted it as the ideal documentation aid for maintenance programmers: "Why, it can be included right there in the listing, alongside the code!" they proclaimed. What the pseudocode enthusiasts failed to realize was that the pseudocode would also have to be *maintained* along with the actual code. Since the pseudocode tended to be nearly as detailed as the code itself, it was almost as tedious to maintain as the actual code. Since it was so verbose, it was a distraction if included in the listing, and thus was kept in a separate folder. Since, unlike real code, it didn't *have* to be maintained, it wasn't maintained. And since it wasn't maintained, everybody knew it was out of date and no longer correct, so they ignored it.*

---

*In 1978, I did an informal survey of 42 shops that used pseudocode. Of those 42, 0 (zero!) found that it had any value as maintenance documentation.

5.4 Designer/programmer communication

In this chapter, we have looked at three ways by which a designer can specify modules to a programmer: by interface specification, by a Structured Analysis specification tool, and by pseudocode (pseudocode being the least desirable option because of its typical closeness to the final code). However, regardless of which method the designer selects to specify a module to a programmer, that specification tool cannot supplant good, old-fashioned human communication. If you build walls between people, you court trouble. Don't separate the programming team from the design team; allow the programmers access to the structure chart before it's finished. Otherwise, there will be misunderstandings, no matter how good the specification tools are.

Exercises

1. Look back at the two examples of pseudocode in Section 5.3. In each of the two examples, do you think that for the modules being specified the dialect of pseudocode shown is too detailed, not detailed enough, or just right?

2. Why might a designer use pseudocode other than to specify a module?

Answers

1. For the particular module being specified, both styles of pseudocode are too detailed. The poor programmer in this situation would be reduced to a mere coder. It would suffice to specify the module by:

    > **for each** customer **in** customer account table:
    >   add his credit and subtract his debit
    >
    > **return** the total

    However, in a more complicated case — such as the procedure for calculating allowable Individual Retirement Account deductions on a tax return — more explicit detail would certainly be called for. Otherwise, the specific method of calculating the deductions could never be divined merely from the interface and a statement of the module's function (which would be "compute Individual Retirement Account deductions"). This detail would probably be contained in a process mini-specification; if not, it would have to be written as pseudocode at design time.

    Another example of a requirement for highly detailed pseudocode might be the specification for a password-checking algorithm in a system with security. No detail of this algorithm could be left up to the programmer.

2. A designer might use pseudocode to test the feasibility of implementation of a module that he has created on his structure chart.

SECTION III
THE QUALITIES OF A GOOD DESIGN

Neither the structure chart, which we explored in *Chapter 3,* nor module specifications, which we considered in *Chapter 5,* by themselves tell us very much about the quality of a particular design. Structured Design is not the structure chart any more than good sculpture is a chisel. The chisel is a tool for chipping that must be used with dexterity to achieve a good result. Similarly, a structure chart is simply a tool for showing a picture of the modules in a system and their relationships to one another.

One of the fundamental principles of Structured Design is that a large system should be partitioned into manageable modules. However, it is vital that this partitioning should be carried out in such a way that the modules are as independent as possible — this is the criterion of *coupling,* covered in *Chapter 6* — and that each module carries out a single, problem-related function — the criterion of *cohesion,* discussed in *Chapter 7.*

Although the complementary measures of partitioning, coupling, and cohesion are central themes in Structured Design, there are many other guidelines that you can use to evaluate and improve the quality of a design. These guidelines are explained in *Chapter 8,* and are summarized in Appendix A.

6

Coupling

In this chapter and in subsequent chapters, we use the structure chart to evaluate the quality of system design. The first way of measuring design quality we'll explore is *coupling*, the degree of interdependence between two modules. Our objective is to minimize coupling; that is, to make modules as independent as possible. Low coupling between modules indicates a well-partitioned system and can be attained in one of three ways:

- by eliminating unnecessary relationships
- by reducing the number of necessary relationships
- by easing the "tightness" of necessary relationships

Before I define what I mean by "tightness," let's return to the analogy of Chapter 1: the stereo system. Visualize a system in which each speaker is directly coupled to the amplifier; without the amplifier, it would be silent. Similarly, the amplifier is directly coupled to the turntable. The speakers, however, are not coupled to each other, because we could unplug one without disturbing the other.

The coupling in this stereo is about as low as we can get. If we removed any of the connections between the modules, the stereo wouldn't work properly. The coupling is also "loose," in the sense that we can detach the modules from one another by pulling out plugs. To detach the turntable from the amplifier, we don't need to disassemble either the turntable or the amplifier, or to burn costly printed-circuit boards (or our fingers!) with a soldering iron. Soldered-in leads, or cords, constitute a tighter coupling.

Let's take this neat and sensible organization and ruin its clean coupling. To make the point, I'll do it in a way that would be a nightmare to any stereo user. First, we will route the power supply for the amplifier through the right speaker. This is an extra piece of coupling between the speaker and the amplifier that, of course, is totally superfluous. Although the stereo will still work perfectly, we've created some diabolical maintenance problems. For example, if we need to send the right speaker away to be fixed, we'll have to do without the amplifier, too. If we want to buy better speakers, we'll have to find a pair whose right speaker has a power supply (a limited market!). The speaker builder has his job made pointlessly more complicated by having to cope with a power supply (which is quite irrelevant to the operation of a speaker).

Second, let's not plug the left speaker into the amplifier — let's drill a hole in the amplifier case and solder the speaker leads directly. By doing this, we've created more problems. For example, we'd better know the design and wiring layout of the amplifier pretty well, because a wire soldered in the wrong place could destroy the speaker or the amplifier or both. Also, changing amplifiers becomes painful. We'll have to do some tedious soldering, and we'll have to learn the internal details of yet another amplifier.

Third, let's abandon all modularity and put everything — speakers and all — into one big box. By doing this, we cause the following to happen: We can't fit the box on one shelf; the speakers are too close to each other for the size of the room; and, unexpectedly, the inductive field from the turntable motor causes a deep hum in the amplifier. The speakers sound terrible in the box, because the sound waves interfere with one another, destroying response at some frequencies. There is very little we can do about these spurious effects of one part of the system on another part — short of chopping the system into modules once again.

Each of the three systems above has worse coupling (and, consequently, worse partitioning) than the original clean system. The original system *is* coupled, of course, which means that connected modules must agree on some details. For example, the speakers and the amplifier must correspond in impedance. Also, the turntable has to have a plug that fits the amplifier's input socket.

However, one of the crucial points of this low coupling is that no module has to worry about the particular internal construction details of any other. Modules are seen by their function and external appearance — that is, as black boxes.

To sum up, we want low coupling because

- The fewer connections there are between two modules, the less chance there is for the ripple effect (a bug in one module appearing as a symptom in another).

- We want to be able to change one module with minimum risk of having to change another module, and we want each user change to affect as few modules as possible.

- While maintaining a module, we don't want to worry about the internal (coding) details of any other module. We want the system to be as simple to understand as possible.

We have established that *low* coupling between modules signifies a well-designed system. Let us now examine the five different types of coupling that may occur between a pair of modules. In order of tightness, they are *

1. data coupling   GOOD, OR LOOSE
2. stamp coupling
3. control coupling
4. common coupling
5. content coupling   BAD, OR TIGHT

Two modules may be coupled by more than one type of coupling, or by the same type a number of times.

6.1 Data coupling

Two modules are *data coupled* if they communicate by parameters, each parameter being either a single field or a homogeneous table (a table in which each entry contains the same type of information).

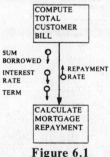

Figure 6.1

---

*Myers first developed this scale of cohesion in *Reliable Software Through Composite Design* (New York: Petrocelli/Charter, 1975). Currently, the theory of coupling is being refined to differentiate between the types of coupling that encourage the ripple effect and the types that make user changes hard to implement.

Data coupling is the necessary communication of data between modules. Since modules *must* communicate, data coupling is unavoidable, and is quite harmless so long as it's kept to a minimum. In the example above, we can't do without any of the four pieces of data: SUM BORROWED, INTEREST RATE, TERM, and REPAYMENT RATE. On the other hand, we don't need anything extra: To send down, say, CUSTOMER NAME would add extra complication without being of use to CALCULATE MORTGAGE REPAYMENT. Keep your interfaces narrow.

Look at the piece of structure chart in Fig. 6.2.

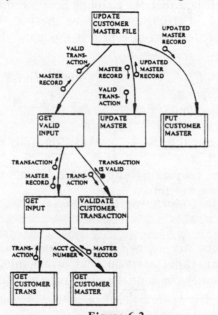

Figure 6.2

At first glance, the coupling in this system looks good. But MASTER RECORD is suspicious. It first enters the system at GET CUSTOMER MASTER, but it takes a roundabout route to reach UPDATE MASTER, where it is used. MASTER RECORD is an example of what I call a *tramp,* a piece of information that shuffles aimlessly around a system, unwanted by — and meaningless to — most of the modules through which it passes. Like a hobo, such tramp data is a nuisance to many modules (for example, GET VALID INPUT), which need extra code in order to drive it out of their neighborhoods toward a module that can make use of it. In addition, the more modules a piece of tramp data travels through, the more likely that it will be accidentally altered.

Tramp data is a symptom of poor organization of modules. In the case of Fig. 6.2, GET CUSTOMER MASTER should be directly subordinate to UPDATE CUSTOMER MASTER FILE. (I show possible causes of tramp data when I address cohesion and decision-splitting in Chapters 7 and 8, respectively.)

6.2 Stamp coupling

Two modules are *stamp coupled* if they refer to the same data structure. By a data structure, I mean a composite piece of data, such as a record consisting of a number of fields. The following figure contains three stamp-coupled modules.

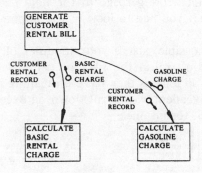

Figure 6.3

In Fig. 6.3, CUSTOMER RENTAL RECORD comprises many fields: LICENSE NUMBER, MERLIN CLUB MEMBERSHIP, MERLIN CLUB NUMBER, GAS USED, CAR TYPE, MILES DRIVEN, and DAYS USED, among others. Although the module CALCULATE BASIC RENTAL CHARGE requires only the last three fields mentioned, it receives the whole CUSTOMER RENTAL RECORD. Any change to this record — either in format or in structure — will affect *all* of the modules that refer to it, *even those modules that don't refer to the actual fields changed.*

As a simple example, let's imagine that the field MERLIN CLUB NUMBER is changed in format. Both the modules CALCULATE BASIC RENTAL CHARGE and CALCULATE GASOLINE CHARGE will have to be changed (at least recompiled), although these modules do not refer to Merlin Club members.

The problem inherent in stamp coupling is that it creates dependencies between otherwise unrelated modules. In addition, other problems exist, as shown in Fig. 6.4:

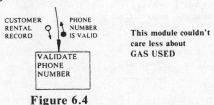

Figure 6.4

VALIDATE PHONE NUMBER is one of those modules you should write only once in your lifetime and then use over and over whenever you get the opportunity. But don't write one like the module in Fig. 6.4! If you wanted to use this module in another system (or even elsewhere in this one), you would have to remember to dummy up a record to look like a CUSTOMER RENTAL RECORD from this *particular* system.

Finally, stamp coupling tends to expose a module to more data than it needs, with possibly disastrous consequences. If a bug in VALIDATE PHONE NUMBER wrote garbage in the field LICENSE NUMBER, how would you guess that you had to look in the phone-number part of the system for the bug?

As much as possible, starve your modules of superfluous data as in Fig. 6.5. But don't reject the idea of using data structures: Data structures are good so long as they have a meaning in the original problem. They are an excellent way to cut down on excessive data coupling, as shown in Fig. 6.6, for instance:

or

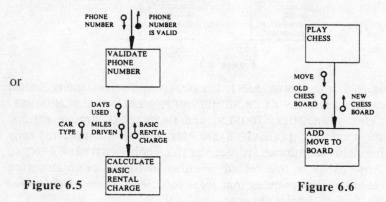

Figure 6.5   Figure 6.6

In Fig. 6.6, CHESS BOARD is the natural data structure for the problem; it wouldn't be very smart to pass down each square of the board separately, because that would yield a total of 65 parameters between the two modules. But take a look at the fragment of structure chart in Fig. 6.7. Could we replace those four parameters by a single structure? A possible solution is to use a data structure called, for example, STUFF, shown in Fig. 6.8:

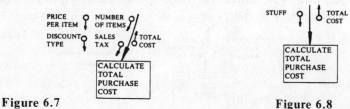

Figure 6.7   Figure 6.8

In COBOL, for example, STUFF might be defined by

```
01 STUFF
   02  PRICE-PER-ITEM
   02  NUMBER-OF-ITEMS
   02  DISCOUNT-TYPE
   02  SALES-TAX
```

This idea of collecting fairly unrelated pieces of data into an artificial data structure is called *bundling.* Doing it offers you nothing but needless obscurity. A common sign that the data structure is not appropriate to the problem is its vague or meaningless name. People bundle data because they think doing so somehow reduces coupling. However, bundling has as much therapeutic effect as a bandage on a pimple.

6.3 Control coupling

Two modules are *control coupled* if one passes to the other a piece of information intended to control the internal logic of the other. Figure 6.9 shows two control-coupled modules:

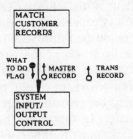

Figure 6.9

The value of WHAT TO DO FLAG indicates to SYSTEM INPUT/OUTPUT CONTROL which record(s) to read as follows: Value 1 means GET NEXT MASTER RECORD; Value 2 means GET NEXT TRANS RECORD; Value 3 means GET BOTH; Value 4 means PRINT PAGE HEADINGS; and so on.

In Fig. 6.9, MATCH CUSTOMER RECORDS explicitly decides which part of the logic of SYSTEM INPUT/OUTPUT CONTROL to use. In order for the calling module to make such a decision, it must know how the logic of the subordinate called module is organized. For example, in order to choose the right value for WHAT TO DO FLAG, MATCH CUSTOMER RECORDS must know the logic of SYSTEM INPUT/OUTPUT CONTROL.

In control-coupled modules, the subordinate module is not a black box. Indeed, as we'll see in the next chapter, on cohesion, a downward passing piece of control usually implies that the receiving module is a disastrously white box.

If the piece of control is heading upward from subordinate to boss, then another kind of faulty partitioning appears: *inversion of authority,* which means that a subordinate gives orders to its boss.

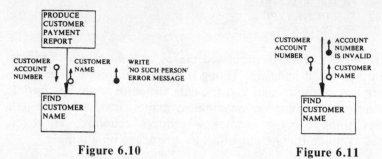

Figure 6.10   Figure 6.11

In Fig. 6.10, FIND CUSTOMER NAME tells PRODUCE CUSTOMER PAYMENT REPORT to print an error message whenever a particular account number cannot be found. This makes a mockery of hierarchy; it's equivalent to a worker's saying: "Boss, do this," or "Boss, don't do that." Another problem is that FIND CUSTOMER NAME assumes that whatever module calls it is capable of writing error messages.

The partitioning could be improved in either of two ways: First, if reporting an error is really a part of the function of finding a CUSTOMER NAME, then FIND CUSTOMER NAME should write the error message. Second, FIND CUSTOMER NAME may not really *know* that an error has occurred. The boss may be able to correct the error in some way unknown to the subordinate. In this case, the subordinate module should just report that no such account number was found.

In this section on control coupling, we've seen that a flag being passed from one module to another for the purpose of control signifies poor partitioning — either a function has been split between the two modules, or a module has to be aware of the detailed internal logic of its subordinate, or a module has to be aware of the specific capabilities of its boss (an inversion of authority).

However, we've also seen that not all flags are equally bad. A flag named WRITE 'NO SUCH PERSON' ERROR MESSAGE was deemed undesirable, whereas a flag named ACCOUNT NUMBER IS INVALID was deemed acceptable. The difference between the two flags is that the first was used to explicitly tell a receiving module what it has to do. This type of flag is called a *control flag.** The second type of flag was used to

---

*This is also colloquially known as a *nag flag,* because it always nags the receiving module into carrying out a certain activity.

describe a piece of data (namely, the ACCOUNT NUMBER). This type of flag is called a *descriptive flag.* It is virtually harmless.

By now, you might feel a little confused about the difference between data, descriptive flags, and control flags. The clue to the distinction is invariably in the name of the piece of information. Data are named by nouns, descriptive flags by adjectives, and control flags by verbs, as shown in Table 6.1:

Table 6.1

Type of Information	Depicted by	Type of Name	Examples
data	o—→	noun	price of eggs age zip code
descriptive flag	●—→	adjective	egg is rotten zip code is numeric transaction file is at end
control flag	●—→	verb	read next record reject this customer rewind master file

Data usually record quantities or amounts that relate directly to the problem. Descriptive flags usually describe data or a situation that has occurred; they are one step removed from the problem. Control flags usually indicate some particular quirk of the implementation and consequently bear no relation to the problem whatsoever. You should therefore strive to remove control flags wherever you possibly can.

Control coupling is not always as explicit as shown above. Sometimes, it's disguised in a form known as *hybrid coupling,** which results from the assignment of several meanings to various parts of the range of a piece of data, and which tends to cause tremendous maintenance problems. If a piece of data were an animal, then hybrid coupling would result in a creature having the front end of a swan, the back end of a camel, and the kidneys of a rhino.

Following is an example of hybrid coupling that occurred at the

---

*Yourdon and Constantine used the term *hybrid coupling* for what essentially is COBOL's ALTER statement. I define the term here in agreement with its current usage. For a comprehensive discussion, see E. Yourdon and L. Constantine's *Structured Design: Fundamentals of a Discipline of Computer Program and Systems Design* (New York: YOURDON Press, 1978), p. 92.

Electric Grunt Book Co. (EGB). Although I've simplified the example, it still retains its original gruesome flavor.

> The EGB Co. is a mail-order company whose customers were assigned account numbers of five digits, ranging from 00001 to 99999. However, there were some rather peculiar account numbers. For instance, those in the range 90000 — 90999 were not account numbers at all! They meant to mail a piece of literature to the region represented by the last three digits. Those customers with account numbers in the range 91000−91999 had a special status. They were allowed an extra thirty days in which to pay their bills. The full range of an EGB account number is shown in Fig. 6.12.

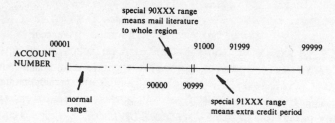

Figure 6.12

As far as I could tell, the supreme benefit of the scheme shown in Fig. 6.12 was that it saved a few bytes of storage in the whole system — a byte of control information for mailing literature, a couple of bytes for the region, and a byte for credit rating.

The maintenance changes that exposed the grotesque nature of these so-called account numbers were as follows: Some customers were to be given a special trade discount. Yes, you guessed it: They were made the 92000 gang. About two days later, it was realized that several of the customers eligible for the special trade discount also were eligible for the additional thirty-day credit period. A few quick-and-dirty changes were made to the code and these people were issued numbers in the 93000−93999 range. As years and personnel went by, business boomed. The highest account number, which had been 30000 for some years, reached 89000, threatening to encroach on the account-number range that signified mailing literature. But the new Manager of Account Numbers was unaware of the 90XXX convention . . . and, since nobody liked him, nobody told him.

Customer number 90000 was welcomed to the Electric Grunt Book Co. with a spectacular event: His bill for $9.57 was circulated to about 2,500 people in New Jersey. The cost of rescinding that bill was huge, especially as some people actually paid $9.57 for goods they had neither ordered nor received!

The EGB Co. solution to that little problem was twofold: to fire the Manager of Account Numbers for "glaring incompetence" and to skip to 94000 as the next available account number. The ridiculous scheme was finally abandoned when the 1001st special-credit customer arrived and there was no available account number for him. To restore sanity required surprisingly extensive and expensive modifications to the code.

6.4 Common coupling

Two modules are *common coupled* if they refer to the same global data area. In Fig. 6.13, FIND PART NAME and REMOVE STOCK are common coupled, because they both refer to PARTS TABLE and ERROR FLAG3, which are global data areas. The term *common* is taken from FORTRAN's COMMON, the area that can be accessed by any SUBROUTINE or FUNCTION. However, globally accessible data areas can be created in most languages. In PL/I, global data is created by the use of the EXTERNAL attribute; in COBOL, a DATA DIVISION in its entirety is global to any paragraph in the PROCEDURE DIVISION.

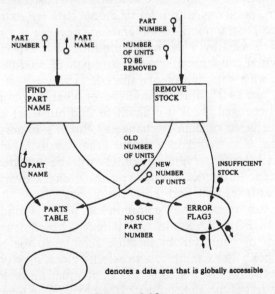

Figure 6.13

Common coupling is bad for six reasons — though it's unlikely that any given pair of common-coupled modules would fall afoul of all six. First, a bug (or programmer malpractice!) in any module using a global area may show up in any other module using that global area, because global data doesn't reside in the protective haven of a module. A common area is a jungle in which a piece of data may be pounced upon and mangled at any moment.

Second, modules that refer to global data usually do so by explicit name. For example, a telephone-number editing module might receive its telephone number from a global piece of data called TEL NO. That module is now committed to the name TEL NO; it can't edit a telephone number that is called something other than TEL NO — either elsewhere in this system or in other applications. Only if you're lucky enough to find an application with a TEL NO can you use this module. By contrast, modules called by parameters aren't tied to specific names in the outside world. The programmers of such modules can pick whatever names they want, thereby freeing them for any particular context or usage.

Third, global areas sometimes may be drastically abused, as, for instance, when different modules use the same area to store quite different pieces of information. In Fig. 6.13, ERROR FLAG3 may mean "insufficient stock," or "no such part number," depending on which module used it last. In this case, maintenance efforts — especially debugging — become as hairy as a werewolf's handshake.

Fourth, programs with a lot of global data are extremely tough for maintenance programmers to understand, because it's difficult to know what data are used by a particular module. It's especially hard to tell what the actual coupling is between any pair of modules, since one has to ascertain what data, if any, are shared.

Fifth, just as it's difficult to discover what data must be changed if a module is changed, so is it difficult to find out what modules must be changed if a piece of data is changed. But it's important to find out. For instance, if a record in a global area has to be changed from 96 bytes to 112 bytes, several modules will be affected. But which? Without a cross-reference listing, you must check every module in the system. That takes time and therefore money.

The sixth reason that common coupling is undesirable applies specifically to FORTRAN. In that language, modules refer to data in COMMON not by name but by location relative to the beginning of the COMMON block. For example, a COMMON block may contain A, B, and C. If a SUBROUTINE wants to access C, it must know how big A and B are in order to get the right offset. If A changes its length, the SUBROUTINE will have to be changed, whether or not it refers to A! This feature compounds common coupling with a kind of stamp coupling among unrelated global items, and explains why seemingly trivial changes to some FORTRAN programs have the maintenance programmer scurrying off to duplicate a particular COMMON card 39 times — once for each SUBROUTINE using that COMMON.*

Modularity calls for constraining a particular item of data as much as possible to a single module or at most to a small group of modules. The overuse of common data degrades this idea of modularity by allowing data to stray outside the strict limits of a module.

COBOL is not particularly strong in this respect. Neither a SECTION nor a PARAGRAPH makes a very self-contained module, for, unfortunately, the whole of the DATA DIVISION is wide open to the use or the abuse of any SECTION or PARAGRAPH in the PROCEDURE DIVISION. The best way to achieve modularity in COBOL is by using CALLed programs. In that way, the interface between modules can be restricted to the LINKAGE SECTION. If the LINKAGE SECTION isn't so wide that Ben Hur could drive a team of horses and a chariot full of bugs through it, then the coupling between the programs is kept low.

6.5 Content coupling

Two modules exhibit content (or pathological) coupling if one refers to the inside of the other in any way; for instance, if one module branches or falls through into another, if one module refers to (or changes) data within another, or if one module alters a statement in another. Such coupling makes nonsense of the concept of black-box modules, since it forces one module to know about the explicit contents and implementation of another one. On the whole, only assembly language allows you to indulge in such sick practices; most higher-level languages offer no way to implement content coupling.

As a quick example to show the dangers of content coupling, imagine that module A has a labeled statement

```
    SRCH:        MOVE 1 TO REG 0
                   .
                   .
                   .
```

and module B has the statement

```
    JUMP TO SRCH
```

Now, the maintainer of module A should have complete freedom to recode the module in any way he sees fit, so long as it still carries out its black-box function. But in this case, he has no freedom. He

---

*The use of small NAMED COMMON areas does largely alleviate this particular problem. In Section 8.8, I show a valid use for such small areas of global data shared between a few modules.

can't change his algorithm; he can't even change label names without fouling up module B. Content coupling brings us back to the tangled mess of non-modular coding.*

6.6 Determining coupling type

Two modules may be coupled in more than one way. In that case, their coupling is defined by the worst coupling type they exhibit. For example, if two modules are stamp *and* common coupled, you characterize them as common coupled. They're still stamp coupled, but that's outweighed by their common coupling.

A good rule of thumb for designing the way a module gets and returns its information is to imagine it as a library module. How would this module be easiest to understand? How would this module be most usable to other people in my shop?

Another way in which one can evaluate the coupling of a design is to suppose that each module will be coded by a different programmer: How independently can the programmers work? Is there any fact, assumption, convention, or implementation decision of which more than one module need be aware? How likely is it that the fact, or assumption, or convention, or implementation will change? Is there any way in which the change could be isolated to one module? Answering these questions will determine which user changes are likely to require modification to a large number of modules.

6.7 Comparison of coupling types

Here is a review of the specific qualities of each type of coupling:

Table 6.2

Coupling Type	Susceptibility to Ripple Effect	Modifiability	Understandability	Module's Usability in Other Systems
Data	variable	good	good	good
tramp	poor	medium	medium	poor
Stamp	variable	medium	medium	medium
bundling	variable	medium	poor	poor
Control	medium	poor	poor	poor
hybrid	medium	bad	bad	bad
Common	poor	medium	bad	bad
Content	bad	bad	bad	bad

---

*I'm not going to offend you by discussing COBOL's ALTER statement. Anyone who's tried to maintain a system sprinkled with ALTERs has already experienced pathology to the point of criminality.

Exercises

1. What type of coupling is indicated by each of the following interfaces from the calling module to a module that prints mailing labels?

    (a)   CALL   PRINT LABEL1   USING   NAME, STREET ADDRESS,
                                                     CITY, STATE, ZIP
    (b)   CALL   PRINT LABEL2   USING   CUST MAILING ADDRESS
    (c)   CALL   PRINT LABEL3   USING   CUST PURCHASE ORDER RECORD
    (d)   CALL   PRINT LABEL4   USING   NZ, SAS, CITY
          (where NZ = NAME + ZIP
                 SAS = STREET ADDRESS + STATE)
    (e)   CALL   PRINT LABEL5
          (in a language other than COBOL)

2. Give an example of a fact, assumption, convention, or implementation decision in a system that might change.

Answers

1. The coupling indicated by each of the interfaces given are

   (a) data

   (b) stamp

   (c) stamp (but presumably with superfluous fields being passed down)

   (d) stamp (but with the weirdest and most unnecessary case of bundling that I've seen for many a moon)

   (e) either common or content, if the language being used permits these forms of coupling

2. FACT: An insurance company might have clients in 52 states (Washington, D.C., and Puerto Rico are included as states). This fact would change if the company gained clients in, say, Guam.

   ASSUMPTION: We already saw in this chapter that the designers of the Electric Grunt Book Co. made an assumption that the company would never have more than 1000 special-credit customers. But one day it did!

   CONVENTION: The color of parts might be recorded by the color's first letter, for example, R for red, G for green, B for blue, and so on. But if parts are ever made in gray or black, then this convention would have to be changed either to a two-letter code or to some arbitrary (and, hence, unnatural) convention.

   IMPLEMENTATION DECISION: The above color convention might be an implementation decision. Another implementation decision would be in a travel application in which the names of all the airlines in the world are ordered alphabetically in a table so that a binary search could be used to find a particular airline. It might be decided later that a linear search would be faster if the table were reordered so that the most popular airlines were at the top of the table.

7

Cohesion

As we saw in the previous chapter, an important way to evaluate the partitioning of a system is by how cleanly the modules are separated from one another: That is the criterion of coupling. Another way to determine partitioning is to look at how the activities within a single module are related to one another: This is the criterion of cohesion. Since coupling and cohesion both are ways of measuring partitioning, you'd expect them to be interdependent. Indeed, they are, in that the cohesion of a module often determines how tightly it will be coupled to other modules in a system.

As an illustration, look at the following map of a pair of cities:

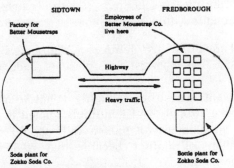

Figure 7.1

The heavy traffic between Sidtown and Fredborough arises because of the way in which the Better Mousetrap Company and the Zokko Soda Company have distributed themselves. Every morning, Better Mousetrap workers leave their homes in Fredborough and beat a path to the door of the Better Mousetrap factory in Sidtown. In the evening, they all return. Day and night, trucks full of bottles rumble from Fredborough to Sidtown to be filled with sparkling, low-calorie Zokko soda. But what if these two companies rearranged their facilities as shown in Fig. 7.2?

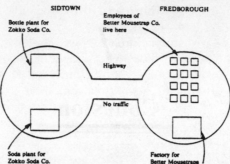

Figure 7.2

Now, each company has restricted itself to one city, resulting in two very boring cities, but also — more importantly — in little or no traffic between the cities. (There may be *some* traffic if Better Mousetrap workers occasionally pause to refresh themselves with Zokko soda.)

The moral of this tale of two cities is that putting strongly associated things in the same city reduces the traffic between the cities. The cities are, of course, thinly disguised modules, and the traffic between them is coupling. The term for "putting strongly associated things in the same module" is cohesion, which brings us to this definition:

> *Cohesion* is the measure of the strength of functional association of elements within a module.

By an *element,* I mean an instruction, or a group of instructions, or a call to another module; that is, any piece of code that accomplishes some work.

What we want are strong,* highly cohesive modules, modules whose elements are strongly and genuinely related to one another. On the other hand, the elements of one module should *not* be strongly related to the elements of another, because that would lead to tight coupling between the modules.

Cohesion, then, is the second way to tell how well we've partitioned a system into modules. Indeed, making sure that all modules have good cohesion is the best way to minimize coupling between the modules. It also ensures that the functions of the system reflect the functions of the original problem.

---

*In fact, a common synonym for module cohesion is *module strength.*

The idea of cohesion came to Larry Constantine* in the mid-sixties. He was interested in learning why people create certain types of modules, and in examining the relative merits and ills of each of the types. The term itself was borrowed from sociology, where it means the relatedness of humans within groups.

From these early studies and later refinements, Stevens, Myers, Constantine, and Yourdon† developed a scale of cohesion as a measure of the black-boxness of a module and, it turns out from experiments, as a good measure of the maintainability of a module.

Scale of Cohesion

	BEST	
Functional	MAINTAINABILITY	black box
Sequential		not-quite-
Communicational		so-black box
Procedural		gray
Temporal		box
Logical	WORST	white or
Coincidental	MAINTAINABILITY	transparent box

In the next seven sections, I will show the good and bad characteristics of each level of cohesion.

7.1 Functional cohesion

A *functionally cohesive* module contains elements that all contribute to the execution of one and only one problem-related task. Examples of functionally cohesive modules are

> COMPUTE COSINE OF ANGLE
> VERIFY ALPHABETIC SYNTAX
> READ TRANSACTION RECORD
> DETERMINE CUSTOMER MORTGAGE REPAYMENT
> COMPUTE POINT OF IMPACT OF MISSILE
> CALCULATE NET EMPLOYEE SALARY

Notice that each of these modules has a strong, single-minded

---

*See E. Yourdon and L. Constantine, *Structured Design: Fundamentals of a Discipline of Computer Program and Systems Design* (New York: YOURDON Press, 1978), pp. 95-126.
†In addition to Yourdon and Constantine, ibid., sources include: W. Stevens, G. Myers, and L. Constantine, "Structured Design," *IBM Systems Journal*, Vol. 13, No. 2 (May 1974), pp. 115-39. [Reprinted in E.N. Yourdon, ed., *Classics in Software Engineering* (New York: YOURDON Press, 1979), pp. 207-32.]

purpose. When its boss calls it, it carries out just one job to completion without getting involved in any extracurricular activity. For example, DETERMINE CUSTOMER MORTGAGE REPAYMENT must do just that; it must *not,* for instance, print out page headings.

You may have observed that some of the functionally cohesive modules above are very simple and would probably be found low on the structure chart (such as VERIFY ALPHABETIC SYNTAX or READ TRANSAC- TION RECORD), while others are complicated and would be found quite high on the structure chart (for instance, COMPUTE POINT OF IMPACT OF MISSILE). READ TRANSACTION RECORD is obviously doing a single func- tion, but how can I claim that CALCULATE NET EMPLOYEE SALARY is do- ing only one job when everyone knows that it's computing gross salary, FICA deductions, federal income tax, state income tax, and so on? The point is that however complicated a module is — and however many subfunctions make up its total job — if you can sum up every- thing that it accomplishes for its boss as *one problem-related* function, then that module is functionally cohesive.*

If you are tempted to think that any module can be summed up as performing *one* function, don't be fooled. There are many kinds of modules whose bosses regard them as doing different jobs that *cannot* be summed up as a single problem-related function. The crucial factor in deciding the level of cohesion of these non-functional modules is how the different activities they perform are related to one another.

7.2 Sequential cohesion

A *sequentially cohesive* module is one whose elements are involved in activities such that output data from one activity serves as input data to the next. To illustrate this definition, imagine that you're about to repaint your bright orange Corvette a classy silver color. The sequence of steps might be something like this:

1. CLEAN CAR BODY
2. FILL IN HOLES IN CAR
3. SAND CAR BODY
4. APPLY PRIMER

This group of four activities cannot be summed up as a single function. That tells us that this "module" is not functionally cohesive.

---

*This is another way of stating the rules: "The outside (function) of a good module is easier to understand than its inside (logic)," and "A good module is easier to use than to write." [R.C. Holt, "Structure of Computer Programs: A Survey," *Proceedings of the IEEE,* Vol. 63, No. 6 (1975), pp. 879-93.]

(If we added a fifth step, PUT ON FINAL COAT, we would have a functionally cohesive module called REPAINT CAR.) To determine the
"module's" level of cohesion, therefore, we must ask: How are these
activities related to one another? The answer is that the output from
one activity serves as input to the next — just like on an assembly line.
And that fits the definition of a sequentially cohesive module.

Here's another example of a sequentially cohesive module,
described first in pseudocode and then shown on a structure chart.

> **module** format and cross-validate record
>> **uses** raw record
>> format raw record
>> cross-validate fields in raw record
>> **returns** formatted cross-validated record
>
> **endmodule**

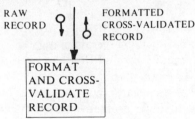

Figure 7.3

In Fig. 7.3, the output from the first activity (formatting) is the
input to the second (cross-validation).

A sequentially cohesive module usually has good coupling and is
easily maintained. Indeed, it is almost as maintainable as a functionally
cohesive module. The only real disadvantage of a sequentially cohesive
module is that it is not so readily reusable in the same system (or in
other systems) as is a functionally cohesive module, because it contains
activities that will not in general be useful together.

7.3 Communicational cohesion

A *communicationally cohesive* module is one whose elements contribute to activities that use the same input or output data.

Suppose we wish to find out some facts about a book: For instance, we may wish to

>> 1. FIND TITLE OF BOOK
>> 2. FIND PRICE OF BOOK
>> 3. FIND CODE NUMBER OF BOOK
>> 4. FIND AUTHOR OF BOOK

These four activities are related because they all work on the same input data — the book — which make the "module" communicationally cohesive.

Another example of a communicationally cohesive module is

    module determine customer details
        uses customer account no
        find customer name
        find customer loan balance
        return customer name, customer loan balance
    endmodule

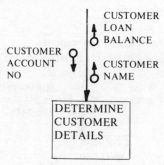

Figure 7.4

In Fig. 7.4, the two activities of finding the customer's name and finding his loan balance use the input of CUSTOMER ACCOUNT NO. The coupling between a communicationally cohesive module and its caller is usually acceptable; typically, it's narrow on one side and arbitrarily broad on the other, depending on the number of functions in the module.

Communicationally cohesive modules are quite maintainable, although there can be problems. In Fig. 7.4, it's possible that another module in the system would need to find out a customer's name but wouldn't be interested in his loan balance. That module would either have to discard the loan balance data (dirty and redundant coupling) or would need its own code for finding the customer name (duplication of function).

Another potential problem with a communicationally cohesive module is the temptation to share code among the activities within it; that can make it tough to change one activity without destroying another. For example, the upper module in Fig. 7.5 is communicationally cohesive: With EMPLOYEE SALARY TABLE, it both generates a report on all of the employees' salaries and calculates their average salary. Because both functions need access to every salary, a programmer may be tempted to put them inside the same loop. It's possible, however, that at some later date a report on only the first twenty employees might

need to be generated. To generate this new report, a maintenance programmer would need to change CALCULATE AVERAGE SALARY by in-
serting a test in the loop to determine when the twentieth employee had
been passed. However, a better solution would be to create a separate
loop for each activity. But in that case, there would no longer be any
point in keeping the two activities in the same module.

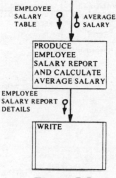

Figure 7.5

Almost always, you'll improve maintainability if you split a communicationally cohesive module into separate, functionally cohesive
ones, as in Fig. 7.6:

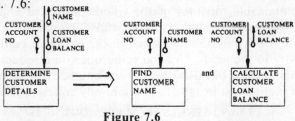

Figure 7.6

Modules with communicational and sequential cohesion seem
quite similar, for they both contain activities organized around the data
in the original problem. They also have quite clean coupling, because
few of their elements are related to elements in other modules. The
main difference between them is that a sequentially cohesive module
operates like an assembly line; its individual activities must be carried
out in a specific order. But in a communicationally cohesive module,
order of execution is unimportant. In the module depicted in Fig. 7.5,
it doesn't matter whether the employees' report is generated before,
after, or at the same time as average salary is calculated.

Sequentially and communicationally cohesive modules can be illustrated in data flow terms, as in Fig. 7.7. This illustration highlights
the fact that the activities are strongly related by the data in the prob-

lem. In Chapter 9, we'll look at the strategy of transform analysis, which is used to derive a good structure chart from a DFD. We'll see that this strategy tends to produce modules of the top three levels of cohesion.

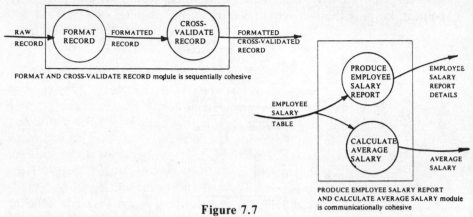

Figure 7.7

7.4 Procedural cohesion

As we reach *procedural cohesion,* we cross the boundary from the easily maintainable modules of the higher levels of cohesion to the less easily maintainable modules of the middle levels of cohesion. A procedurally cohesive module is one whose elements are involved in different and possibly unrelated activities, in which control flows from each activity to the next. (As you remember, in a sequentially cohesive module not control but data flows from one activity to the next.) Here is a list of steps in an imaginary procedurally cohesive module.

1. CLEAN UTENSILS FROM PREVIOUS MEAL
2. PREPARE TURKEY FOR ROASTING
3. MAKE PHONE CALL
4. TAKE SHOWER
5. CHOP VEGETABLES
6. SET TABLE

SET TABLE is the last step listed for this "module." But GET DRESSED or MAKE ANOTHER PHONE CALL would be equally valid candidates for step 6, because the activities on this list are related only in that they may well happen in this order during a particular day. They make up, if you like, a piece of someone's daily flowchart. They are related by order of excution rather than by any single problem-related function.

At the top of the next page is another example of a procedurally cohesive module (shown as part of a structure chart in Fig. 7.8):

module write read and edit somewhat
   uses out record
   write out record
   read in record
   pad numeric fields of in record with zeros
   return in record
endmodule

Figure 7.8

Procedurally cohesive modules tend to be composed of pieces of functions that have little relationship to one another (except that they're carried out in a specific order at a certain time). However, these pieces of functions probably have quite a lot to do with pieces of functions in other modules. WRITE, READ, AND EDIT SOMEWHAT finishes dealing with the last transaction (by writing OUT RECORD), and starts to deal with the next one (by reading and somewhat editing IN RECORD). It's typical of a procedurally cohesive module that the data you send to it and the data it sends back have little relationship. It's also typical that such a module passes around partial results (e.g., a partially edited IN RECORD), flags, switches, and so on.

Procedural cohesion could be nicknamed cop-out cohesion, as a procedurally cohesive module tends to do only part of a job.

7.5 Temporal cohesion

A *temporally cohesive* module is one whose elements are involved in activities that are related in time. Picture this late-evening scene:

1. PUT OUT MILK BOTTLES
2. PUT OUT CAT
3. TURN OFF TV
4. BRUSH TEETH

These activities are unrelated to one another except that they're carried out at a particular time: They're all part of an end-of-day routine.

The classic example of temporal cohesion is an initialization module, as shown in Fig. 7.9. Temporally cohesive modules, like procedurally cohesive ones, tend to be composed of partial functions whose *only* relationship to one another is that they all happen to be carried out at a certain time. The activities are usually more closely related to activities in other modules than they are to one another, a situation that leads to tight coupling.

```
module initialize
    updates a-counter, b-counter, items table,
            totals table, switch-a, switch-b
    rewind tape-a
    set a-counter to 0
    rewind tape-b
    set b-counter to 0
    clear items table
    clear totals table
    set switch-a to off
    set switch-b to on
endmodule
```

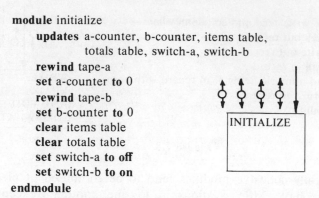

Figure 7.9

In Fig. 7.9, the module INITIALIZE initializes many different functions in a mighty sweep, causing it to be broadly related to several other modules in the system — a condition that is reflected by broad coupling to its caller. A temporally cohesive module also has some of the same difficulties as a communicationally cohesive one. The programmer is tempted to share code among activities related only by time, and the module is difficult to reuse, either in this system or in others.*

For instance, if a maintenance change later requires you to put out the cat in the middle of the afternoon, you'd be obliged to put out the milk bottles, brush your teeth, and turn off the TV, all of which may be highly inconvenient. In Fig. 7.9, if you want to re-initialize TAPE B elsewhere in the system, then you're faced with two unfortunate choices: To avoid resetting the whole system to zero, you could either introduce flags to indicate to INITIALIZE which part(s) of it should be executed, or write another piece of code for dealing with TAPE B. Both of these solutions degrade maintainability.

Procedural and temporal modules are quite similar: They can be created by taking scissors to a flowchart. The degree of their black-boxness, or coloring, varies from dark gray to light gray, since it is not very easy to state simply the function of such a module without listing its internal details. They are similar as well in that the coupling to procedural and temporal modules ranges from mediocre to poor. The difference between them is like the difference between sequential and communicational cohesion: The order of execution of activities is more important in procedurally cohesive modules. In addition, procedural

---

*Clearly, initialization and termination must be done. In Chapter 8, I discuss the best way to organize these tasks.

modules tend to share loops and decisions between functions, whereas temporal modules tend to contain more straight-line code.

7.6 Logical cohesion

A *logically cohesive* module is one whose elements contribute to activities of the same general category in which the activity or activities to be executed are selected from outside the module.

Keeping this definition in mind, let's look at an example: If you were contemplating a journey, you might compile the following list:

1. GO BY CAR
2. GO BY TRAIN
3. GO BY BOAT
4. GO BY PLANE

What relates these activities? They're all means of transport, of course. But a crucial point is that for any journey you must choose a specific subset of these modes of transport: You're unlikely to use them *all* on any particular journey.

A logically cohesive module contains a number of activities of the same general kind; to use the module, we pick out just the piece(s) we need. Thus, a logically cohesive module is a grab bag of activities. The activities — although different — are forced to share the one and only interface to the module. The meaning of each parameter depends on which activity is being used; for certain activities, some of the parameters will even be left blank (although the calling module still needs to use them and to know their specific types).

The activities in a logically cohesive module fall into roughly the same category, having some similarities as well as differences. Unfortunately, this leads the programmer into knotting together the code of the activities by allowing activities to share common lines of code. So not only does a logically cohesive module have an ugly exterior with maybe a dozen different parameters fighting to use four accesses, but its inside resembles a plate of spaghetti mixed with noodles and worms. The resulting module is neither easy to understand nor to maintain.

Try understanding the code for the logically cohesive module in Fig. 7.10. (This is an example from real life rewritten to eliminate the original GOTOS, which made it totally incomprehensible.)

The example represents not so much the sharing of code as the sharing of buffer space, exploiting such facts as TRAN FILE2 and MASTER FILE1 records both are 120 characters long and are never read together. Notice that RECORD-A sometimes is read, sometimes is written, and sometimes acts as a flag — a ghastly piece of hybrid coupling.

```
module general io routine
    uses input flag   /* to choose which function */
    updates record-A
    define record-B as 80 char   /* working */
    define record-C as 120 char   /* storage */
    if input flag = 1
    then write record-A to new master file
        read tran file1 into record-B
    elseif input flag = 2
    then if record-A = all spaces
        then read tran file1 into record-B
        endif
        read tran file2 into record-C
    elseif input flag = 3
    then read tran file1 into record-B
        read master file1 into record-C
        read master file2 into record-A
    endif
    return record-B, record-C
endmodule
```

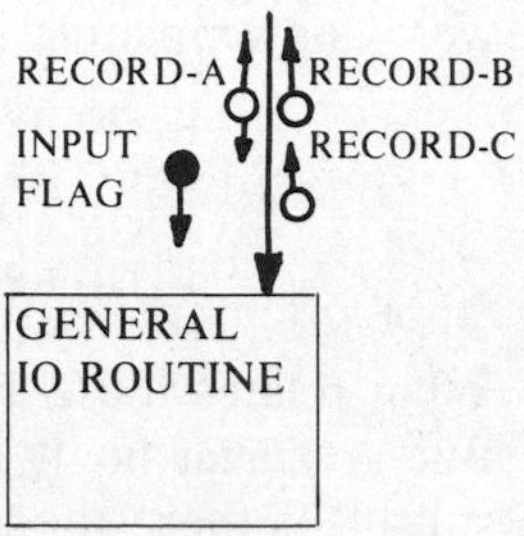

RECORD-A ↕↑ RECORD-B
INPUT ○○ ↓↑ RECORD-C
FLAG ● ↓ ○

GENERAL
IO ROUTINE

Figure 7.10

Have you got that? Or would you like some clarification?

```
/* Clarification of GENERAL IO ROUTINE:
    RECORD-B and TRAN FILE records are 80 chars
    RECORD-C, TRAN FILE2 and MASTER FILE1 records are 120 chars
    RECORD-A, MASTER FILE1 and NEW MASTER FILE records are 142 chars
```

The effect of the module depends on the value in INPUT FLAG:

```
    when INPUT FLAG = 1
            RECORD-A is written to NEW MASTER FILE
            RECORD-B is set to the next TRAN FILE1 record
            RECORD-C is undefined
    when INPUT FLAG = 2
            RECORD-A is used as an auxiliary input flag
            RECORD-B is set to the next TRAN FILE1 record
                (But only if RECORD-A had been set to SPACES;
                otherwise RECORD-B is undefined)
            RECORD-C is set to the next TRAN FILE2 record
    when INPUT FLAG = 3
            RECORD-A is set to the next MASTER FILE2 record
            RECORD-B is set to the next TRAN FILE1 record
            RECORD-C is set to the next MASTER FILE1 record
*/
```

If you understand this module, then you're doing better than I did when I had to maintain it. But let's see how you fare with a few changes.

First, can you modify GENERAL IO ROUTINE so that if INPUT FLAG = 3, TRAN FILE2 instead of TRAN FILE1 is read? Sorry, can't do it. A TRAN FILE2 record (120 chars) won't fit into RECORD-B (80 chars), into which the TRAN FILE1 record is currently being placed. RECORD-C (120 chars), which *would* fit, is already in use for the MASTER FILE1 record.

Can you change the module so that if INPUT FLAG = 2, RECORD-C is written to NEW MASTER FILE? No go, I'm afraid. Remember that RECORD-C is being used as a funny flag when INPUT FLAG = 2? It can't be used to hold "real" information.

Is it possible to lengthen a TRAN FILE2 record (120 chars) to 132 chars? I hate to be difficult, but where on earth would we put it? The only possibility is RECORD-A (142 chars) with a ten-space padding (ugly), but we can't even do that because RECORD-A is being used for so many other weird things.

The only reason that people create logically cohesive modules is to overlap parts of functions that happen to have the same lines of code or the same buffers. You can imagine, I'm sure, that if code as well as buffers had been shared in the above example, the result would have been functions so inextricably intertwined that Harry Houdini himself would have had difficulty untangling them. And if nothing can be overlapped between functions, then logically cohesive modules have no point whatsoever. A better name for logical cohesion would be *illogical cohesion!*

7.7 Coincidental cohesion

A *coincidentally cohesive* module is one whose elements contribute to activities with no meaningful relationship to one another; as in

1. FIX CAR
2. BAKE CAKE
3. WALK DOG
4. FILL OUT ASTRONAUT-APPLICATION FORM
5. HAVE A BEER
6. GET OUT OF BED
7. GO TO THE MOVIES

A coincidentally cohesive module is similar to a logically cohesive one: Its activities are related neither by flow of data nor by flow of control. (One glance at the above list should convince you that you'd be unlikely to carry out all seven activities at one time!) However, the activities in a logically cohesive module are at least in the same category; in a coincidentally cohesive module, even that is not true.

The following pseudocode and structure chart will illustrate why coincidental cohesion is considered to be the worst level of cohesion:

```
module miscellaneous functions
    uses func flag, operator message
    updates matnum, acc
    define trans record as 80 char
    define error switch as switch
    if func flag = 1
    then clear matnum to 0        /* matnum is a matrix */
        set acc to 1
    elseif func flag = 2
    then rewind tape-B
        print customer headings
    elseif func flag = 3
    then rewind tape-B
    elseif func flag = 4
    then read trans record
        if eof
        then set error switch to on
        endif
    else display operator message
    endif
    return trans record, error switch
endmodule
```

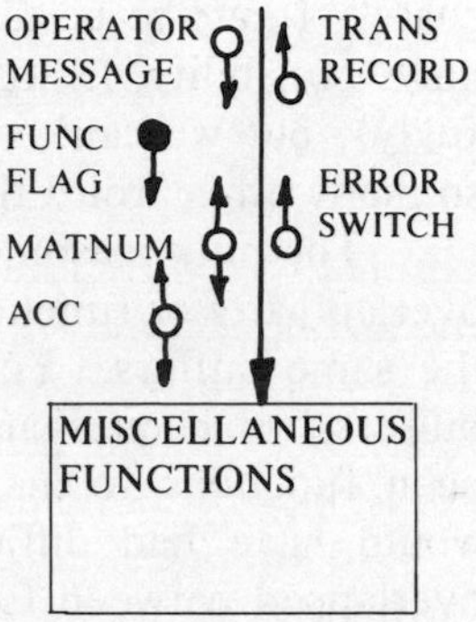

Figure 7.11

If you think that the module shown in Fig. 7.11 has very little going for it, you are absolutely right. All the nasty things I described about logically cohesive modules hold true for coincidentally cohesive modules, and then some!

For instance, if, while you were attempting to debug a piece of code, you saw a call to a logically cohesive module like this

CALL GENERAL IO ROUTINE USING 3, RECORD-A, RECORD-B, RECORD-C

you'd at least get the feeling that it was doing some kind of input and/or output, and you might be able to continue debugging without having to look at the actual code of GENERAL IO ROUTINE. But if you stumbled across *this* call* while doing midnight maintenance, you might think you were asleep and having a nightmare:

CALL MISCELLANEOUS FUNCTIONS USING 4, BLANKS, DUMMY 1, DUMMY 2,
                            TRANS RECORD, ERROR SWITCH

---

*Note: This code is intended to signify nightmare code; it is not an example of correct COBOL syntax.

The only way you could possibly figure out what's going on is to dig down among the actual code of MISCELLANEOUS FUNCTIONS and work out just which activity the module is carrying out on this occasion. MISCELLANEOUS FUNCTIONS — like all coincidentally cohesive modules — is a joke module, a white box whose insides are glaringly visible. Such modules make systems less understandable and less maintainable than systems with no modularity at all!

Coincidental cohesion, fortunately, is rare. Among its causes are the misguided attempts of morons to save time or memory (both usually unsuccessful); the shoveling of existing monolithic code arbitrarily into modules; and the ill-considered maintenance changes to modules with mediocre (typically temporal) cohesion, leading to the addition of flags.

Logical and coincidental modules are similar in their schizophrenia: Such modules have no well-defined function, so the boss module must send a completely artificial flag to tell them what to do. This violates the principle of independent black boxes, since the boss needs to know the internal details of the subordinates. The coupling to both kinds of module is horrendously obscure.

Both logical and coincidental modules are such white boxes that to distinguish between them is quite subjective. But you could say that a coincidental module is a box of a whiter shade of pale.

7.8 Determining module cohesion

In this chapter, I have defined, described, and given examples of each level of cohesion. But how does one actually set about determining the level of cohesion of a particular module? One good way is to write a short sentence that accurately, honestly, and fully names the module and describes its function. Usually, the structure of the sentence reveals fairly accurately the level of cohesion of the module.

Let's take a look at some examples:

Functional cohesion. A module doing one function can be summed up by a precise verb-object name; for example,

strong imperative verb	*specific singular direct object*
READ	CUSTOMER TRANSACTION RECORD
CALCULATE	NORMAL AUTO INSURANCE PREMIUM
DEDUCT	FEDERAL TAXES

Sequential cohesion. A number of assembly-line functions show sequential cohesion, as in

VALIDATE TRANSACTION AND [USE IT TO] UPDATE MASTER RECORD

Communicational cohesion. A number of non-sequential functions working on the same data are the clue here; for example,

> CALCULATE AVERAGE AND MAXIMUM EMPLOYEE SALARY

Procedural cohesion. Look for procedural or "flowcharty" names; for example,

> LOOP ROUTINE or SWITCH MODULE

or, in worse cases, even less meaningful names.

Temporal cohesion. Time-related names are a giveaway; for example,

> START UP, END OF JOB, or BEFORE . . .

Logical cohesion. The name is an umbrella or general-purpose one; for example,

> INPUT ALL or EDIT MODULE

and to use the module, a flag is needed.

Coincidental cohesion. The name is silly or meaningless; for example,

> FRUNK-MODULE, PROCESS-ROUTINE, X-100-RTPQ-ROUTINE

and to use the module, a flag is needed.

7.9 A decision tree for module cohesion

Some people prefer to use a decision tree in order to determine the level of cohesion of a module. To use the tree, start at the left and proceed toward the right. When you answer a question about the module, follow the path indicated by your answer. You will eventually arrive at the level of cohesion for that module.

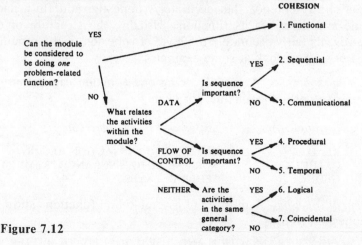

Figure 7.12

7.10 Finding the level of cohesion

Cohesion is a measure of module strength, and acts somewhat like a chain, holding together the activities in the module. If all the activities of a module are related by more than one level of cohesion, the module has the strength of the strongest level of cohesion; this is the chains-in-parallel rule.* If activities *within* a module are held together by different levels of cohesion, the module has the strength only of the *weakest*. This is the chains-in-series rule.†

For example, a module may contain some activities related procedurally, while other activities may be merely coincidentally related. In this case, the module *as a whole* is only coincidentally cohesive.

However, what about the case of a module called GET RECORD, FORMAT IT, AND EDIT IT? This appears to indicate that the module is sequentially cohesive. But if it's renamed GET VALID RECORD, it suddenly appears to be functionally cohesive, because all those activities make up the single problem-related function of getting a valid record. But the same chains-in-parallel rule applies: The best that we can say of this module *as a whole* is that it's functionally cohesive.

The level of cohesion of a module depends on the activities it carries out for its boss and is independent of where the module appears on the structure chart. For example,

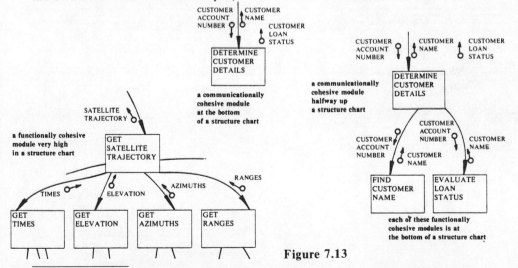

Figure 7.13

*Think of a chain capable of supporting twenty pounds tied in parallel with a chain capable of supporting only ten pounds. The resulting fat chain can hold at least twenty pounds.
†Think of the twenty-pound chain tied in series with the ten-pound chain. The resulting long chain can hold only ten pounds.

There are no tradeoffs between cohesion and coupling; they work together. Better (more) cohesion leads to better (less) coupling, which leads to better (more maintainable) systems.

7.11 Comparison of levels of cohesion

The following table presents a summary of the specific qualities of each type of cohesion:

Table 7.1

Cohesion Level	Coupling	Cleanliness of Implementation	Usability in Other Programs	Modifiability	Understandability
Functional	good	good	good	good	good
Sequential	good	good	medium	good	good
Communicational	medium	good	poor	medium	medium
Procedural	variable	medium	poor	variable	variable
Temporal	poor	medium	bad	medium	medium
Logical	bad	bad	bad	bad	poor
Coincidental	bad	poor	bad	bad	bad

Exercise

Each of the modules below is accompanied by a short sentence describing its activities. Determine as well as you can (without seeing each module as a structure chart) each module's level of cohesion:

AFTIN1   after input, add control items and verify totals

AFTIN2   after input, write proof tape, add control items, verify totals

GENREPT   produce report: either a sales report, a project status report, or a customer transaction report

SYNCH   check syntactic correctness of space-vehicle guidance parameters

OUTTRAN   print transaction and copy it to tape

UPCREDOUT update current credit record and write it to disk

STARTIT   open files, obtain first transaction and first master record, and print page headings

NEWTRAN   update record on file and get next transaction

CIRCDISP from an electrical connection matrix, produce a circuit diagram on a plotter

Answer

AFTIN1   sequential (if the added control items are the totals being verified)

AFTIN2   we know that AFTIN1 was sequential, but "write proof tape" is an activity whose strongest relationship to the other two is that it's done at the same time (that is, "after input"). Since "write proof tape" could be done either before or after the other two activities, the strongest cohesion for the whole module is *temporal*. This is an example of the chains-in-series rule.

GENREPT   logical

SYNCH   functional

OUTTRAN   communicational, also temporal, but since these two types of cohesion apply to the module *as a whole,* the stronger applies. This provides an example of the chains-in-parallel rule.

UPCREDOUT   sequential

STARTIT   temporal (not coincidental, because the activities are all done at one time)

NEWTRAN   procedural

CIRCDISP   functional (a complicated function high in the structure chart, no doubt, but a single problem-related function nonetheless)

8

Additional
Design Guidelines

Clearly, we need more than the criteria of coupling and cohesion to design maintainable systems. For example, if we relied on coupling alone, we would always produce systems consisting of a single module. And, we could hardly say that that module was tightly coupled to other modules, for there would be no other modules! Cohesion wouldn't help much either, because the cohesion of that single module would probably be quite high. Therefore, we need to take other design guidelines into account; this chapter explores twelve such elements: factoring, decision-splitting, system shape, error reporting, editing, state memory, matching structures, informational clusters, initialization and termination modules, restrictivity/generality, fan-out, and fan-in.

8.1 Factoring

Factoring is the separation of a function contained as code in one module into a new module of its own. It may be done for any of six reasons:

1. to reduce module size
2. to get the modular advantages of classic top-down design: making the system easier to understand and making modifications to the system more localized and straightforward
3. to avoid having the same function carried out by more than one module
4. to separate work (calculating and editing) from management (calls and decisions)
5. to provide more generally useful modules
6. to simplify implementation

The six sections that follow elaborate on each of these reasons.

8.1.1 Reducing module size

Factoring is a very effective way to deal with a module that is too large. A good size for a module is about half a page of a listing (30 lines or so), coded in a normal high-level language. Certainly, all the code of a module should be visible on one page of the listing (a requirement that sets an upper limit of 60 lines) or on two facing pages (120 lines). Experiments by Gerald Weinberg* show that our ability to understand a module and to find bugs in it depends on our being able to comprehend the whole module at once. Tom DeMarco maintains that the clarity of a program is inversely proportional to the number of fingers you need to read it.† He said this in condemnation of the oft-persecuted GOTO, but it applies to module size as well. A module that has to be on two back-to-back pages must be twice as hard to understand than one that is all on one page, because you need at least two fingers to keep track while you are reading it.

Thirty lines per module is certainly not a rigid standard; some modules will have fewer than ten lines, while a few may have more than one hundred lines. Then, at what point should you stop factoring modules?

- Stop factoring when you can't find a well-defined function to factor out. Don't pull out random lines of code, because together they would probably form a procedurally or temporally cohesive module.

- Stop factoring when the interface to a module is as complicated as the module itself (unless the module will be an often-used, "utility" module). A thousand-line module is bad because too many issues are confused within it — but a thousand one-line modules are worse, because you can't keep track of any single function without hopping from module to module and across interface after interface. But at design time, don't worry unduly about having modules that are too small, for it's better to be too detailed than to be too vague — and, anyway, it's easy to back off by using the "hat" or "unfactoring" symbol, as shown in Fig. 8.1.

---

*G. Weinberg, *The Psychology of Computer Programming* (New York: Van Nostrand Reinhold, 1971).
†T. DeMarco, private communication.

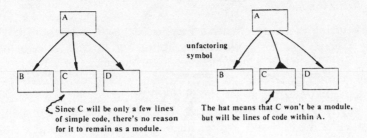

Since C will be only a few lines of simple code, there's no reason for it to remain as a module.

unfactoring symbol

The hat means that C won't be a module, but will be lines of code within A.

Figure 8.1

If a module is expected to be about thirty to fifty lines long, reducing its size clearly is not advantageous unless one of the other reasons for factoring applies.

8.1.2 Clarifying the system

To see how factoring gives us the modular advantages of classic top-down design, look at the module CALCULATE NET PAY FOR HOURLY WORKER in Fig. 8.2:

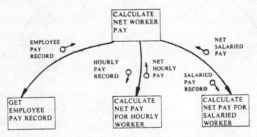

Figure 8.2

Inside this module, we know, will be both the code for calculating the worker's gross pay and the code for calculating the worker's deductions. If we wish to change one of these functions, then we have to be very careful to change only the desired one without interfering with the code for the other function.

Top-down design tells us to pull out each function into a module of its own (see Fig. 8.3). Now either function can be modified with little risk of accidentally destroying the other one, so long as the coupling to each module is low. The best way to get low coupling is to ensure that the factored-out modules have functional (or, at worst, sequential or communicational) cohesion.

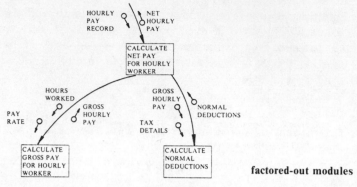

Figure 8.3

8.1.3 Minimizing duplication of code

Look at the effect of factoring on the whole piece of the structure chart in Fig. 8.4:

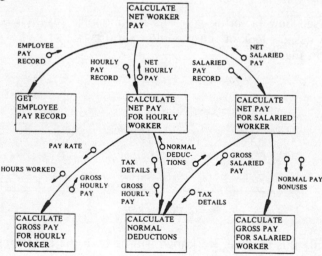

Figure 8.4

CALCULATE NORMAL DEDUCTIONS appears only once now, although its code was originally in two modules: CALCULATE NET PAY FOR HOURLY WORKER and CALCULATE NET PAY FOR SALARIED WORKER. This is a tremendous advantage, for the function of calculating normal deductions would originally have needed maintenance in two places — a tedious and error-prone duplication.

But what if, in the future, CALCULATE NET PAY FOR SALARIED WORKER requires abnormal instead of normal deductions? Shall we send a flag to CALCULATE NORMAL DEDUCTIONS telling it whether to be normal or abnormal? Definitely not! That would reduce it to being logically cohesive. Instead, we would add a new module called CALCU-LATE ABNORMAL DEDUCTIONS used only by CALCULATE NET PAY FOR SALARIED WORKER. (Any function that appears as code in both the NORMAL and ABNORMAL modules could be factored out to another, lower module if desired.)

8.1.4 Separating work from management

You may wonder why I bothered to factor out both CALCULATE GROSS PAY FOR HOURLY WORKER and CALCULATE NORMAL DEDUCTIONS from CALCULATE NET PAY FOR HOURLY WORKER, when factoring either one would have achieved the effect of separating the functions. But not only have I separated functions, I've also separated work (calculating and editing) from management (decisions and calls to other modules). (Remember I said in Chapter 1 that a manager in a well-organized company should coordinate the work of subordinates rather than *do* the work?)

The result of this kind of organization is a system in which modules at medium and high levels of the structure chart are quite simple to implement, because they get their work done by manipulating willing and trusty servants at lower levels. This is not to say that modules above the bottom level do nothing. They make coordinating decisions — and typically, the higher a module is in a system, the more important or global are its decisions.

The separation of work from management greatly improves maintainability. A change to a system is usually either a control change (part-time workers no longer get a lunch allowance, for example) or a work change (the formula changes for computing contributing insurance). It is rarely both.

8.1.5 Creating useful modules

Another advantage of factoring is that it often creates generally useful modules.

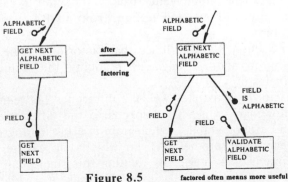

Figure 8.5   factored often means more useful

In Fig. 8.5, VALIDATE ALPHABETIC FIELD can now be used by any part of the system (or even systems yet to be developed) to check state or city names or whatever, whereas when it was code within GET NEXT ALPHABETIC FIELD, it was not accessible to any other module.

8.1.6 Simplifying implementation

Factoring can also ease programming problems. Imagine that text comes into a system on eighty-character cards and that we want to separate it into its constituent words. How about the solution shown in Fig. 8.6?

Since words are of various lengths, GET NEXT WORD is not easy to program, especially if words can cross card boundaries. If GET NEXT WORD is factored, as shown in Fig 8.7, then it's quite easy to implement, as it has only to combine characters into words.

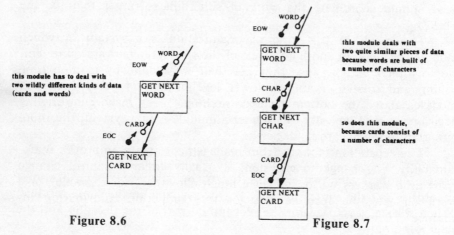

Figure 8.6

Figure 8.7

GET NEXT CHAR has the fairly easy job of getting the next character from the input. This arrangement is also more flexible, since now GET NEXT WORD (the "intelligent" part) is not tied to cards; it would work quite happily, without modification, from a CRT, paper tape, or any input medium.

In Section 8.11, we'll see that factoring can be used to ease programming in another way: by reducing the number of immediate subordinates of a module.

Factoring illustrates well the difference between a structure chart and a flowchart, which is analogous to the difference between a hologram and a photograph. A hologram is a fascinating device (created by laser beam interferometry) from which you can re-create an original three-dimensional image. By rotating this single holographic plate, you can see the front, sides, or even the back of a subject. Now, I don't want to digress too far into physics, but there's an even more fascinating property of a hologram: If you break off just a piece of it, you can still re-create the *whole original image,* although the details will be less well defined.

Look back at the structure chart in Fig. 8.2. Cover a part of it: the bottom three modules. You can still see the whole picture — calculating the net pay of a worker — although some of the details have gone. However, cutting part of a flowchart is like cutting part of a photograph: You lose some of the overall picture completely. If your structure chart has proper top-down characteristics, you should always be able to cut across the bottom (not the top!) and it will still show the whole scene, but without so many details.

8.2 Decision-splitting

A decision has two parts: recognition of what action to take, and execution of that action. These two parts are very different. For instance, recognizing that you have to get up and actually getting out of bed are certainly not the same!

Here's a pseudocode example:

if customer account number is not known   RECOGNITION
then reject whole customer record
endif   EXECUTION

Notice that the data used by the recognition part (customer account number) and that used by the execution part (whole customer record) aren't the same, and may not be available in the same module. When the data required for the recognition part of the decision and the data required for the execution part are *not* available in the same module, a *decision-split** occurs. A decision-split is the separation of the two parts of a decision.

Avoid decision-splits as much as possible. The execution part of a decision should be kept as close as possible to the recognition part, so that the recognized information doesn't have to travel a long way (usually as an undesirable tramp flag) to be acted upon. A severe decision-split — although sometimes unavoidable — is usually a symptom of poor organization of modules. If you notice that a decision has been split, rearrange the modules to bring recognition closer to execution. You shouldn't do this in a cavalier way, but you should pay attention to

---

*For further reading, see S. McMenamin, "The Perils of Decision-Splitting," *The YOURDON Report,* Vol. 3, No. 5 (October-November 1978), pp. 2-3.

cohesion and coupling — although curing a decision-split usually improves both cohesion and coupling.

For example, consider the portion of an interactive system for updating a file with transactions in Fig. 8.8:

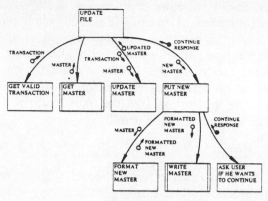

Figure 8.8

ASK USER IF HE WANTS TO CONTINUE recognizes the user's response, but UPDATE FILE is the only module with the power to execute that decision. The decision-split is the gap between the two modules. One symptom of the decision-split is the tramp flag CONTINUE RESPONSE, which passes through the uninterested module PUT NEW MASTER. Another symptom is the cohesion of PUT NEW MASTER, which, of course, should be called PUT NEW MASTER AND ASK USER IF HE WANTS TO CONTINUE. Its cohesion is procedural; its two activities are related only because one follows the other on a flowchart, and they cannot be summed up as a single function.

The cure for this decision-split is simple. The module ASK USER IF HE WANTS TO CONTINUE should be made directly subordinate to UPDATE FILE. But, two warnings about decision-splitting are in order. First, factoring tends to produce minor decision-splits, as shown in Fig. 8.9, for example. GET VALID TRANSACTION executes differently depending on whether VALIDATE TRANSACTION has recognized a particular TRANSACTION as valid or as invalid. Putting a hat on VALIDATE TRANSACTION would cure the decision-split — but it would also violate the rules of factoring. So, we would not do it.

A second warning is that some decision-splits are impossible (or very undesirable) to remove. A classic example is the recognition of the end of a sequential file. Although the end-of-file can be detected only by the READ NEXT RECORD module, the execution may be system-wide: Many modules may have to "shut up shop" when the end of the file is reached. Contorting the whole system to remove that decision-split would be foolish. It would violate not only the rules of factoring but also the very important criterion of system shape, discussed in Section 8.3.

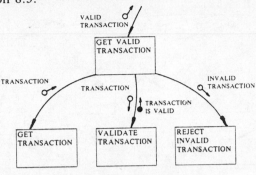

Figure 8.9

8.3 System shape

Some characteristics of the structure chart as a whole give us important clues as to the quality of a system. But before we look at the shape of the entire system, we need to look at the individual module types, because the distribution of these types is what we mean by a system's shape.

Modules consist of four basic types, determined by the direction that data flows through them. The types are: afferent, efferent transform, and coordinate, as shown in Fig. 8.10.*

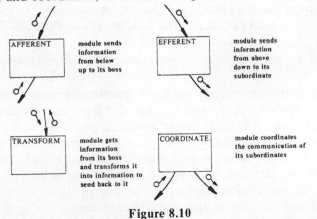

Figure 8.10

---

*Of course, many modules combine more than one of these basic flows.

By tradition, we group modules on a structure chart as much as possible as shown in Fig. 8.11:

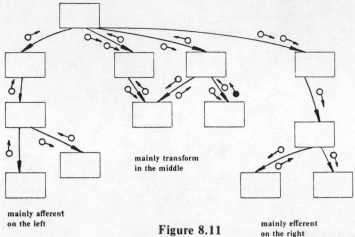

mainly afferent
on the left

mainly transform
in the middle

mainly efferent
on the right

Figure 8.11

Perhaps you're wondering why I burdened you with yet more jargon for something that's clearly "input-process-output." The problem is that "input" and "output" mean "read" and "write" to some people, and "what you give to a module" and "what you get back from it" to other people; and no doubt they have yet other meanings to other people. Not all afferent modules read anything; neither do many efferent modules write anything. The terms are taken from anatomy, which defines an afferent nerve as sending information toward the brain and an efferent nerve as sending it away from the brain.*

Now that we've arranged the modules in a standard way on the structure chart, we can look at the system's overall pattern or shape.

8.3.1 Physically input-driven systems

A *physically input-driven* system is one that does too little processing on its afferent (input) side so that the top modules have to deal with raw, physical, unedited, "dirty" data.

As a simple example, let's imagine that our input is a transaction from a CRT, which is to be applied to some master file. The transaction is made up of fields, each field occupying one or more CRT lines, with a special character at the end of the line to show continuation. A rough structure chart to do that might be that shown in Fig. 8.12:

---

*My own mnemonic is that an affluent person is on the way up, and effluent is on its way down.

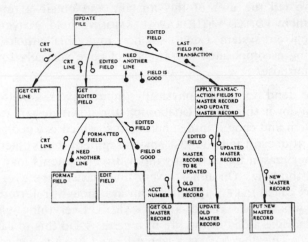

Figure 8.12

This is a physically input-driven system, because the boss, UPDATE FILE, has to deal with data that's physical (it has the specific characteristics of the CRT) and dirty (a line may contain a partial field and some fields may be incorrect). A physically input-driven system has been likened to a bum wandering into the president's office, without even a receptionist to greet him. In general, GET CRT LINE would be any module named GET A GRUBBY PIECE OF INPUT DATA.

Having derided physically input-driven systems, I should come up with concrete reasons for claiming that they are bad. There are several:

- Coupling is usually poor in such systems, because of decision-splitting problems. Notice in Fig. 8.12, for example, that FORMAT FIELD (a minor module in the organization) is sending control ("boss, I need another line") right up to the top of the chart.

- Many modules at the top of the system are concerned with the physical format of the input. A large and important part of the system would be badly hurt by a minor specification change (especially to a physical input format).

- In a physically input-driven system, modules that produce edited input may not be readily usable by other modules in the system. For example, imagine that the structure chart of Fig. 8.12 is part of a banking system and that UPDATE MASTER RECORD discovers that a field is in error — perhaps a withdrawal amount exceeds the previous balance. UPDATE MASTER RECORD might like

to tell the user of this mistake and obtain a replacement EDITED WITHDRAWAL AMOUNT field. Given the
current system, I don't see how to do this without writing a complicated extra piece of code specially for the
purpose.

People tend to create physically input-driven systems through
unaided top-down thinking. Unadorned top-down design tells you to
take a problem and chop it into subproblems, which is a good idea. Unfortunately, it doesn't tell you just *how* to segment the problem.

Another reason for physically input-driven systems may be residu-
al flowchart-thinking. On almost every flowchart I have ever seen, following a box called HSKPING (which I always thought referred to a town
in China) was a box called READ CARD. Everything else in the
flowchart read like a day in the life of a card: "Do this to card." "Do
that to card." The flowchart as a whole looked like the gastro-intestinal
tract of a card-eating monster. This practice virtually guaranteed a
card-driven system, in which a change to the format of the card would
bring disaster.

More rare — but just as bad — are physically output-driven systems. In this case, the boss gets hung up with the exact physical format
of the output. Such systems, being the mirror-image of physically
input-driven systems, have almost identical problems.

8.3.2 Balanced systems

A *balanced system* is one in which the top modules deal with data
of a logical, rather than a physical, nature. On the afferent side, the
data is edited and unblocked so that it's no longer dependent on the
way it happened to come into the system. On the efferent side, the
data is quite independent of any particular report format, for example,
that the user may want.

A balanced system, therefore, can be defined as one that is neither physically input-driven nor physically output-driven. An example
of a well-balanced system is shown in Fig. 8.13, in which the physical
characteristics of the input and output data have been relegated to the
bottom of the afferent and efferent branches, respectively.

Not only are balanced systems easier to implement because of
their cleaner coupling, but they're also very adaptable to specification
changes — especially changes to physical devices or formats. If, for example, we change the input medium to cards, or to paper tape, or to
anything else, the modification is confined to the humble module GET
TRANSACTION FIELD.

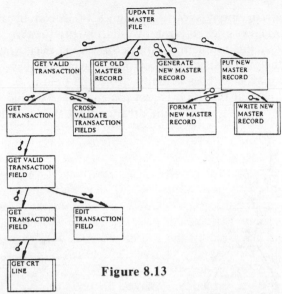

Figure 8.13

A balanced system provides generally useful low-level modules. Remember that in the input-driven system shown in Fig. 8.12 we had great difficulty getting an edited replacement field. About the only piece of data we could get easily was a CRT line. But in Fig. 8.13, we have the opportunity for GENERATE NEW MASTER RECORD or one of its subordinates to call GET VALID TRANSACTION FIELD for a valid replacement field. It's quite likely that even a module on the afferent side would offer this flexibility. For example, CROSS-VALIDATE TRANSACTION FIELDS would probably like to call GET VALID TRANSACTION FIELD to replace any inconsistent fields. It could also call GET VALID TRANSACTION to get a whole new transaction. And, if it really wanted a CRT line, it could still call GET CRT LINE.

A stunted afferent or efferent side of a structure chart is often a sign of imbalance. But I must emphasize that balance is NOT a visual characteristic. A system is balanced if and only if it deals with logical data at its top. Balanced systems may — and often do — *look* quite asymmetrical. The shape of the structure chart is dictated by the problem and not by aesthetics.

8.4 Error reporting

Errors should be reported from the module that both detects an error and knows what the error is. For example, let's say that we want to collect an input record, field by field, and to check the validity of each field as it is read.

The arrangement shown in Fig. 8.14 is bad because it restricts VALIDATE ALPHABETIC FIELD to validating CITY NAME only. Another way to look at this problem is to ask how VALIDATE ALPHABETIC FIELD can *know* that there's been an error. Maybe its boss can correct the problem or maybe its boss actually *wants* the field to be non-alphabetic. VALIDATE ALPHABETIC FIELD is just too menial to decide such matters.

At the other extreme is the arrangement shown in Fig. 8.15.

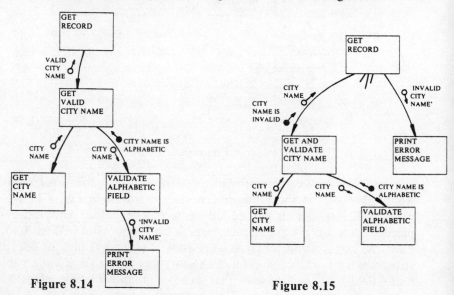

Figure 8.14   **Figure 8.15**

In Fig. 8.15, the error is being reported at some distance from where it's being detected. This causes extra coupling (the CITY NAME IS INVALID flag) to be passed to GET RECORD so that it knows whether to invoke PRINT ERROR MESSAGE.

The happy medium is shown in Fig. 8.16:

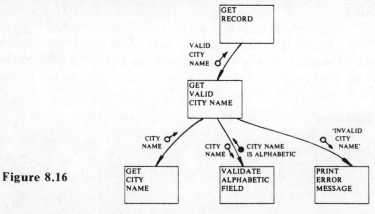

Figure 8.16

GET VALID CITY NAME is the lowest module that is aware of the error. If the system is an on-line one, the module can also easily obtain a replacement field if one is required.

A question that sometimes arises is where the text of error messages should be placed. The two major choices are to sprinkle the messages around the system so that each error message belongs to the module detecting the error, or to keep them all in one place. There are several advantages to keeping error messages together:

- It's easier to keep the wording and format of messages consistent. Users get very confused by receiving two slightly different messages for the same error when the error occurs in two different parts of the system.

- It's easier to avoid duplicate messages.

- It's easier to update messages and even to translate them all to a foreign language.

There are, however, two minor disadvantages. If you keep messages in one module, you'll need an artificial error message number to access them:

This module holds *all* of the error messages.

Each module that calls PRINT ERROR MESSAGE has to know which message number to send down. That makes it very difficult to reorder the messages and generally to keep them tidy.

Another disadvantage is that the code in the system isn't so readable as it is with the message text located where it's used.

8.5 Editing

I'm often asked in what order the editing of a piece of input data should be done. To illustrate my general guidelines, imagine the name of an American state being entered at a CRT.

- *Edit known before unknown.* If the person entering the field realizes he's made a mistake, then give him a chance either to correct it or to cancel the entry. For example, NE;ADA [CANCEL] should be graciously ignored.

- _Edit syntactic before semantic._ This simply means checking the data's format before checking its sense. For example, NE;ADA would be syntactically incorrect, whereas NEXADA would be syntactically correct, but semantically incorrect.

- _Edit single before cross._ Cross-validate only those fields that are individually correct. Obviously, a state name of NEVADA with a zip code of 10036 would be rejected, even though the components are individually correct. On the other hand, it would be useless to try to cross-validate NEXADA and T0Q36, because each component is incorrect in itself.

- _Edit internal before external._ Make sure that you verify everything in a given record before you try to apply that record to something else. For example, you should affirm that an amount of $200 in a withdrawal request record is syntactically and semantically correct and agrees with all the other fields on the record. Then you may reject it if the account balance on the customer's master record is only $152.

A generalized structure chart for editing is shown in Fig. 8.17.

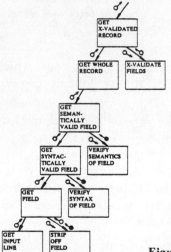

Note: In systems design, this generalized structure chart would be modified to show two things: First, error messages would also be issued from the appropriate modules. Second, external editing would be done when the X-VALIDATED RECORD is applied to another record.

Figure 8.17

A popular approach to editing, which Structured Design neither condemns nor condones, is table-driven editing. Table-driven processing is a useful technique for cutting down simple but repetitive coding. However, Structured Design offers an alternative editing technique that also reduces repetition but is more flexible than table-driven editing. This is transaction-centered editing, which is covered in Chapter 10.

8.6 State memory

When an ordinary module returns to its boss after carrying out its function, the module dies, leaving only the result as a legacy. When the same module is called upon again to do its duty, it's as if it is born for the first time. The module has no memory of anything that happened in its previous lives; indeed, like ourselves, it has no idea whether it even had a previous existence.

However, there's a kind of module that *is* aware of its past, through what is known as state memory. *State memory* is data internal to a module that survives unchanged from one invocation of that module to the next. (It is known in some languages as *static data*.)

A simple example of the need for state memory is shown below.

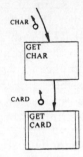

Figure 8.18

If we want to obtain our input character by character, although it enters the system on cards, we should have a module GET CHAR to pick off characters one by one, and to read a new card whenever necessary. But GET CHAR needs state memory. It has to save the current card intact from call to call, and it has to keep a pointer to the next character to be delivered from one invocation to the next. (The alternative − to hand all this information to the boss and get it back again on the next call − is undesirable. The very reason for a GET CHAR module is to hide such details from the boss.)

A module with state memory is generally unpredictable, which means that, although called with identical inputs, the module may act differently and/or produce a different output each time it is called. The GET CHAR module, although called with no inputs, sometimes reads a card and sometimes doesn't, depending on the value of its pointer. Another classic example of an unpredictable module is, of course, a random-number generator.

The module below collects fields until it has a whole transaction, which comprises twenty fields:

FIELD   TRANS

TRANS IS COMPLETE

BUILD
TRANS

BUILD TRANS may have to be called twenty times before it's ready to hand back the whole transaction to its caller. BUILD TRANS is unlikely to be usable in more than one place in the system. If another module calls BUILD TRANS, there's a risk that BUILD TRANS will not have a clean slate: It may contain a partially constructed transaction that could be mutilated by the second caller. The only sense in which BUILD TRANS is still generally useful is as a library module.

Maintenance programmers seem to have more trouble handling modules with state memory than they have with ordinary modules. This may be because a bug associated with a state-memory module can be intermittent and dependent on the current state of the module.

Because of their added complication, modules with state memory should be avoided wherever possible. But there are a number of places within most systems where they're unavoidable. In the next section, I offer a rule by which you can determine where you need state memory.

8.7 Matching program structure to data structure

The programming of many modules is made easier if the structure of the system follows the structure of the data. To illustrate data structure in this section, I use the graphic form of the data dictionary (see Chapter 4).

As a simple example, let's suppose that a line containing 120 characters is required for processing. However, the input comes from a device that delivers, not lines, but single characters. Therefore, we must build the lines ourselves (see Fig. 8.19):

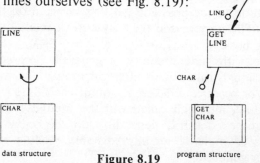

LINE

CHAR

data structure

Figure 8.19

LINE

GET
LINE

CHAR

GET
CHAR

program structure

The logic in GET LINE is trivially simple. When GET LINE is called, it calls GET CHAR 120 times, putting each CHAR received in the next available position in a buffer, LINE. Then it returns LINE.

But let's take the opposite situation, discussed in the previous section. Although single characters are required, the input arrives on 80 character cards that we have to segment (see Fig. 8.20).

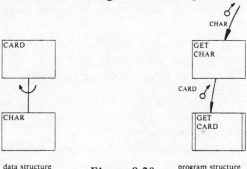

data structure   **Figure 8.20**   program structure

The logic in GET CHAR is not entirely trivial, because each time GET CHAR is called it has to deliver exactly one character from a group of 80. Therefore, between calls, GET CHAR has to hold any undelivered characters as well as a pointer to the character in the card to be delivered next. This, of course, is state memory. State memory almost always arises when the arrangement of the modules in a system is upside down with respect to the data that the modules are processing.*

Here's another example — from the efferent side of the system this time:

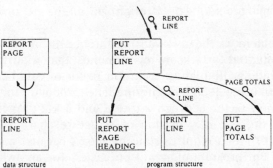

data structure   program structure

Figure 8.21

*Michael Jackson, one of the pioneering investigators of data structure, called this phenomenon *program inversion.* [See M. Jackson, *Principles of Program Design* (New York: Academic Press, 1975).]

In Fig. 8.21, the state memory is needed in PUT REPORT LINE to remember how many lines have been printed on the current page and to accumulate the totals for that page.

Things become rather more complicated as the differences between the types of data being processed increase. So far, we've been looking only at turning N items into one item or one item into N items. What if we have to turn N items into M items (what Jackson calls a structure clash[†])?

Let's say that a transaction record contains 19 fixed-length fields. However, the physical input is on cards, and each card contains as many fields as will fit (but always between three and seven fields). Graphically, in Fig. 8.22 we have:

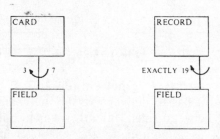

Figure 8.22

To obtain a record in the way shown in Fig. 8.23 would make the programming of GET RECORD very difficult. There's no telling how many CARDS make a RECORD: It might be three, six, or even four and a half.

The problem is the awkward difference in structure between a CARD and a RECORD. Jackson recommends that a structure clash be resolved by finding the highest common factor of data between the two structures and using it as an intermediate product. In this case, the highest common factor between a CARD and a RECORD is easy to find: It's a FIELD. So, our new portion of structure chart is shown in Fig. 8.24. Now, GET FIELD requires state memory, because a card comprises many fields. But programming will be easier, for an awkward problem has been split into two simpler ones.

[†]According to Jackson, ibid., two items of data exhibit a structure clash when there is no integral fit between one item and the other.

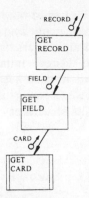

Figure 8.23   **Figure 8.24**

You may have noticed that this is identical to the kind of factoring we did in Section 8.1.6. It also leads to balanced systems, in which potentially difficult or changeable physical aspects of data are pushed down to the bottom of the structure chart, where modifications would have a minimal effect on the overall system. These all are manifestations of Beneficial Wishful Thinking,* a design philosophy that advocates

- Keep the data structures around a module (or DFD bubble) as similar as possible. If the available data structures are not similar, then change them by introducing new structures and modules (or bubbles).
- Don't ask a single module to do too much.

Beneficial Wishful Thinking sums up a number of design criteria and guidelines that we've already seen:

- factoring for ease of programming
- editing in levels, whereby only syntactically correct data is checked for semantic corrections
- creating balanced systems, whereby the top modules deal with refined, edited, logical data and the bottom modules deal with unedited, physical data. This has its equivalent in a DFD, in that the innermost bubbles deal with processing logical data, whereas the outermost bubbles "protect" the innermost ones from the brutal physicalities of the outside world (see Fig. 8.25).

---

*T. DeMarco, private communication.

We've also seen how data structure helps not only with Beneficial Wishful Thinking, but also with spotting state-memory requirements.

Jackson and others have tried to make the data structure approach a stand-alone design strategy. In its present state of development, I haven't found it very successful in designing a whole system, but I have found it extremely useful in sorting out knotty problems caused by difficult data structures.

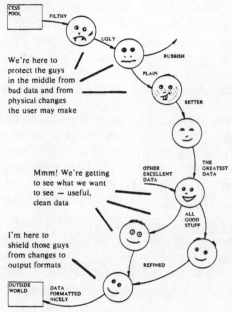

Figure 8.25

8.8 Informational clusters

An *informational cluster** is a set of modules used for every access to data that has a complex structure or sensitive security. To illustrate the use of an informational cluster, I present the following example: When you make a long-distance telephone call, you sometimes reach a wrong number or get a line that's so bad it sounds as if you're communicating with a Voyager space probe. In such a case, you probably hang up, call the operator, and grumble about the state of today's utility companies. If you convince the operator that the utility was at fault, then your call will be canceled with no payment due.

---

*D. Parnas, "Information Distribution Aspects of Design Methodology," *Proceedings of the 1971 IFIP Congress,* Booklet TA-3 (Amsterdam, The Netherlands: North-Holland Publishing Co., 1971), pp. 26-30.

As you might expect, most such cancellations are made within a couple of minutes of the offending call. So, phone companies delay writing a long-distance call record on to a permanent file pending an immediate cancellation. If the cancellation comes, then it can annihilate the call, and both call and cancellation can vanish without a trace.

In theory, the phone company has to hold on to an infinite number of call records while waiting for a possible cancellation. But since, as we saw, most cancellations arrive soon after the call, holding on to about one thousand records will usually suffice.

The best way to organize these thousand or so records is in a circular buffer, where the oldest call record is the first to be written out to make room for a new call record. A cancellation will knock a record out if it's in the buffer; otherwise, the cancellation will have to be written to a special cancellation file for later credit.

Figure 8.26 shows the set of modules that might be used to access a temporary call area:

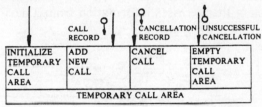

Figure 8.26

The notation in Fig. 8.26 means that there is an area of data called TEMPORARY CALL AREA (containing the delayed call records), which can be accessed by only four modules in the whole system: INITIALIZE TEMPORARY CALL AREA, ADD NEW CALL, CANCEL CALL, and EMPTY TEMPORARY CALL AREA. Each access to TEMPORARY CALL AREA is made via one of these four modules; no behind-the-scenes fiddling with this data is allowed by any other module.

The major benefit of an informational cluster of modules like this is that knowledge of the specific layout of TEMPORARY CALL AREA is hidden from all but four modules in the system. So the area could be implemented by a single physical area with two pointers, or by a linked list, or by any other weird and wonderful scheme. The problem of the "hole" created when a call is canceled could also be tackled in a number of ways that are irrelevant to this discussion.

The undesirable alternatives to hiding TEMPORARY CALL AREA behind an informational cluster are to pass it as a parameter between the modules that need it, or to keep it in a global area. The first alternative has all of the problems of stamp coupling, in that each module using a part of TEMPORARY CALL AREA needs to be aware of the naked structure of all of it. And furthermore, fairly complex data access logic will have to be duplicated in several modules. Common coupling has the same problems as stamp coupling; in addition, even modules not using TEMPORARY CALL AREA would have unrestricted access to it.

The most general way to implement an informational cluster is as one routine (a COBOL program, for example) with a separate entry point for each module in the cluster. But make sure you obey Structured Programming principles by having a separate RETURN or GO BACK for each entry point and that there is no code shared among the entry points. A bad alternative — calling a single module with a function flag — would have all the problems of logical cohesion (parameters with meanings that vary from call to call, and so on). A good alternative, if your language (like FORTRAN) has the facility, is a labeled COMMON area. This is an area that is "partially global" in that only modules with specific permission written into them can access it.*

Another use for informational clusters is in improving the performance of a system that accesses information from a data base. Consider the simple example presented in Fig. 8.27.

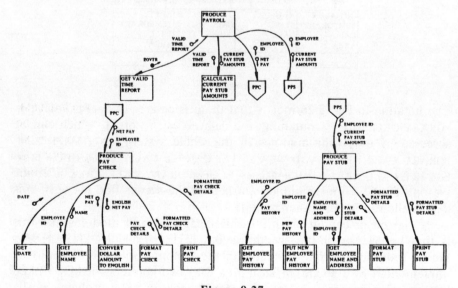

Figure 8.27

---

*If you're a data-base aficionado, you've already seen the idea of informational clusters in the notion of data independence, which says that application programs should be blissfully ignorant of the physical layout of the data they use. Data bases also like to restrict access to data for security. This could be implemented in an informational cluster in a rudimentary way by requiring that a password be used as one parameter in each call.

If the EMPLOYEE DETAILS FILE looks like this

employee details file = {employee ID + employee name + employee address}

then it has to be accessed twice for each employee: once by GET EM-
PLOYEE NAME and once by GET EMPLOYEE NAME AND ADDRESS. That
might increase the run time of the system considerably — especially if
each access to the EMPLOYEE DETAILS FILE causes the mechanical seek
of a disk head.

The best solution to this problem — short of passing EMPLOYEE
NAME AND ADDRESS all around the system as a tramp (which, in general, leads to diabolical coupling) or keeping it in a common area — is
to use a *cache*.* In the example of Fig. 8.27, the cache would look like

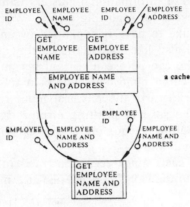

Figure 8.28

Let's say that PRODUCE PAY STUB wants the EMPLOYEE NAME and the
EMPLOYEE ADDRESS. It calls GET EMPLOYEE NAME, which inspects the
cache. Then, one of two events may occur: The name and address for
that employee may already be in the cache, in which case GET EMPLOY-
EE NAME will send back the EMPLOYEE NAME immediately. That will
save a data-base call. Or, there may be nothing for that employee in
the cache, in which case GET EMPLOYEE NAME will have to issue a data-
base call. In that event, we've gained nothing. But the next time a
name or address for that employee is needed, there will be no need for
another data-base call.

The cache can be extended to hold a group of records, rather than
just one. This improves run time or response time even more; but it

---

*A cache is a method for reducing access time to data stored in a large, slow medium, by
retaining the most often accessed data in a smaller, faster medium.

does require an ability to predict roughly what information you will need and to retrieve it efficiently in one attempt from your data base. This technique is known as *anticipatory retrieval* (on input) or *deferred storage* (on output). It is closely analogous to input/output buffering in operating systems.

What I've said about data-base usage in the last few paragraphs implies that, as a designer, you must have a reasonably clear idea of how your data bases are organized. The best way to find that out is to go to your data-base administrator or data-base design group if the data base is being developed in parallel with your system. Ask them what problems your data-base accesses might cause you, and how you can improve your design for the sake of their data base.

Yet another use of informational clusters (similar to using a cache for data-base accesses) is for reporting errors. When an error is detected, the user would like to have it explained by an error message, and very often he would also like to see the current physical input record printed out so that he can peruse it to find his mistake. However, an error could be discovered almost anywhere in the system. Does that mean that you have to carry the physical input record all around the system merely for the sake of printing error messages? Clearly, that would be such a violation of coupling and of Beneficial Wishful Thinking that it cannot be allowed.

Instead, when each input record is read in, it should be kept where it is available to the PRINT ERROR MESSAGE module, as in

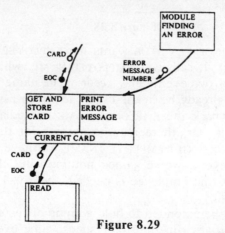

Figure 8.29

When an error is detected, the current card can be displayed alongside the error message.

If you think that a module with separate entry points is going a bit far to implement a method of displaying the current input record, then relax. No one says you have to implement an informational cluster as a module with separate entry points: It just happens to be the best way to do it in most languages. An alternative is simply to put the current input record into an area of working-storage common to all modules. That alternative is less desirable because of the exposure of the input record to too much code. However, it does have the advantage of simplicity.

8.9 Initialization and termination modules

I hinted in Section 7.5 on temporal cohesion that initialization and termination modules would be difficult to maintain because of their mediocre cohesion and high coupling. Initialization and termination must be done somewhere, but they shouldn't be allowed to create the problems of temporal cohesion. For example, see Fig. 8.30.

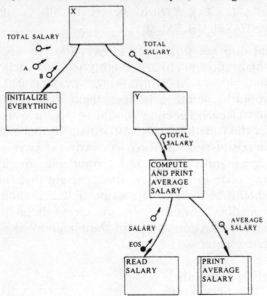

Figure 8.30

This system has a large initialization module, which initializes everything in the system in one magnificent blast. In particular, it clears TOTAL SALARY for a module called COMPUTE AND PRINT AVERAGE SALARY. I've shown TOTAL SALARY being passed through very many modules as tramp data. In reality, most designers would slap it into a common area and hope for the best.

There are several problems with the arrangement in Fig. 8.30:

- Initialization of TOTAL SALARY is far away from the rest of the function of calculating an average salary, both on the structure chart and in the final code. Surprisingly often, the initialization is forgotten or mishandled.

- COMPUTE AND PRINT AVERAGE SALARY isn't a very useful module. Let's imagine another module, Z, wants to compute and print the average salary. It can't merely use the existing module COMPUTE AND PRINT AVERAGE SALARY because this module doesn't do any initialization.

- INITIALIZE EVERYTHING is not very useful either, because each time it is called it resets everything in the system to its initial state. Therefore, Z could not use INITIALIZE EVERYTHING before it calls COMPUTE AND PRINT AVERAGE SALARY.

We could improve INITIALIZE EVERYTHING by factoring it into a number of initialization modules, roughly one for each function being initialized. But, if we split INITIALIZE EVERYTHING into separate modules, it would be pointless to keep them all in one place. Instead, the initialization of each function should be placed where it belongs — with the rest of the function being initialized. In this example, clear TOTAL SALARY in COMPUTE AND PRINT AVERAGE SALARY.

Although big initialization and termination modules do package "housekeeping" code in one place, the rules are that for each function initialization should be done as late as possible and should be terminated as soon as possible.* Another way to express these rules is, Initialize and terminate each function as low in the hierarchy as possible without introducing state memory.

8.10 Restrictivity/generality

Don't make your modules too restrictive or too general. This bland statement sounds reasonable, but what do "restrictive" and "general" mean? A _restrictive module_ has one or more of the following characteristics:

- _It performs a needlessly specific job._ I once encountered four pieces of code in a system that generated weather statistics: One generated the mean, mode, and median

---

*P.J. Plauger, private communication.

for 28 temperatures; another did the same for 29 temperatures; another for 30; and another for 31. This is the most ludicrous example of restrictivity I've ever seen. What was needed was a *single* module that generated mean, mode, and median for any length of month. The length of the month could be passed to it as a parameter rather than being hard-wired in.

- *It deals with restrictive data values, types, or structures.* A simple example might be a COMPUTE NET PROFIT module that could handle only positive numbers — optimistic, but restrictive!

- *It makes assumptions about where or how it's being used.* For example, look at the arrangement in Fig. 8.31:

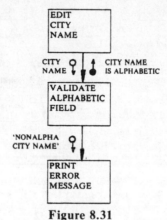

Figure 8.31

VALIDATE ALPHABETIC FIELD must be assuming that it's always called by EDIT CITY NAME, since it's sending a specific error message to PRINT ERROR MESSAGE.* This is a shame, because VALIDATE ALPHABETIC FIELD is a potentially useful module for validating state names, person names, and so on, although now it's being restricted to validating only city names. One solution would be to have a less specific error message; but a better solution would be to rid VALIDATE ALPHABETIC FIELD of any involvement with error messages, and have PRINT ERROR MESSAGE be called by EDIT CITY NAME.

The problem with restrictive modules is that they are hard to reuse. Maintenance is slow and tedious when each of a dozen modules

---

*No module has the right to this assumption. As a child doesn't get to choose its parents, so a module doesn't get to choose its superordinates.

is doing an esoteric variation on the same theme and the theme has to be changed. Whenever you must create a new module to do a function almost identical to one being done by an existing module, it's often worth making the old one general enough to handle both variations of the function, as long as that doesn't create logically cohesive modules.

A subtle case of restrictivity is created by tying a module to a specific input or output stream. This means that afferent and efferent modules aren't so reusable as their transform equivalents. For example, look at the comparison in Fig. 8.32.

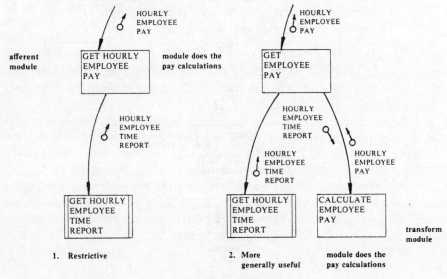

Figure 8.32

In case 1, the pay calculations are tied to hourly paid employees. In case 2, they are not. Therefore, in case 2 we would be able to use CAL-CULATE EMPLOYEE PAY to calculate the pay of part-time workers, for example.*

At the opposite extreme to a restrictive module, an *over-general module* has one or more of the following characteristics:

- *It performs a ridiculously broad job.* An example is a date-editing routine that accounts for the year 1752, in which many countries removed 13 days from September in order to adjust the calendar from Julian to Gregorian.

---

*This example of restrictivity, as you may have realized, is simply a restatement of the fifth advantage of factoring — creating generally useful modules (Section 8.1.5).

- *It deals with too many data types, values, or structures.* For example, to use a real number rather than an integer to keep track of the number of bolts in a stockroom would be over-general.

- *It reads in, or takes as a parameter, data that is unlikely to change.* A module that reads in the number of days in a week is certainly general; it's also ludicrous.

Over-general modules typically have poor coupling and cohesion. The extra code for the more baroque parts of their functions has to be maintained even though it's probably "dead weight" code that will never be used. Recent college graduates are notorious for producing over-general modules and large software vendors are notorious for producing over-general systems. In a fanatical effort to please or impress people, they give their modules the ability to deal with combinations of events that won't arise until the year 2525.

Generalizing by allowing more flexibility of data is usually less dangerous than generalizing to allow more flexibility of function. Increasing flexibility of function tends to lead to more code, more complexity, worse coupling, and even perhaps to worse cohesion.

A fairly harmless way to generalize is to delay *binding time* (alias *commitment time),* which is the time that a piece of data is given an actual value. It can occur at various times, from coding through execution.

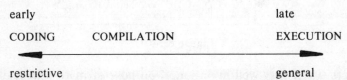

Binding a value to a piece of data at coding time usually means writing in a raw literal, such as 2.71828 or 30. It is very restrictive. Binding a value at execution time (for example, reading in the price of eggs) is very general. You must choose what is right for the problem. In a payroll system, it would not be right to hard-code in the number of employees in a company or their salaries, since these values are continually changing. Neither would it make sense to read in the number of cents in a dollar. Often the best compromise is to bind a value at compilation time (in effect, with a COBOL VALUE or with a FORTRAN DATA statement). The number of days in a week could be set as

DAYS-IN-WEEK   VALUE 7   PIC 9.

Then, instead of a possibly ambiguous 7 in the code, the instantly meaningful DAYS-IN-WEEK would appear.

8.11 Fan-out

The *fan-out* from a module is the number of immediate subordinates to that module. An example is shown in Fig. 8.33.

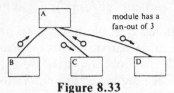

Figure 8.33

In the 1960s, when modularity — the "maintenance savior" of the future — first became popular, a software design technique known as main-line design made its debut on the systems development stage to thunderous applause and wild cheering. Main-line design called for a single boss (the "control" or "main-line") module, with every other module in the system as its subordinate (see Fig. 8.34).

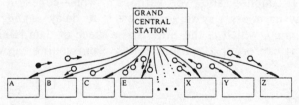

Figure 8.34

There was a very well-intentioned purpose of main-line design: to reap the benefits of modularity by isolating a single change to a single module. It did that, all right! Almost every non-trivial change that was made to the system required a change to — yes, you guessed it! — the main-line module, simply because almost every non-trivial function in the system was being carried out by that unhappy module. Even from the structure chart in Fig. 8.34 alone, you can visualize that the main-line module must contain a maelstrom of code, for all the pieces of data in the system are dashing in and out like Keystone Kops.

The adulation of main-line design turned to sneers, and the bouquets of roses to cabbages. Main-line design was booed off the software stage and almost dragged modularity with it.

So, to avoid repeating such a tragedy, you should try to limit the fan-out from a module to no more than seven. A module with too many subordinates can be easily cured by the old familiar remedy of factoring. Separate each subfunction within a main-line module into a module of its own, as shown in Fig. 8.35:

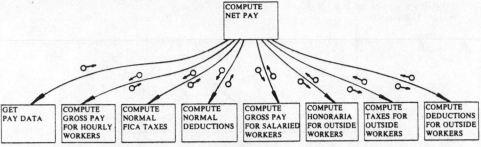

Figure 8.35

The figure looks like a "pancake," a symptom of a missing intermediate level. High fan-out is rectified by factoring out middle-management modules with strong cohesion and loose coupling (see Fig. 8.36).

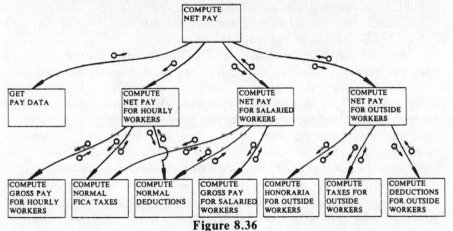

Figure 8.36

Why should the limit on the number of immediate subordinates to a module be seven and not seventeen or twenty-seven? Does this mean that if you design a module with eight other modules reporting to it that you'll be struck by lightning? No, of course the number seven is not an unbendable standard, although if you have a fan-out of more than seven from any module, warning bells should sound in your mind.

Seven is a very important number in human psychology.* Have you ever tried doing more than seven activities at once? If you have,

---

*G.A. Miller, "The Magical Number Seven, Plus or Minus Two: Some Limits on Our Capacity for Processing Information," *Psychological Review,* Vol. 63 (March 1956), pp. 81-97.

I'm sure you have found yourself becoming very flustered and prone to making errors. Reasonably scientific experiments have yielded the results shown in Fig. 8.37.

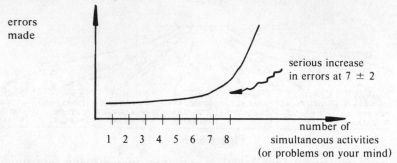

Figure 8.37

Everyday life seems to bear out the graph. For example, a person has difficulty memorizing more than seven digits (which, interestingly, is the length of a North American telephone number). Air traffic controllers handle about seven planes at a time.

Several tentative explanations for this human limitation* have been put forward. The most attractive one is that the brain's "central processor" uses seven "registers," each one of which can hold a "node of information" (a concept, if you like). When you have to tackle more than seven problems at once, the brain must "page" information into and out of the registers. This process isn't quite error-free, apparently. In the extreme case, "thrashing" sets in, and the whole "system" comes crashing down in a mélée of distracted confusion.

Someone programming a module with seven subordinates must have at least seven issues on his mind. Although I can't say that this is bound to make him err, it will bring him too close to his hrair limit for comfort.

Low fan-out is acceptable, although it's rather like a department with one boss and one worker. Such a case may be a hint to factor out a module from the boss, as VALIDATE TRANS has been factored in the example in Fig. 8.38.

---

*This limitation is not solely human. This phenomenon has been observed in several animal species. For example, Richard Adams in his delightful heroic tale *Watership Down* (New York: Macmillan, 1974) relates how rabbits count: "one-two-three-four-hrair." Numbers greater than four are just too large for them to distinguish between. Their conceptual counting limit (or *hrair* limit) is four.

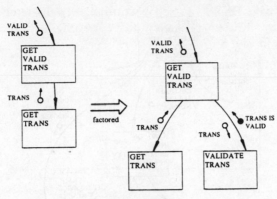

Figure 8.38

8.12 Fan-in

The *fan-in* to a module is the number of immediate bosses it has.

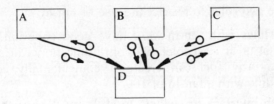

Figure 8.39

High fan-in is the reward for intelligent factoring and the removal of restrictive modules. At programming time, having one function called by several bosses avoids the need to code practically the same function in several places. Hence, at maintenance time, duplicate updating to a function is eliminated.

Don't be afraid of the situation shown in Fig. 8.40, in which a module's bosses are at different levels. If a module has a truly useful function, then it can be used by a module anywhere in the system.

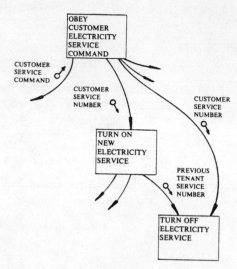

Figure 8.40

There are two rules to restrict the use of fan-in:

● <u>Modules with fan-in *must* have good cohesion</u>: functional or at least tolerably communicational or sequential. Any fool can create a coincidentally cohesive module with a fan-in of 100.

● <u>Each interface to a single module must have the same number and types of parameters</u>. For example, this makes no sense:

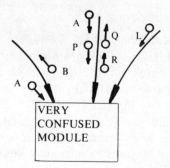

8.13 Table for design criteria

Here is a table summarizing the twelve design criteria discussed in this chapter, plus cohesion and coupling, which were discussed in Chapters 6 and 7.

Criterion	Guideline
cohesion	make each module functional or, at the least, sequential or communicational
coupling	keep the coupling between modules loose (data, stamp, and descriptive flags are acceptable)
data structure	match the program structure as much as possible to the data structure
decision-splitting	keep the recognition part of a decision close to its execution
editing	edit in successive levels, with the simplest editing done at the lowest level
error reporting	have the same module that recognizes the error as such report the error
factoring	keep it high
fan-in	make it high
fan-out	restrict the number of subordinates to a module to fewer than seven
informational cluster	use an informational cluster to avoid the problems of stamp or common coupling (or both)
initialization/termination modules	initialize as late as possible; wrap up as soon as possible
restrictivity/generality	don't make a module too restrictive or too general
state memory	avoid state memory wherever possible
system shape	make the system balanced (neither physically input-driven nor physically output-driven)

This brief list/table presents only a simplification of the criteria. In the actual design process, it is necessary to take into consideration all of the details presented in the body of this chapter; used carefully, these criteria are your basic tools for evaluating and refining a design.

Exercises

1. Does the cohesion of a module's subordinates have any effect on the permissible fan-out from that module?

2. DeMarco's Law — the clarity of a program is inversely proportional to the number of fingers you need to read it — was coined to draw attention to the incomprehensibility of large chunks of spaghetti code. However, DeMarco's Law seems to imply a condemnation of Structured Design too, for in order to understand a single module one also has to "put one's fingers" on the code for all that module's subordinates, and possibly even for each of their subordinates as well. Is there a fallacy in the previous sentence, or does DeMarco's Law really run counter to Structured Design?

3. Suppose you are required to construct a record (comprising ten fields) from fields that are read in with random sequence. Using the field number that accompanies each field, you should place each field in its appropriate slot in the record. (Duplicate fields should be rejected with an error message.)

   The portion of a structure chart that would effect this requirement is shown below:

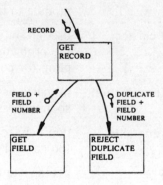

The criterion of factoring might lead to the structure chart shown below:

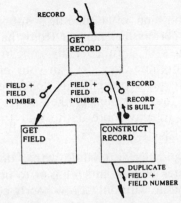

Does the structure chart shown in the second figure have any disadvantages that the one shown in the first figure avoids?

4. In Section 7.5, on temporal cohesion, and again in Section 8.9, on initialization and termination modules, I emphasized the dangers of large initialization modules invoked at the start of a program. Can you think of *any* valid use for such an initialization module?

5. Can you suggest a reason for deliberately giving a module a fan-out of more than 7 ± 2?

Answers

1. Indeed the cohesion of a module's subordinates does have an effect on the permissible fan-out from that module. One of the great advantages of a functionally cohesive module is that you need to use only one "register" in your brain to think about the module. However, a procedurally cohesive module that contains pieces of, say, four functions is likely to tie up four mental "registers" — and probably more if the four functional fragments are related in an obscure way.

    Therefore, in practice, a module with a dozen functionally cohesive subordinates may be much easier to understand and to maintain than a module with only a few poorly cohesive subordinates.

2. The fallacy lies in the fact that to understand the function of a module's subordinate, it should not be necessary to "put one's finger" on that subordinate's code. Instead, the function of any strongly cohesive module should be readily apparent from its name and the details of the subordinate's code should be irrelevant to the calling module, so long as the subordinate actually accomplishes its stated function.

    However, if a system contains a bug, one cannot be sure that a subordinate *does* accomplish its intended function. Therefore, while debugging, one may have to keep a finger on the code of the calling module at the point where it calls its subordinate, and use another finger to trace through the logic of the suspect subordinate.

    This process may have to continue through further levels of invocation until the bug is found. For most systems, even this should require only a handful of fingers; and, regardless of the number of fingers one needs, the clarity of the code remains high because at all times it's obvious where you came from last and where you will arrive next. The problem that DeMarco highlighted in code with wild and random GOTOS — that of needing an exponentially increasing number of fingers and of very quickly losing track of the system's logic — simply does not arise.

3. Yes, there are disadvantages in the factored structure chart. The module CONSTRUCT RECORD requires state memory, which is not required by any module on the first structure chart. The state memory is needed to remember the partially constructed record from call to call of CONSTRUCT RECORD. Furthermore, CON-

STRUCT RECORD has to return a flag to indicate to GET RECORD whether the record is complete.

In this example, factoring has achieved little: It has merely removed the complexity of constructing a record from GET RECORD to the new module CONSTRUCT RECORD. However, this new module is harder to understand than the original GET RECORD was, because CONSTRUCT RECORD has state memory and an awkward interface.

(The moral of this exercise is that whenever you apply a Structured Design guideline you should think about what the application will buy you and what it will cost you.)

4. Almost every system needs state memory in a few modules. In most languages this state memory has to be initialized from outside the module. Although state memory — like everything else — should be initialized as late as possible, for a great deal of state memory this initialization cannot be postponed beyond the start of a program. Thus, it is worthwhile to introduce a module (called, for example, INITIALIZE STATE MEMORY) to open files, set a page counter to 0, set a line counter to 1, set a transaction count to 0, and so on.

However, such a module should not contain any superfluous initialization. It should not look like the traditional "housekeeping" module, which typically contained a miscellany of initialization, including very often the printing of column headers for the first page of a report. The printing of column headers has nothing to do with system initialization: It's part of a module called, perhaps, THROW PAGE.

5. There are two special cases in which a module may have a high fan-out and still be acceptable. One is at the top of a transaction center; this case is covered in detail in Chapter 10. The other is when a part of the design is based on the data structure of the problem and the data structure itself has high fan-out.

For example, let's say that we want to input a customer transaction consisting of fourteen fields from a CRT.

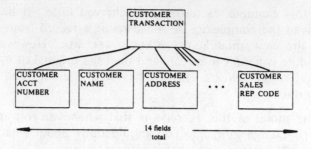

The part of the structure chart that gets the customer transaction is depicted below:

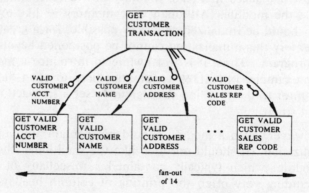

Of course, whenever possible, data structures with high fan-out should be avoided, for the same reasons that modules with high fan-out should be avoided.

SECTION IV
DESIGN STRATEGIES

If all we had for designing systems were a set of tools for depicting, evaluating, and refining a design, then reaching a design that was worth implementing would be a long, tedious process. Fortunately, however, Structured Design offers us two major strategies for quickly deriving a good design. From this good design, the evaluation and refinement guidelines can swiftly take us toward an excellent design. Without such strategies, we would all too often have to play the part of an infinite number of monkeys scratching away at structure charts and hoping that sooner or later we would turn out something close to good.

Chapter 9, covering the design strategy called transform analysis, provides the main link between Structured Analysis and Structured Design (or, if you prefer, between the data flow diagram and the structure chart). The chapter shows how the structured specification from Structured Analysis can serve the designer as a tremendous aid in the smooth development of a well-designed system.

The overall structure of systems tends to fall into recognizable patterns. One of the most common patterns in commercial systems is the so-called transaction-centered system. Transaction analysis, the subject of *Chapter 10,* is a specific strategy for designing this type of system.

9

Transform Analysis

Transform analysis (or transform-centered design, as it is also known) is the major strategy for designing balanced systems, which — as we saw in Section 8.3 — are easier to develop and cheaper to maintain than physically input- or output-driven systems. The whole point of transform analysis is to convert the DFD of analysis to the structure chart of design.

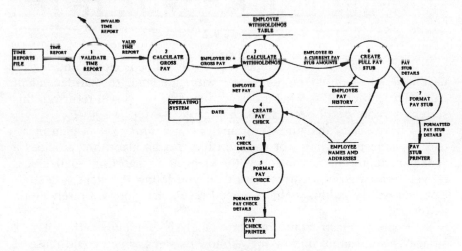

Figure 9.1

The application of transform analysis to the DFD shown above in Fig. 9.1, depicting an hourly workers payroll system that prints pay checks and pay stubs, would yield a balanced structure chart of the same payroll system as pictured in Fig. 9.2:

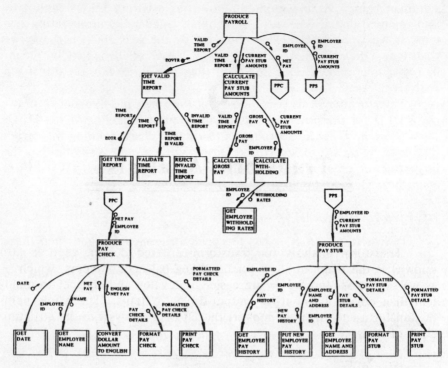

Figure 9.2

Notice that the top modules deal with refined, clean, and logical data while the bottom modules deal with unedited, format-dependent data. That, after all, is what a balanced system is. (I will return to this system in more detail later in this chapter.)

I have stated that transform analysis is a *strategy* — a plan of attack, a game plan. It is not an algorithm, for an algorithm provides a cookbook approach. If you follow the steps of an algorithm meticulously, you're assured of a correct result. If you follow the steps of a strategy, you will get within sight of a good result, but you will rarely attain perfection.

When you carry out transform analysis, remember that it is a strategy. You cannot unthinkingly follow its steps as you could those of an algorithm. From time to time, to stay on the right track, you must bring to bear your knowledge of what the system is supposed to accomplish. And, when you derive your first structure chart, you must use all the design criteria you have learned to improve it.

One day, transform analysis may become an algorithm. But if it does, the structure chart will disappear and the DFD will be implemented directly, for a machine can obey an algorithm much better than can a human being. At the moment, however, arbitrary DFDs cannot be implemented directly, because, in general, languages and operating systems are just not sophisticated enough.* By the year 2000, perhaps, we shall see DFDs being executed on a horde of dynamically reconfigurable microprocessors. But until then, we must rely on transform analysis.

Transform analysis is composed of the following five steps: drawing a DFD for the problem, finding the central functions of the DFD, converting the DFD into a rough-cut structure chart, refining this structure chart by means of Structured Design criteria, and verifying that the final structure chart meets the requirements of the original DFD. I explain these steps and their sub-topics below.

9.1 Step 1: Draw a DFD

If Structured Analysis has preceded Structured Design, then there will be a set of rigorous DFDs in the structured specification. If not, then it's worth the time it takes to sketch out some DFDs from the verbal outpourings of the functional specification.

Not only will the DFDs be the input to transform analysis, but drawing them will help to clarify the specification. Don't go to such a level of detail that you have more bubbles than you know what to do with. Stay at a level that has a few dozen bubbles at most. If you find you need more detail (or less detail) in a particular area, then go down (or up) a level in that area.

9.2 Step 2: Identify the central transform

The central transform is the portion of the DFD that contains the essential functions of the system and is independent of the particular implementation of the input and output. It can be found in either of two ways. The first way to identify the center of the DFD is just by looking at it. For example, study Fig. 9.3 on the next page.

---

*However, the UNIX† operating system and the ADA programming language have made some dramatically successful advances in directly implementing simple DFDs. (†UNIX is a registered trademark of Bell Laboratories.) For more information about ADA, see P. Wegner, *Programming with ADA* (Englewood Cliffs, N.J.: Prentice-Hall, 1980), especially Chapters 4 and 5.

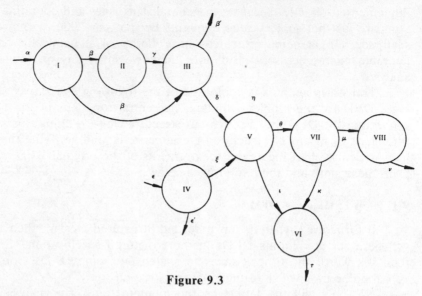

Figure 9.3

The DFD in Fig. 9.3 is atrocious.* Its bubbles are named so badly that we have only its shape to help us to identify the central transform. Where is its center? V? VII? No one knows for sure, but it's reasonable to assume V, VI, and VII are in or near the central transform.

A second, better way to find the central transform is to identify the center of the DFD by pruning off its afferent and efferent branches. You do this by following three steps: First, trace each afferent stream from the outside of the DFD toward the middle. Mark the data flow that represents the input in its most logical form. In other words, mark the stage at which the input has been thoroughly refined, but has not yet been used for actual processing. Second, trace each efferent stream from the outside of the DFD toward the middle. Mark the data flow that represents the output at its most logical form. In other words, mark the stage at which the input has just been produced, but has not yet been formatted. Third, join all the marks in a closed curve.

Let's look at Fig. 9.3 to determine how we would use the second method to identify the DFD's central transform. First, however, we'd better put real names on it, as in Fig. 9.4.

---

*This DFD's author has been banished to Baffin Island with only a COBOL ABEND dump for companionship.

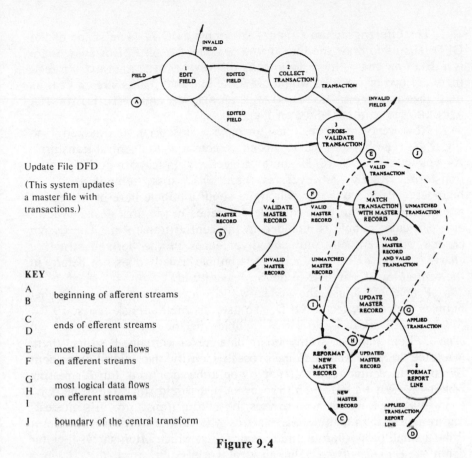

Update File DFD

(This system updates
a master file with
transactions.)

KEY

A B	beginning of afferent streams
C D	ends of efferent streams
E F	most logical data flows on afferent streams
G H I	most logical data flows on efferent streams
J	boundary of the central transform

Figure 9.4

A and B mark the beginnings of the two afferent streams, which we have to follow toward the center of the DFD. The data flow VALID TRANSACTION (at point E of Fig. 9.4) represents stream A at its most logical. A TRANSACTION, for instance, is not as refined as a VALID TRANSACTION. Conversely, we can't continue further toward the center in our search for more refined input because the bubble MATCH TRANS-ACTION WITH MASTER RECORD actually seems to be processing both afferent streams.

Similar reasoning tells us that VALID MASTER RECORD (at point F of Fig. 9.4) represents stream B at its most logical. So, we can now mark the most logical points of the afferent streams, as shown in the figure. C and D are the ends of the two efferent streams, which we have to follow back toward the center of the DFD. The data flow AP-PLIED TRANSACTION (at point G of Fig. 9.4) represents stream D at its most logical. (UPDATE MASTER RECORD, the next bubble inward, is do-ing the processing that generates APPLIED TRANSACTION.)

The efferent stream C is not so simple as D is. The shape of the DFD tells us to draw the line at NEW MASTER RECORD. However, there is a data flow that is more logical than is NEW MASTER RECORD. In fact, there are two of them! I would draw the line that marks stream C at its most logical across UNMATCHED MASTER RECORD and UPDATED MASTER RECORD (see points H and I on Fig. 9.4).

Now we connect the lines to make a closed curve (marked J on Fig. 9.4). The bubbles inside this curve comprise the central transform. As you can see, there is some subjectivity in choosing the central transform. Rarely, however, is there *much* disagreement about its boundary. People typically will argue about a bubble here or there, but it generally turns out to make little difference in the final design whether a particular bubble is included in the central transform. The design criteria will eventually pull any divergences in the derived structure charts together. However, a dubious bubble usually does not belong in the central transform — if in doubt, leave it out.

People often use the "ideal-world" method to determine what bubbles are central to the DFD. To use this method, ask yourself: "If this were an ideal world, what bubbles in the DFD would just go away?" For example, if the input data never contained errors, there would be no need for validating processes. If the user didn't care about the format of his reports, there would be no need for formatting processes. What's left — the processes that would still have to be done even in an ideal world — comprises the central transform. It's interesting to note that in commercial systems, the central transform turns out to be a small proportion of the overall DFD, which often shows how far commercial EDP is from being an ideal world!

9.3 Step 3: Produce a first-cut structure chart

Remember that the purpose of transform analysis is to turn a DFD into a structure chart. The main difference between a DFD and a structure chart is that a structure chart depicts bosshood.* In a DFD, there are no bosses. The bubbles are like happy workers in an idyllic commune, each one attending to its own work and sending its product to the next worker in line. But, the application of transform analysis introduces the shocking news that in the future the commune is to have bosses — and, in particular, one chief for the whole organization.

---

*The hierarchy of levels of a set of DFDs represents a hierarchy of detail; on a structure chart, the hierarchy of modules represents control as well as detail.

In the real world, we would have two choices about where to find this head honcho: We could promote someone from within the organization, or we could hire a new boss from outside the organization.

Transform analysis gives us the same two choices: A bubble in the central transform may stand out as a potential boss. One feature setting it apart from other bubbles may be that it does little processing but a lot of "traffic cop" activity, sending data hither and thither. That's equivalent to coordinating the work of other bubbles. Another feature setting it apart from other bubbles could be termed geometric: A bubble in the center of a spider's web of data flows is likely to have good coordinating abilities.

There may be two or three bubbles that each look worthy for promotion. If so, try each one in turn to see which gives the best initial design. However, it's very possible that there is *no* obvious candidate for boss, in which case you would have to choose a boss that is not presently in the DFD at all.

To sum up Step 3:

IF there is a good candidate for boss (in the central transform)

THEN pick up the boss and let all the other bubbles hang down

OTHERWISE hire a new boss, consider the central transform as one DFD bubble, and hang the central transform and each afferent and efferent branch from the new boss

Let's examine the promote-a-boss approach first. Picture the DFD as a set of ping-pong balls tied together with pieces of string.

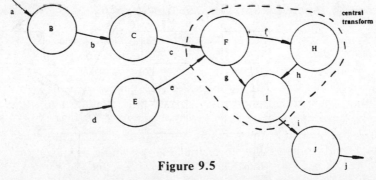

Figure 9.5

Choose one ping-pong ball from the central transform as boss. Now imagine that you pick up this boss ping-pong ball, and let the other ping-pong balls dangle. The DFD represented by our ping-pong balls is on its way to becoming a structure chart, as depicted in Fig. 9.6.

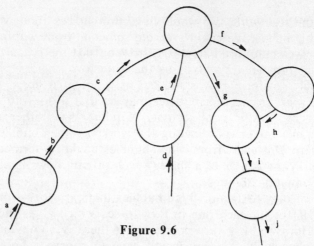

Figure 9.6

There's plenty of work still to do to complete this metamorphosis. Notice that I removed the arrowheads from the data flows. That's because DFD arrowheads won't necessarily correspond to structure chart arrowheads; direction of data flow isn't the same thing as direction of call. Next, the arrowheads for calls need to be added and the oval bubbles need to be redrawn as square modules. Names of modules won't necessarily correspond to names of bubbles, either; a module's name has to sum up the activities of its subordinates, while a bubble's name describes only its own activity.

Adding read and write modules gives the diagram in Fig. 9.7, a first-cut structure chart.

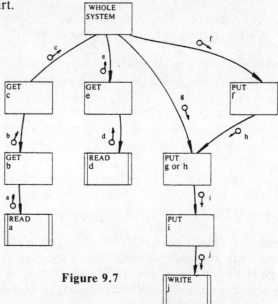

Figure 9.7

Let's follow the promote-a-boss method to Step 4.

9.4 Step 4: Revise the first-cut structure chart

The simple structure chart in Fig. 9.7 is good, but not great. It's a first cut that will benefit from the application of the design criteria — especially factoring and cohesion. In order to produce a better design, the following revision to the structure chart should be made:

- Add read and write modules (with keys if necessary) for accessing sources, sinks, and files.

- Factor and reorganize the afferent and efferent modules — but keep the system balanced.

- Factor the central transform (if necessary) using the DFD as a guideline. The levels of the DFD are useful in this regard.

- Add error-handling modules.

- Add initialization and termination details (if required).

- Ensure that all modules have names in keeping with their hierarchical roles.

- Show all flags that are necessary on a structure chart but not on a DFD (for example, "end of stream" information).

- Check all the design criteria and be prepared to improve the design in *keeping with those criteria.* Look first at system shape, factoring, cohesion, and decision-splitting.

Although an abstract example emphasizes the many mechanical aspects of transform analysis, it is also important to see the technique used in a real example. Let's repeat this process on a real example, the Update File DFD, as shown in Fig. 9.4. From the central transform, I've chosen MATCH TRANSACTION WITH MASTER RECORD as a potential boss, because that bubble makes a matching decision that coordinates the activities of the bubbles around it.

The next step in the strategy is to remove the data flow arrowheads and the names of the bubbles, and to lift the whole mass by MATCH TRANSACTION WITH MASTER RECORD. The result is Fig. 9.8.

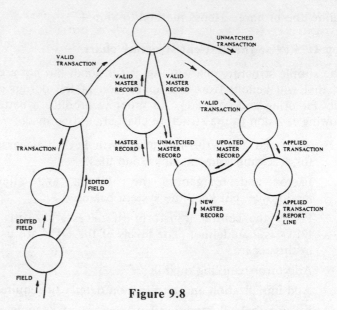

Figure 9.8

Adding some structure chart details gives us Fig. 9.9:

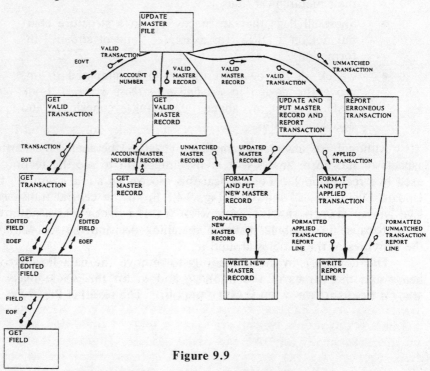

Figure 9.9

The module with the worst cohesion is UPDATE AND PUT MASTER RECORD AND REPORT TRANSACTION, which is communicational (to be precise, sequential and communicational in series). I'll try splitting this module and factoring out some of its functions (see Fig. 9.10):

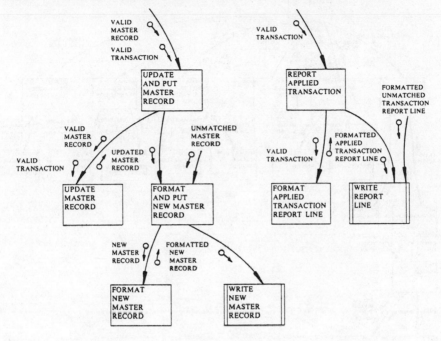

Figure 9.10

Now, no module has less than sequential cohesion. The module FOR-MAT AND PUT NEW MASTER RECORD is sequentially cohesive and trivial (two simple lines of code). I would be tempted to place a hat on it, except that it is used by another module — UPDATE MASTER FILE — to output an UNMATCHED MASTER RECORD (see Fig. 9.9).

UPDATE AND PUT MASTER RECORD is also sequentially cohesive and trivial. But I *will* put a hat on this module. The only penalty I pay in getting rid of the module is the increased fan-out of the boss module, UPDATE MASTER FILE.

Now we have a second cut, shown in Fig. 9.11. My reason for not putting a hat on FORMAT AND PUT NEW MASTER RECORD (the reason being that it had fan-in) no longer holds true. Since I put a hat on UP-DATE AND PUT MASTER RECORD, FORMAT AND PUT NEW MASTER RECORD is called only by UPDATE MASTER FILE. I could now put a hat on this sequentially cohesive and trivial module. However, the fan-out from UPDATE MASTER FILE would then increase from six to seven. Worse, the whole system would become physically output-driven, for the boss would have to worry about the details of a FORMATTED NEW MASTER RECORD. So, FORMAT AND PUT NEW MASTER RECORD remains factored.

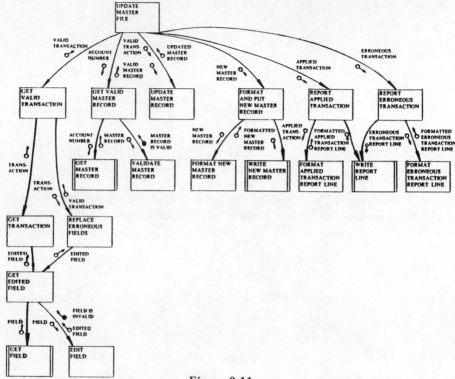

Figure 9.11

In the example above, we have accomplished Steps 3 and 4 of the transform analysis strategy: We have developed a rough structure chart, based upon the DFD of a problem (by "promoting" a bubble), and we have revised that first, rough structure chart to develop an improved design. In our example for Step 3, we chose the THEN alternative (promoting a boss), rather than the OTHERWISE alternative (hiring a new boss). Hiring a new boss generally produces a better first-cut structure chart — although problems with both approaches will be resolved by an application of the design criteria. (Hiring a new boss also eliminates the need to choose one.)

So, let's backtrack and explore the OTHERWISE of Step 3, the hire-a-new-boss approach, and follow it through Steps 3 and 4. We start with the abstract DFD in Fig. 9.12.

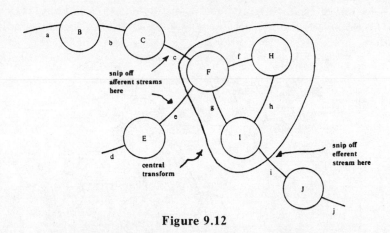

Figure 9.12

Find the central transform as before. Snip off all the afferent and efferent streams where they join the central transform. In this case, the DFD falls into four pieces. Tie each of these four pieces under the new, hired bubble, as shown in Fig. 9.13.

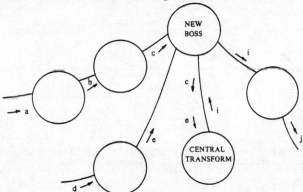

Figure 9.13

Once again, pick up the boss, and let the incipient structure chart dangle. The result is shown in Fig. 9.14 on the next page. Notice that in Fig. 9.14, I've taken an early opportunity to factor three modules from the central transform. These modules are the bubbles F, H, and I. It was easy for me to factor them out, since I knew that they were concealed in the central transform.

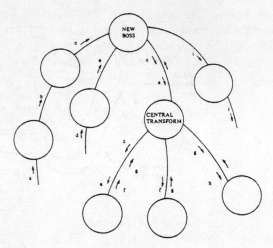

Figure 9.14

Figure 9.15 is the first-cut structure chart:

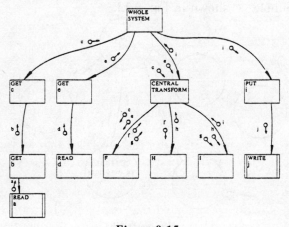

Figure 9.15

We've hired a new boss and — what do you know — the boss has brought its own lieutenant. The CENTRAL TRANSFORM module is needed on the structure chart merely to limit the fan-out from the boss. If we hadn't included it now, we'd probably have been obliged to do so later to reduce the fan-out from the boss. On the other hand, the boss module now may be so trivial that it acts as a mere messenger boy for c, e, and i. If that's so, we would put a hat on CENTRAL TRANSFORM and perhaps try factoring other subfunctions from the boss.

Let's try the hire-a-boss approach on a real example.

We start, as before, by finding the central transform on our familiar Update File DFD, shown earlier in Fig. 9.4. Next we snip off the afferent and efferent streams and hang them with the whole central transform under the new boss (see Fig. 9.16):

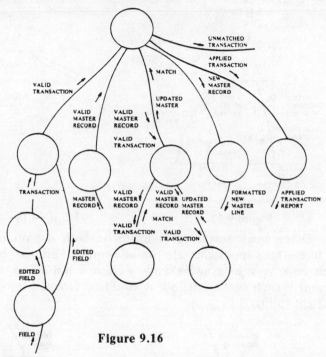

Figure 9.16

Figure 9.17 shows a first-cut structure chart that is much closer to the final design than was the first-cut produced by the promote-a-boss approach. The only real problem with this design is a decision-split. We could partially rectify this decision-split by putting a hat on the central transform module. I've called that module ?, because I can't think of a better name for it. That fact, together with the fact that it does almost nothing, makes it worth unfactoring. Once module ? has been removed, the decision-split is reduced to a single level. But neither UP-DATE MASTER FILE nor MATCH MASTER WITH TRANSACTION has very complicated logic; indeed, MATCH MASTER WITH TRANSACTION is trivial. The decision-split can be eliminated entirely by unfactoring one step further and pushing MATCH MASTER WITH TRANSACTION into the boss module, to give Fig. 9.18. A beneficial result of this last step is that the fan-out from UPDATE MASTER FILE is reduced from seven to six.

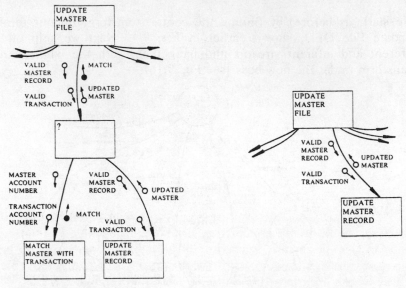

Figure 9.17   **Figure 9.18**

Other areas worthy of factoring in both the promote-a-boss and the hire-a-boss approaches are the afferent and efferent branches, which often look very long and skinny. There's not much wrong with the afferent branch at the left, but it could be factored into the diagram at the right in Fig. 9.19.

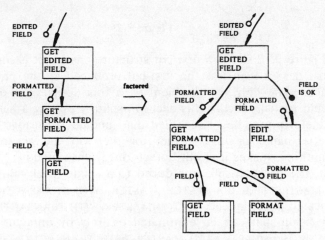

Figure 9.19

Now that we've factored out two useful modules, EDIT FIELD and FORMAT FIELD, we have two very trivial modules named GET EDITED FIELD and GET FORMATTED FIELD. It's reasonable to put a hat on GET FORMATTED FIELD to give Fig. 9.20:

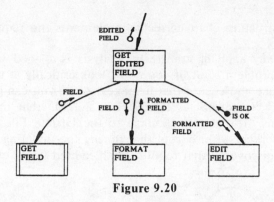

Figure 9.20

Don't carry out this process ad absurdum or you'll be left with a physically input-driven system that has some intolerable fan-outs. Already in this reasonable broadening of an afferent branch, we've lost a potentially useful module, GET FORMATTED FIELD. A good rule of thumb comes from our discussion of factoring in Section 8.1.6: When unfactoring the afferent or efferent branches of the structure chart, don't force a module to handle more than two different data structures. In this case, GET EDITED FIELD handles only one data structure, FIELD, although GET EDITED FIELD does encounter FIELD as a "raw" FIELD, as FORMATTED FIELD, and as EDITED FIELD.

Once the afferent and efferent modules are factored and slightly reorganized, the structure chart obtained by hiring a new boss looks very like that obtained by promoting a boss. Typically, the approach you take and the particular boss you choose become almost irrelevant once you've applied the design criteria.

9.5 Step 5: Make sure the design works

The final step in the strategy is crucial: Make sure it works! The purpose of transform analysis is not to *do* transform analysis. The purpose is to attain quickly a structure chart that, first, implements the problem specification correctly and, second, lives up to the criteria for a maintainable system. People doing transform analysis sometimes forget this and, after having produced an excellent and correct structure chart, worry themselves silly about whether they drew the right boundary to the central transform or whether they chose the right boss.

The end is more important than the means. You can even discard transform analysis entirely if you can clearly see your way from the DFD to the final structure chart. Indeed, with a little practice, you should be able to do exactly that for many DFDs. But whatever approach you take to derive the structure chart, it's a good idea to have the author of the DFD review the structure chart derived from it to ensure that the structure chart correctly implements the requirements of the DFD.

Mechanically applying transform analysis is a good way to get a handle on any problem. But, if you don't look critically at the structure chart you produce and ensure that it makes sense, you can get some ludicrous results. For example, Fig. 9.21 is a DFD that updates a file with transactions. It's almost identical to the Update File DFD we've already been working with, except that during the updating of a record, errors may be discovered that require fresh, edited fields to replace the erroneous ones.

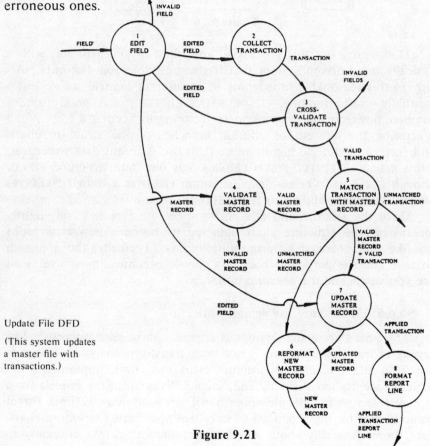

Update File DFD

(This system updates a master file with transactions.)

Figure 9.21

It is not obvious merely by looking at the DFD whether UPDATE MASTER RECORD should call GET EDITED FIELD or vice versa. The call could be either way (see Fig. 9.22).

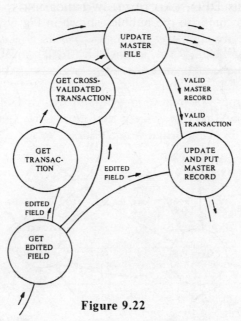

Figure 9.22

However, common sense tells us that UPDATE AND PUT MASTER RECORD has to call GET EDITED FIELD since it is UPDATE MASTER RECORD that *wants* EDITED FIELD.

In more subtle cases, it might be necessary to look at the mini-specs for the bubbles to determine which module calls which.

9.6 Questions about transform analysis

So far in this chapter, in describing the basic transform analysis strategy, I have ignored several details and complications that may occur in practice. Below I cover these points in a question-and-answer format.

Q: How do I factor the central transform?

A: Levels of the DFD provide a good guide for factoring any part of the system. For example, study the DFD in Fig. 9.23.

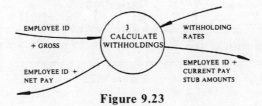

Figure 9.23

Bubble 3 of this DFD, CALCULATE WITHHOLDINGS, might at a lower level be seen to comprise the bubbles shown in Fig. 9.24:

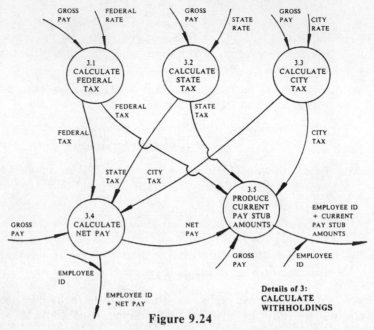

Figure 9.24

The factoring of the module CALCULATE WITHHOLDINGS is determined from the leveling of the bubble CALCULATE WITHHOLDINGS and is shown in Fig. 9.25.

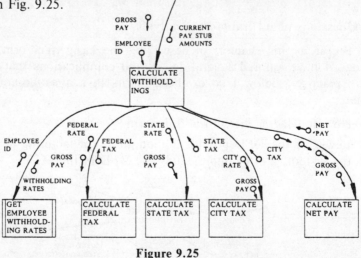

Figure 9.25

Four ways in which my factoring of the structure chart differs from the leveling of the DFD are

- I put a hat on PRODUCE CURRENT PAY STUB AMOUNTS, since in the DFD, it was just a dummy bubble drawn to bring together a number of data flows to form CURRENT PAY STUB AMOUNTS.

- CALCULATE NET PAY involves a trivial piece of arithmetic which in COBOL would be:

    COMPUTE NET PAY = GROSS-PAY − FEDERAL-TAX
    − STATE-TAX − CITY-TAX

    Since the module has only one boss and is unlikely to prove useful in the future, I can put a hat on it, too.

- The DFD in Fig. 9.23 says I should have CALCULATE WITHHOLDINGS return EMPLOYEE ID with CURRENT PAY STUB AMOUNTS. I don't do that because the boss already knows the information in EMPLOYEE ID; he must, because he sent it down!

- CALCULATE WITHHOLDINGS doesn't return NET PAY, although the DFD says it should. However, NET PAY is included in CURRENT PAY STUB AMOUNTS, a point that can be gleaned only from the data dictionary.*

Q: What if I hire a new boss and then discover that the job he has to do is utterly trivial? Or, what if I decide on the promote-a-boss approach and I pick the wrong bubble?

A: This question is an example of what I call the "Las Vegas" mentality exhibited by some designers. When you carry out transform analysis, you don't have to stake everything on a single throw. You should try out two or three different bosses. It takes only a few minutes to sketch the top of the structure chart. By the time you have completed the sketch, you can tell which approach will give you a design that is most easily improved by means of the Structured Design criteria.

---

*The data dictionary is an essential tool in creating a DFD (to check that Bubble 3 tallies with the detailed breakdown of Bubble 3, for example). A data dictionary is also essential in using a DFD because, without it, a complex DFD hardly makes sense.

However, I will answer the question as posed. The usual symptom of having chosen the wrong boss is a decision-split in which the rightful boss of the structure chart passes a flag up to the nominated boss telling it what to do. You can improve the decision-split by pushing the real boss up to "usurp" the pretender to the throne. But a better approach is to learn from the mistake and to try promoting the bubble that *wants* to be boss. (By the way, you'll never completely remove decision-splits from an average system. When you cure a decision-split, remember that cohesion, factoring, and balanced systems are more important criteria to follow than avoiding decision-splits: Don't jeopardize them.)

Q: How can I apply transform analysis to large systems?

A: It's unlikely that applying transform analysis alone will work on a large system, for you will find that seventy-five percent of the DFD seems to be central transform, and that there are dozens of afferent and efferent streams. The best way to tackle a complex DFD is to break it down by transactions. (I discuss this method in Chapter 10 on transaction analysis.)

Each transaction that a system accepts will use perhaps one or two afferent streams and two or three efferent streams. Treat the bubbles between the relevant afferent and efferent streams as a separate subsystem for the purpose of transform analysis. You can exploit any commonality among the subsystems as shared modules with fan-in when you put all the subsystems together into one structure chart.

Q: At which level of the DFD should I apply transform analysis?

A: Apply it at a fairly high level. If you try using it at a level of detail that forces you to deal with twenty or thirty bubbles per transaction, you'll soon get into a tangle. It's better to tackle at most ten to twenty higher-level bubbles first, and then to use the details from the lower levels as an aid in factoring.

9.7 Summary

In this chapter, we have seen how a DFD, the major product of Structured Analysis, can be used to derive a structure chart, the major product of Structured Design. That the transformation from DFD to structure chart is reasonably straightforward should not surprise you, for the aims of Structured Analysis and Structured Design are almost identical. Both disciplines seek to control the complexity of a system by partitioning the system in a top-down manner and with minimal interfaces between the components of the system, by striving for black-box functions whenever possible, by suppressing procedural details, and by minimizing redundancy.

However, there are some differences between the DFD and the structure chart: The DFD is intended to be a tool whose chief purpose is to tackle the problem — the requirements of the system — whereas the chief purpose of the structure chart is to tackle the solution to the problem — the design of a computer implementation of the system. The strategy of transform analysis enables us to bridge the gap between the network of processes that comprises a DFD and the hierarchy of modules that forms a structure chart, and hence to use Structured Analysis as a tremendous aid to quickly deriving a reasonable Structured Design.

Exercises

1. Try to develop the structure chart for the hourly workers payroll system, which I showed at the beginning of the chapter in Fig. 9.2. Here again, in the figure below, is the DFD for the system, accompanied this time by a data dictionary. (If you've forgotten how to use the data dictionary, reread Chapter 4.) You're unlikely to produce *exactly* the same structure chart as shown in Fig. 9.2, but you should produce one that comparably satisfies the criteria of good design.

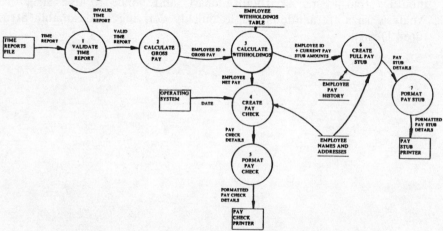

Data Dictionary: HOURLY WORKERS PAYROLL SYSTEM

cumulative pay stub amount	=	gross pay + net pay + federal tax + state tax + city tax
current pay stub amounts	=	gross pay + net pay + federal tax + state tax + city tax
employee names and addresses	=	{employee ID + name + address}
employee pay history	=	{employee ID + cumulative pay stub amounts}
employee withholding table	=	{employee ID + withholding rates}
pay check details	=	employee ID + employee name + date + net pay + English net pay
pay stub details	=	employee ID + employee name + cumulative pay stub amounts + current pay stub amounts
time report	=	employee ID + {hours worked + hourly rate}
withholding rates	=	federal rate + state rate + city rate

2. Loops in afferent and efferent streams sometimes cause difficulty to designers attempting to convert a DFD into a structure chart. Using the example below, suggest a method by which this difficulty can be alleviated. Assume that the single bubble FILL CUSTOMER ORDER is the whole central transform.

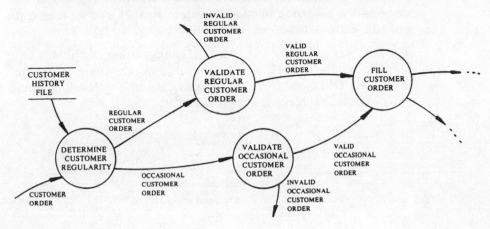

Answers

1. I chose CALCULATE GROSS PAY and CALCULATE WITHHOLDINGS as the bubbles of the central transform and I hired a new boss to preside over them. The structure chart shown in Fig. 9.2 is factored on the afferent and efferent sides. Next, I would factor CALCULATE WITHHOLDINGS — as shown in Fig. 9.25.

2. The best way to handle any awkward configuration of bubbles on a DFD is to draw a single new bubble around the tangle — to "unlevel" the DFD, so to speak. In this case, the unleveling would yield just two bubbles, as shown below:

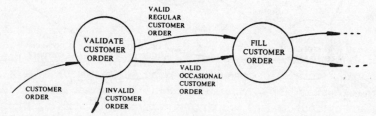

These bubbles would transform initially to the simple structure chart shown below on the left. Note that the descriptive flag, CUSTOMER REGULARITY, can be eliminated unless FILL CUSTOMER ORDER needs to know whether a customer has been determined to be regular or occasional. Then using the original DFD to guide the factoring, we arrive at the solution shown at right:

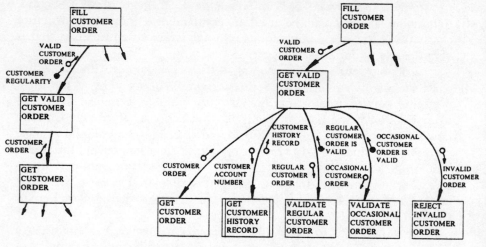

10

Transaction Analysis

Transform analysis, which we have just examined in Chapter 9, is the major strategy for converting a DFD into a structure chart. However, a supplementary technique called transaction analysis (or transaction-centered design) is extremely valuable in deriving the structure chart for a system that processes transactions.

Transaction analysis has two main uses: First, it can be used to cleave a large, complicated DFD into smaller DFDs — one for each transaction that the system processes. These smaller DFDs are then simple enough to be converted by transform analysis into a number of small structure charts. (This part of transaction analysis, which I call "route-mapping," is covered in Appendix E, the case study.) Second, transaction analysis can be used to combine the individual structure charts for the separate transactions into one larger structure chart that is very flexible under user changes.

I devote much of this chapter to the organization of the structure chart for maintainable transaction-processing systems. This is the most profound part of transaction analysis, for it marks a radical departure from traditional methods of handling transactions. If you understand how a well-organized transaction-centered structure chart should appear, then you will find the DFD representation of transactions and the transition from a transaction-centered DFD to a transaction-centered structure chart very straightforward. So in this chapter, I reverse the order of topics of the last chapter and cover the structure chart before I cover the DFD.

A transaction, in its broadest, most formal sense, is a stimulus to a system that triggers a set of activities within the system. Examples of transactions are a signal to a space vehicle to fire its retro engines, a coolant-temperature alarm in a fission reactor, or a clock interrupt in an operating system. The activities associated with these transactions would be, respectively, the firing of the space vehicle's retro engines, the shutting down of the reactor, and the starting of a new time slice.

The above definition of a transaction is broad enough to apply to real-time systems, such as process-control or operating systems. However, a definition that is valid for most other purposes is: A *transaction* is a single item or − more often − a collection of input data that can fall into one of a number of types. Each type of transaction is processed by a specific set of activities within the system.

Commercial data processing has thousands of examples of transactions. A transaction in a utility company system, for instance, might contain the information for adding a new customer, deleting an old customer, changing a customer's address, or billing a customer. Every customer transaction entering the system would carry a *tag* (alias *transaction code)* − for example, ADD, DELETE, BILL − to indicate its type. By referring to the tag, the system would determine what processing each respective transaction required and would make sure that the transaction was handled by the appropriate lines of code.

10.1 The difficulties with conventional transaction processing

Before the development of transaction analysis, the design of transaction-processing systems was notoriously ad hoc and haphazard. The systems that resulted were typically inflexible, error-prone, and difficult to understand. These problems arose because each type of transaction normally needs to be processed differently, and yet the processing for all types of transactions is often very similar. Consequently, programmers would use all manner of tricks to share common code between transactions.

For example, each of the transaction types described above would need to have its fields validated similarly and would need to access a customer master file. However, in other respects, the processing for each type of transaction would be quite different. So, traditionally, programmers would identify which lines of code could be shared among different types of transactions and which lines of code were peculiar to a specific type of transaction. Then they would set flags and switches − often in very obscure ways − to force each type of transaction to take the appropriate path through monolithic chunks of shared code. Thus, each transaction would meander through line after line of code until it hit a line that might be inapplicable to it. There, it would encounter a test something like the code example that follows:

IF TRANSACTION IS A 'CHANGE,' 'CORRECT,' OR
   'DELETE' TRANSACTION
THEN GO TO CCD-12.

which would cause a skip over perhaps twenty lines of inapplicable
code.

A system that has to process fifty, one hundred, or even two hundred transactions soon becomes a tangle of code if it is "designed" in
this way; but the fact that all the different types of transactions are tied
into a Gordian knot is not exposed until the user changes the way in
which he handles one or two transactions. When modifications to those
transactions are made, other transactions somehow develop mysterious
bugs, since they no longer find their way through the correct lines of
shared code. It takes a lot of effort for the maintainers of a system to
restore it to completely correct operation for every type of transaction.

10.2 Transaction-analysis principles

Bell Telephone of Canada, in a response to the slapdash methods
of conventional transaction processing, cut the Gordian knot by
developing a new technique called SAPTAD (for "System, Analysis,
Program, Transaction, Action, and Detail").* Transaction analysis,
which is a refinement of SAPTAD, has this fundamental principle:

> Using the tag, separate the various transactions by *type* and
> not by any common processing requirements.

In other words, regardless of how similar or different the types of
transaction might be, there should be a separate module responsible for
the processing of each type. These modules are called *transaction
modules*; there are, of course, as many of them as there are transaction
types. There is another module that determines the type of each transaction entering the system (by inspecting its tag) and routes it to its ap-
pointed transaction module. This is called a *transaction-center* module.

Applied to our example of the utility company transaction, transaction analysis leads to the design shown in Fig. 10.1. The modules AP-
PLY ADD-CUSTOMER TRANSACTION, APPLY DELETE-CUSTOMER TRANS-
ACTION, and APPLY BILL-CUSTOMER TRANSACTION are the transaction
modules. With their subordinates, they ensure that their respective
transactions are processed. The module APPLY CUSTOMER TRANSACTION
is the transaction-center module, which is responsible for discovering

---

*P. Vincent, "The System Structure Design Method," *Proceedings of the 1968 National
Symposium on Modular Programming,* ed. by Tom O. Barnett (Cambridge, Mass.: Information & System Press, 1968 — out of print).

the type of each transaction and for sending it to its appropriate trans-action module.

A diamond symbol at the bottom of a module signifies that the module calls *either* subordinate A *or* subordinate B *or* one of the other subordinates connected to the diamond, depending on the result of a test. (The test in APPLY CUSTOMER TRANSACTION would be the inspection of the transaction tag.) This construct is referred to as a *transaction center* and would be implemented by a case construct in the calling module (e.g., GOTO DEPENDING ON in COBOL, COMPUTED GOTO in FORTRAN, SELECT in PL/I, **case** in Pascal).*

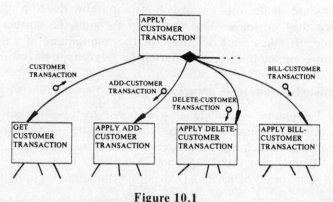

Figure 10.1

The advantage of this design over the shared-code approach is that the processing for all of the transaction types is cleanly partitioned, so that any change to the processing for one type of transaction will not affect that for any other type.

The penalty we've apparently paid for this cleanliness is having identical code in many different modules, since many transaction types require similar processing. Fear not, however. In the next section, we see how factoring comes to our rescue to eliminate this problem.

10.3 Factoring transaction modules

A less obvious example of a transaction than that in Fig. 10.1 — but one that nevertheless satisfies the definition of a transaction — is a field from a record. In Table 10.1, I show the processing (specifically validating and formatting) that each of seven types of field requires:

---

*The case construct is an n-way test and can be thought of as an extension to the IF-THEN-ELSE construct, which is a two-way test.

Table 10.1

FIELD NUMBER (TAG)	FIELD TYPE	PROCESSING REQUIRED (VALIDATING AND FORMATTING)
01	account number	validate numeric check length of 6
02	customer name	validate alphabetic left-justify pad with spaces check length of 20
03	customer street address	validate alphanumeric left-justify pad with spaces check length of 30
04	customer city	validate alphabetic left-justify pad with spaces check length of 30
05	customer state	validate alphabetic check length of 2 ensure valid state
06	customer zip code	validate numeric check length of 5
07	customer balance	validate numeric right-justify pad with zeros

The transaction-centered design for the piece of a system that validates and formats these fields is shown in Fig. 10.2. As the figure shows, there is one module to validate and format each type of field, plus one to report any field numbers that are out of range. Now, if the user should change the validating or formatting rules for the customer name, for example, then those changes could be addressed in the VALIDATE AND FORMAT CUSTOMER NAME module. The changes would have almost no chance of disturbing the correct operation of, say, VALIDATE AND FORMAT CUSTOMER CITY NAME.

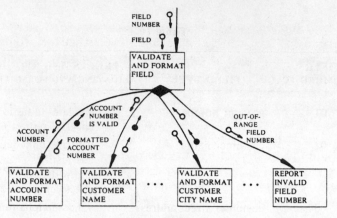

Figure 10.2

So far, we've accounted for the differences in processing each type of field by having a separate module for validating and formatting each type of field. But, as Table 10.1 clearly shows, many of the processing details are identical from field type to field type. How can we make use of that fact? Simply by factoring out common functions into new modules at a lower level (this is the application of factoring discussed in Section 8.1.3 — the sharing of common functions).

In this example of validating and formatting fields, we'll need the seven modules shown in Fig. 10.3:

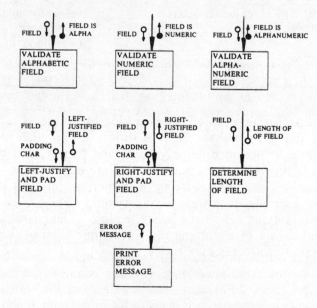

Figure 10.3

These modules would be called as appropriate to validate and format each field. (Of course, in a high-level language, some of these modules could be single statements in the validating routines.) We've now gained a lot of flexibility, because if the validation criteria for a field change, we simply call on a different set of bottom-level modules. If a new field is introduced, all of the modules needed for its validation probably already exist.

To emphasize the value of transaction analysis, it's worthwhile contrasting the transaction-centered design of Figs. 10.2 and 10.3 with a more conventional approach to validating and formatting fields. A common way to organize the editing of a field is to have an EDIT ALL ALPHABETIC FIELDS module, the code for which might be

```
check field is alphabetic
if field number = 2 or field number = 4
then left-justify field
     pad field with spaces
     if field number = 2
     then check length = 20
     else check length = 30
     endif
elseif field number = 5
then check length = 2
     check field against state table
elseif . . .
     . . .
endif
```

(or some even worse code containing GOTOs). Not only is this code difficult to understand but it would also be difficult to change if the user decided that, in the future, customer names would be alphanumeric. Implementing that change would require major internal surgery to both the EDIT ALL ALPHABETIC FIELDS and the EDIT ALL ALPHANUMERIC FIELDS modules.

The difference between the transaction-centered philosophy and the conventional transaction-handling philosophy should now be apparent. Transaction analysis assumes that each transaction will be processed totally differently and regards any similarities in function between transaction modules as pieces of good fortune that can be exploited by factoring. The conventional approach assumes that many transactions will be processed similarly and herds similar-looking transactions into the same module, leaving the code of that module to take care of the many differences that exist among the transactions. The transaction-centered approach leads to far more general and flexible systems than does the conventional approach because it avoids depending on similarities, which are susceptible to change.

Transaction analysis seems to violate the guideline of fan-out. For example, if the record in Fig. 10.2 contained 25 fields, then the VALI-DATE AND FORMAT FIELD module would have had a fan-out of 26. Although 26 is well beyond human hrair (about 7), neither the original programmer nor the maintenance programmer should have any problem in understanding the module, for he will never have to think about all 26 subordinates at one time. Indeed, since a transaction center is essentially a case construct, he will have to consider only *one* subordinate at a time.

10.3.1 Another example of factoring modules

As a result of factoring, it is possible — and quite legal — for a transaction module for one type of transaction to be called upon by a transaction module for another type. Indeed, in many commercial applications, this is a frequent occurrence. For example, Fig. 10.4 shows part of the Customer Service System of the Consolidated Volts and Amps Company:

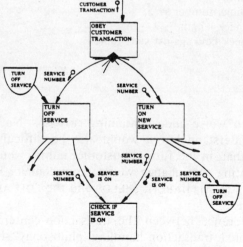

Figure 10.4

To turn on the electricity service for a new tenant, the company first may have to turn off the previous tenant's service. TURN ON NEW SERVICE checks whether service is already on. If it is, then the transaction module TURN ON NEW SERVICE calls TURN OFF SERVICE, which is itself a transaction module.

10.4 Transaction centers in on-line systems

A kind of transaction center often found in on-line systems is one in which the user is given a menu of options from which to select one. An example would be in a system to direct a missile-bearing ship from a CRT:

Table 10.2

COMMAND TAG	COMMAND TYPE	PROCESSING REQUIRED
TURN	turn ship	turn ship from present angle by specified amount
SET	set ship course	set ship to absolute course
FIRE	fire missile	fire missile in specified direction
SCUTTLE	self-destruct	blow up ship after specified time

The transaction center to implement this system is shown in Fig. 10.5.

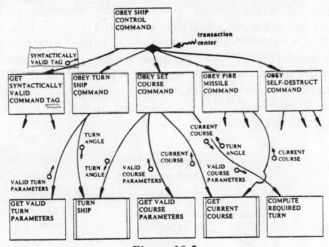

Figure 10.5

The interesting feature of the transaction center in Fig. 10.5 is that the top module calls each of the transaction modules with no data at all. This isn't a mistake; each transaction-processing subsystem is responsible for obtaining its own input and delivering its own output. Separating the respective inputs and outputs of each subsystem in this way leads to much greater flexibility than was provided in Fig. 10.1, in which the top module collects the input, hands it to the appropriate transaction module, and accepts the transaction module's output. That method required the top module to be aware of the syntax of almost all of the information in the system. Since the top module doesn't need any of that information, we'd have a case of "tramp stamp" coupling! Worse, it would be difficult to modify the system to permit each subsystem to enter into its own conversation with the user or to obtain data from its own data base.

The ship system has fan-in to TURN SHIP from OBEY TURN SHIP COMMAND and OBEY SET COURSE COMMAND. The two subsystems for turning the ship and for setting a course are very similar: The main difference is that OBEY SET COURSE COMMAND must determine the ship's direction and how much it must turn the ship before it can call TURN SHIP. Almost certainly, there would be no fan-in between the OBEY SELF-DESTRUCT COMMAND subsystem and any other (except perhaps to some very low-level editing modules).

10.5 Cohesion of a transaction center

What is the cohesion of a transaction center? Well, it varies. Most transaction centers have high cohesion, but it's possible for a perfectly good transaction center to have coincidental cohesion. The cohesion of the top of a system is always at the mercy of the user. Imagine, for example, a system that does inventory, bullion-futures forecasting, and missile tracking: If the user insists, you will have to implement this system despite your abject cries of "coincidental cohesion!" But the application of transaction analysis would lead to a clean system, in which the strange bedfellows are separated at the top of the structure chart, as in Fig. 10.6:

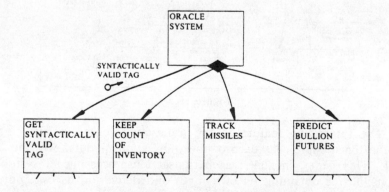

Figure 10.6

10.6 Identifying transactions on DFDs

Very often, it's extremely easy to recognize transactions, transaction centers, and transaction-processing bubbles on a DFD by the shape of the diagram alone. Wherever a data flow enters a bubble that determines its type, and routes it in one of several directions depending on its type, you can be sure that you've located a transaction entering a transaction center. The DFD for the editing field transaction center represented as a structure chart in Fig. 10.2 is shown in Fig. 10.7:

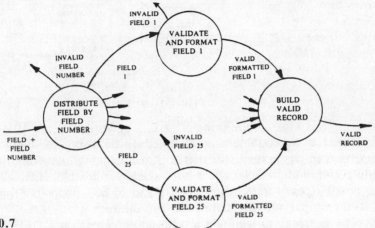

Figure 10.7

(I've assumed that all the fields, having been validated and formatted, are collected into a single record.) The bubble DISTRIBUTE FIELD BY FIELD NUMBER contains the transaction center, which, acting like a railroad switching yard, sends each field along its appropriate line to the bubble that validates and formats it. However, the manifestation of transactions on a DFD is often more subtle (see Fig. 10.8).

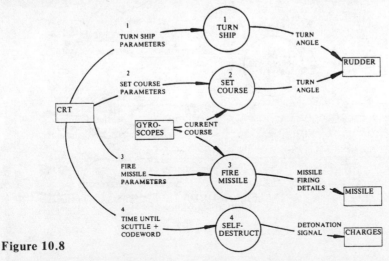

Figure 10.8

I've numbered the types of transactions entering this system 1, 2, 3, and 4. The bubbles that will become transaction modules on the DFD are also numbered 1, 2, 3, and 4. But where is the transaction-center module to be found? Clearly, it is nowhere on the DFD.

Some people are tempted to insert a bubble that routes the input, as shown in Fig. 10.9:

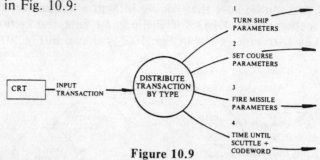

Figure 10.9

However, this violates the principle I laid down in Section 10.4 that no single module (or bubble) should need to be aware of every type of transaction in the system, for that would needlessly overcomplicate the module and would render the whole system inflexible. Instead, wherever possible, each transaction module should be responsible for obtaining its own input and dispatching its own output.

The best way to highlight a transaction center on a DFD is shown in Fig. 10.10:

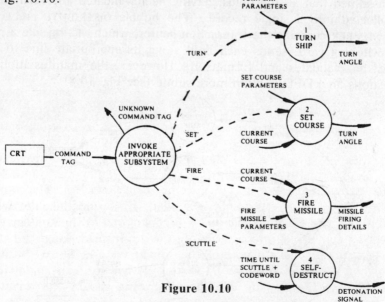

Figure 10.10

In the figure, I've shown dotted lines radiating from INVOKE APPROPRI-ATE SUBSYSTEM. They are, blatantly, lines of control that simply invoke the appropriate subsystem to handle the type of command the user has specified by the command tag. To show these as solid lines would be dishonest, for they bear no data. The transaction center of this DFD is clearly at INVOKE APPROPRIATE SUBSYSTEM. To transform the DFD into the structure chart of Fig. 10.5, you can simply pick up the bubble IN-VOKE APPROPRIATE SUBSYSTEM as if you were carrying out transform analysis.

Because of the graphic difficulties of showing a transaction center as explicitly as Fig. 10.10, most designers simply omit the bubble IN-VOKE APPROPRIATE SUBSYSTEM and work directly from Fig. 10.8, but with an image of Fig. 10.10 in their minds. That's what I have done in Appendix E (the case study), which shows how an apparently compli-cated system can be broken into subsystems, each of which handles the processing of a single type of transaction. (Appendix E also shows transform and transaction analysis being used in tandem.)

Partitioning a DFD into subsystems by transaction can go awry because of the temptation not only to route the input for every type of transaction through a single bubble, but also to combine bubbles that are similar or identical in function but belong to different transactions. Figure 10.11 illustrates the case in which a single process is being used to edit the customer name from two distinct types of transaction:

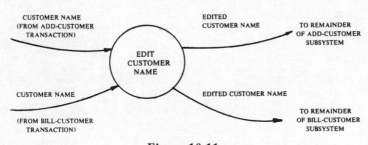

Figure 10.11

Resist the temptation to pull together data flows from afar simply because some of their processing is similar. If you do this, the DFD will soon look like a cat's cradle and will never yield to any strategy that attempts to convert it into a structure chart. Instead, keep the data flows separate and make a note of the similar features of any bubbles (possibly by a shared mini-spec). During design you can exploit any commonality of function by intelligent factoring and by the resultant fan-in to shared modules. Transaction analysis echoes once again the familiar theme of Structured Design: Divide and conquer.

Exercise

The Cosmopolitan Indemnity Fund and Mutual Assurance Company sells automobile insurance. It computes automobile premiums for most states of the U.S. by a standard method. However, it computes insurance premiums for two states (Montana and New York) by two other methods. The module that computes the automobile insurance premiums is shown below:

Using transaction analysis and the information given above, derive the modules that are subordinate to COMPUTE AUTO INSURANCE PREMIUM.

Answer

My solution is shown below:

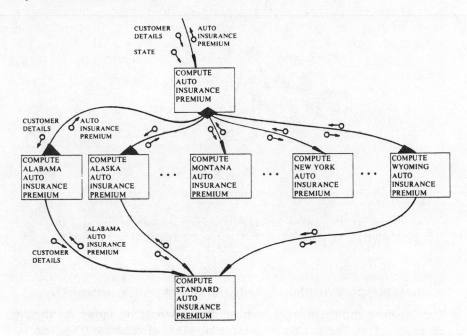

Notice that this transaction center has the characteristic shape of high fan-out at the top and high fan-in at the bottom, where COMPUTE STANDARD AUTO INSURANCE PREMIUM is called by many (46, to be precise) modules.

Notice also that many modules (COMPUTE ALABAMA AUTO INSURANCE PREMIUM, for instance) have hats. Since each of these modules contains only a single line of code (namely, CALL COMPUTE STANDARD AUTO INSURANCE PREMIUM), it's pointless for them to be distinct modules. Each of these single lines can be placed in the appropriate arm of the case construct within COMPUTE AUTO INSURANCE PREMIUM. In general, a transaction-processing module containing only a few CALLs can justifiably be compressed into its superordinate by having a hat placed on it.

You may have noticed, too, that I wasn't able to fit all fifty modules of the transaction center on the page. A graphic device that is sometimes used to solve this problem is shown on the next page.

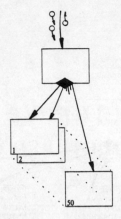

Key

1 COMPUTE ALABAMA AUTO INSURANCE PREMIUM (see page 10)
2 COMPUTE ALASKA AUTO INSURANCE PREMIUM (see page 10)
.
.
.
50 COMPUTE WYOMING AUTO INSURANCE PREMIUM (see page 17)

The modules and their subordinates (if any) would be shown on the cited pages. This device also solves the problem of crossing lines that often accompanies high fan-out followed by high fan-in.

SECTION V
BEYOND STRUCTURED DESIGN

Most of Structured Design quite rightly dwells on ensuring that the logical design of the system is sound. But in doing that, it almost entirely ignores the existence of the computer. *Chapter 11,* on packaging, describes how the logical system must be organized into jobs, job steps, or programs, so that it can be run on a particular machine. Some of this packaging is actually best done before the start of Structured Design, during the transition from Structured Analysis; the remainder is done at the end of Structured Design (or occasionally after programming has been completed).

Chapter 12, describing the implementation phase, covers the various strategies by which coded modules might be integrated to gain the greatest benefits in testing, in using resources, and in providing feedback to the user.

Optimization, that oft-neglected consideration of Structured Design, is the subject of *Chapter 13.* This chapter shows that Structured Design does not necessarily produce inefficient systems. Indeed, a structured system can usually be timed more easily than an unstructured one and yet return the essential quality of maintainability.

11

Packaging

The development of a computer system should be a more or less steady progression from a logical representation (a data flow diagram) to a concrete implementation (0's and 1's within a machine). One of the tenets of all the structured disciplines is that each stage of physicalization — each particular means of implementation, if you like — should be postponed for as long as possible. In that way, the system's developers can concentrate on the system's basic requirements before they have to choose a particular means of implementing those requirements.

So far in this book, we've followed the progress of a system from a DFD representation to a structure chart blueprint. But before we can begin the next step of developing the system — programming — we have to consider some of the practical constraints of a real computer environment. This chapter* explores ways of, and specific reasons for, packaging a system into implementation units without betraying its good logical design.

By *packaging,* I mean the set of decisions and activities that subdivide a system into implementation units.† Implementation units come in all shapes and sizes; here are some of the most common ones with their definitions:

system = one or more application-related jobs
job = a sequence of one or more job steps

---

*Parts of this chapter are based on an article coauthored with T.R. Lister, "Principles of Packaging," *The YOURDON Report,* Vol. 4, No. 4 (September-October 1979), pp. 5-7.
†See also L.A. Rose, "Packaging," *The YOURDON Report,* Vol. 3, No. 6 (December 1978), pp. 2-3, 7.

> job step   = one main program with (optionally) a hierarchy of one or more subprograms*
>
> program   = a hierarchy of one or more structure chart modules
>
> load unit = a hierarchy of one or more programs whose calls are linked before execution

There are two major stages of packaging, the first of which precedes design, and the second of which follows it:

- At the end of analysis, package the system into separate jobs and into job steps.

- At the end of design, package each job step into possibly further job steps, load units, and programs.[†]

The sections below describe how each type of packaging is accomplished, and indicate when the packaging should be done.

11.1 End of analysis: Packaging into jobs

Packaging a system into jobs is done at the end of analysis for three reasons: First, it requires some information from the user — information most readily available after analysis has been completed. Second, DFDs developed during analysis are useful to show where data flows cross job boundaries. And third, it facilitates the designer's job. Being able to see the system as a network of distinct jobs is more helpful than having to deal with the system as one huge job. Attempting to derive a single structure chart for the whole system is extremely difficult since most systems do not comprise a single hierarchy.

Packaging a system into jobs is done by drawing three types of physical boundaries on the DFD.[‡] The parts of the DFD on each side of a boundary will become different jobs.

- *hardware boundaries* — Different parts of the system may be implemented on different machines. For example, an analyst may decide that the overall cost of a system would be reduced if each of a user's branch offices had its own STOIT 30 mini-computer that edit-

---

*A *main program* is a program that is called by the operating system; a *subprogram* is a program that is called by another program.

[†]After programming, this second stage of packaging may be revised to take into account actual program size. This packaging may also be revised during system testing to decrease run time or response time if the system failed a performance test.

[‡]Another physical boundary has already been drawn on the DFD during analysis: the manual/automated boundary. (See Chapter 4.)

ed local data and transmitted it in a summarized form to the main central LOOMIS 9000. The alternative of centralizing everything, although initially cheaper, might incur higher running costs.

I encountered another hardware boundary in a weapons-monitoring system: an analog/digital boundary. In this case, the designers had to compromise between making most of the system analog, which would have increased its speed, and making most of the system digital, which would have decreased the error rate during telemetry transmission. The DFD enabled the designers to optimize this tradeoff between speed and accuracy.

- *batch/on-line/real-time boundaries* — The passenger reservation and inquiry parts of an airline reservations system, for example, must be on-line. However, the report-generation part of the system will be batch. Similarly, telephone or process-control systems will be partly batch, partly on-line, and partly real-time. At the end of analysis, it is usually obvious enough which part is which.

- *cycle (alias periodicity) boundaries* — It makes little sense to put the yearly IRS report-generating portion of an accounting system, for instance, in the same job as the nightly run portion of that system. Jobs run with different cycle times should be packaged separately.* Not so obviously, it makes little sense to package a biweekly payroll job with a biweekly accounts payable job.

Two jobs run with the same cycle time should also be packaged separately if the only relationship between them is temporal. The problems with temporally cohesive jobs are similar to those with temporally cohesive modules. The designer must be concerned with what the coupling will be between the job and the tapes and disk packs; what the operators' instructions

*Occasionally and regrettably, practical considerations weigh against this rule. For example, suppose a master file is too large to be passed twice in one night. Then, a monthly job that uses this file would have to be packaged with a nightly job using the file, in order to avoid the difficulty of trying to pass the file twice during the last night of the month.

will look like; and what happens if one part of the job changes its cycle, or keeps the same cycle but shifts it forward by one day.

At this stage of packaging a system into jobs, you should ask certain questions each time a data flow crosses any physical boundary. The answers to these questions will determine, among other things, the implementation and running costs of the system. For example,

- What volume of data crosses this boundary?
- What frequency of data is likely?
- Do any outputs have to be produced within a critical time after an input is received?
- On what device is this data captured/displayed?
- Do any extra files have to be introduced?
- Are any special data access methods needed?
- How easy is it for different jobs to share files?
- What machine/machine protocol is necessary?
- What human/machine dialogue is called for?
- What validation requirements are there (on input)?
- What format requirements are there (on input or on output)?
- What users will be affected? How?
- What is the value of the data to the organization?
- What security checks must be performed on the data?

Clearly, the above considerations will add to the complexity of the system and to the amount of hardware required to run the system and hence to the overall cost of the system.

11.2 End of analysis/beginning of design: Packaging into job steps

Partitioning a job into job steps is best done at the end of analysis by means of the DFD. (It can be done at the end of design; however, it is more awkward to partition a structure chart into job steps than it is to partition a DFD.) The rule for creating job steps is: Partition the DFD for a job into as few job steps as possible. The reason for this is to reduce the number of intermediate files needed — and so to reduce the complexity of the system — and to decrease the run time of the system. (The reading and writing of intermediate files can significantly increase the run time of a job.)

There are three considerations in splitting a job into job steps:

- *Commercial software packages* may be used to implement some of the functions of the system. Such packages are rarely callable as subroutines and so cannot therefore be easily integrated into a structure chart. On the other hand, there is little point in making each package a separate job. Thus, the best compromise is to make each package into its own job step.

- *Safety or defensive requirements* may call for the introduction of otherwise unnecessary job steps and/or intermediate files. Examples would be audit, security, backup, recovery, or checkpoint-restart requirements. For instance, you would be unwise to run a ten-hour job as a single step on hardware whose mean time between failures is seven hours. Instead, you would create intermediate results in one step and use those intermediate results in a second step to create the final output. If the machine went down during the second step, then only the second step — not the whole job — would have to be repeated.

  The user may have business security requirements that are best effected by means of separate job steps. For example, banks periodically produce a confirmation of the balance in each of their accounts. These confirmations are issued to the owners of the accounts. However, before the confirmations are printed on the official forms, the bank must audit them to prevent inaccurate balances from being printed on official forms. Therefore, the confirmations are printed on plain paper and also stored on disk as one job step. Then, as a second job step, an audit program scans the output from the first job step. Finally, if the audit finds nothing wrong, a third job step prints out the confirmations on the special forms. The audit has to be a separate job step because its value as an independent safeguard would be lost if it were combined with the other job steps.

- *Resources* may be insufficient to run the job all at once. If an entire job cannot be held in the machine at one time, then it will have to be cut into pieces that can be executed one at a time. Nowadays, a lack of memory is unlikely; but other resources may be lacking. For example, if a job requires information from three tapes

but your shop has only one tape drive, then some preliminary transfer of data (on to, say, disk files) will be
necessary. Such transfers are best carried out by
means of separate job steps.

11.3 End of design: Packaging into programs and load units

By the end of design, each job step will be represented by a structure chart.* A Structured Design fanatic might try to convince you that
every module on a structure chart should become a separate program.
In a language such as COBOL,† the smallest physical unit in which data
can be protected from the rest of the system is the program. Therefore, in order to retain the full maintenance advantages of Structured
Design (e.g., isolating bugs to a small region), each module on the
structure chart *ideally* should become a separate COBOL program. But
such an ideal is hardly practical because of the overhead of having to
write out all four DIVISIONS for every module; hence, many modules
will become SECTIONS or PARAGRAPHS.

An often-heard objection to using called programs in COBOL is
the execution overhead of the CALL statement. This objection,
although based on mythology, does have *some* truth to it. The overhead of a CALL to very frequently executed modules (which are usually
located at the very bottom of the structure chart) may be significant.
But more likely to be significant is the overhead of calls between
different load units (*dynamic* calls).‡ Therefore, frequently executed
calls should be kept within the same load unit (*static* calls) by linking
together the appropriate structure chart modules before execution.

The preceding paragraph implies that for greatest efficiency all
modules should be linked into the same load unit. While this is true, it
has two drawbacks: First, most operating systems impose a limit on
load unit size. Second, each time a module in a load unit is recompiled, the whole load unit has to be relinked. This tedious process
reduces the flexibility of a system.

✔*For background reading on this as well as on programs and load units, see J.C. Emery,
"Modular Data Processing Systems in COBOL," *Communications of the ACM,* Vol. 5, No.
5 (May 1962), pp. 263-68.
†Most references to programs in this chapter — though relevant to many languages —
pertain specifically to COBOL programs. In a language like PL/I, data can be made
"private" within a unit much smaller than a program — namely, a PROCEDURE. In
PL/I, therefore, each job step would generally become a separate program and each structure chart module would become a separate procedure.
‡A dynamic call causes the loader to look for the load unit in memory, and, if it isn't
there, to load it from the load library and to resolve its external references.

The strategy for choosing which modules should be linked into a single load unit depends on how often each pair of modules in the system will be called within a short time of each other. Those modules frequently called one after the other should be grouped together; those modules that rarely execute together are good candidates for isolation into separate load units.*

This packaging for the sake of efficiency is an art that often depends on a sound knowledge of how the system is likely to execute for a typical set of data, and of what a typical set of data will look like. Consequently, this packaging may have to wait until the system is in production. However, Myers[†] has found that the intelligent packaging of a modular, loosely coupled system can reduce expensive operating system intervention by about five to one.

Figure 11.1 shows a structure chart for a simple job step that summarizes customer payments and that we wish to package in an efficient way. In Fig. 11.1, the small, arc-like arrow symbol means that, for instance, B invokes C iteratively — that is, in a loop.

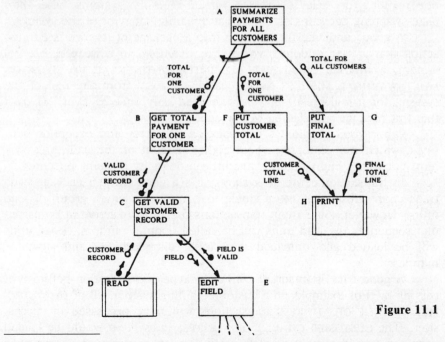

Figure 11.1

*Exactly the same strategy applies to grouping modules into a single page in a virtual memory system.

[†]G.J. Myers, *Reliable Software Through Composite Design* (New York: Petrocelli/Charter, 1975), p. 127.

Let's assume that there are a thousand customers, five payment records for the average customer, and ten fields on each record. This is how often each module will be invoked per run:

A	1	E	50000
B	1000	F	1000
C	5000	G	1
D	5000	H	1001

This table very quickly tells us what modules to package together in order to cut overheads. The first priority is to package C and E (which will turn 50,000 DYNAMIC CALLS into 50,000 STATIC CALLS if the packaging is into one load unit; or it will eliminate 50,000 page faults if the packaging is into one page). The second priority is to package B and C (and D, of course).

In this example, I based my packaging on the assumption that the average customer has five payment records. My optimal packaging might have to change if the actual number turned out to be 1.3 or 10.9. (However, if we are considering packaging into pages, even this might not matter, for today's smarter virtual-memory systems base their page-swapping decisions on the actual dynamic behavior of the system.)

A good candidate for isolation into a package of its own is a transaction that a user seldom invokes. For example, in a weapons-control system, a module called FIRE ALL INTERCONTINENTAL 100 MEGATON MULTI-WARHEAD MISSILES can be packaged away from the rest of the system, for it will presumably be executed only once — ever! (I trust that this package will also be well wrapped in security.)

Other good candidates for isolation are error and exception routines, which may comprise about eighty percent of the code of a system, but which, individually, have little probability of being executed.

In transaction-centered systems, it's a good idea to package each transaction subsystem into a single load unit or a small group of load units. However, since input transactions presumably arrive in no particular sequence, the load units will be called upon at random. Load units will be loaded and unloaded in a most disorderly — and slow! — manner.

A good trick is to sort the input by type of transaction before processing it. For example, in a customer-billing system, all of the CUSTOMER CHANGE OF ADDRESS transactions would be processed in succession. The CUSTOMER CHANGE OF ADDRESS subsystem would be loaded once and would remain in place until the last transaction of that type had been dealt with. Next, all the CUSTOMER PAYMENT transactions could be processed. And so on.

11.4 Preserving design quality during packaging

Nothing you do while packaging should menace the Structured Design criteria that most of the design effort is devoted to meeting. Indeed, you should use the same criteria that yielded a good logical design to attain a good physical design. For example, the criterion of cohesion dictates that you shouldn't package random structure chart modules into a single program or load unit. Instead, you should look for a single branch of modules on a structure chart to group into a physical package. In that way, you will also minimize the coupling between the packages. Similarly, jobs should have at least sequential cohesion. Even communicational cohesion can sometimes lead to complicated coupling between jobs, or between a job and the resources that it uses.

Beneficial Wishful Thinking in packaging leads to creating coupling (such as intermediate files) between packages that is as free as possible of the particular physical formats in which data happens to enter and leave the system. In this way, intermediate files are protected from changes in input and output formats — changes that the user is all too likely to make.

11.5 A packaging example

Figure 11.2 depicts the payroll DFD of Chapter 9 slightly modified to show that the TIME REPORTS are entered and validated by an intelligent terminal, and then sorted and processed by a batch job.

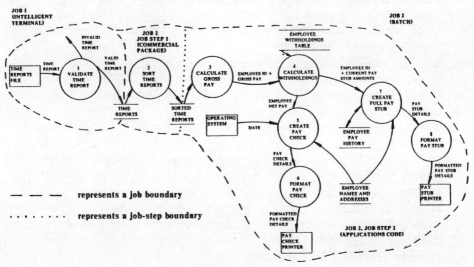

— — — represents a job boundary

· · · · · · · · represents a job-step boundary

Figure 11.2

This DFD yields two jobs: the intelligent terminal job and the batch job. Additionally, the SORT may be best implemented by a commercial package that requires a separate job step, so the second job will divide into two job steps. The net result of this packaging is three structure charts, as shown in Fig. 11.3.

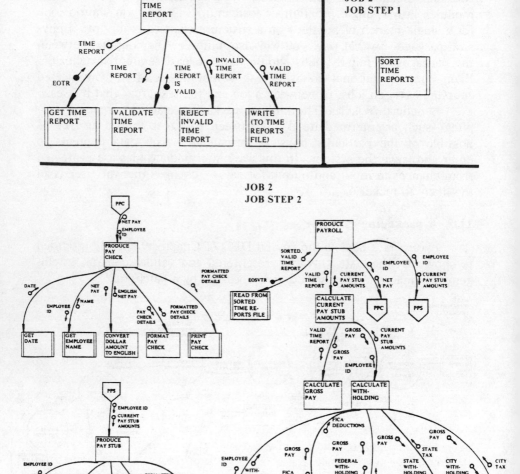

Figure 11.3

Finally, we can depict the system by a systems flowchart, as shown in Fig. 11.4.

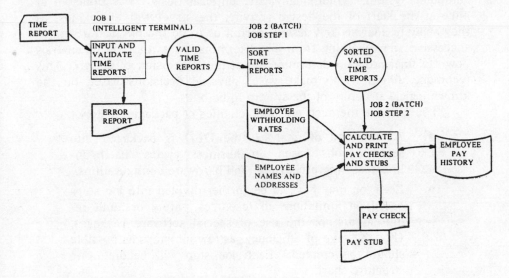

Figure 11.4

Are you surprised to see a systems flowchart in a book on Structured Design? You may have heard a rumor that Structured Design is against systems flowcharts. That's not true; but it *is* true that Structured Design wants to change the way in which systems flowcharts are currently used. If you saw someone banging a nail into a plank with the head of a screwdriver, I'm sure you'd be deeply offended, but you wouldn't seek to rid the world of "that accursed screwdriver."

In the past, people have packaged a system into job steps (the old favorites being input, edit, sort, process, and output) before they figured out what was being packaged (input what? edit what?). Notice that we developed the systems flowchart in a much saner way: We worked out the functions of the system first and then packaged them as necessary and appropriate. Had we started development with a systems flowchart, we would soon have become committed to it — even if it was wrong! It is very difficult to turn a poor systems flowchart into a better one. However, with DFDs and structure charts, we have many options — including preserving the whole job as a single step.

In its correct context, however, the systems flowchart is an indispensable tool. That context is neither analysis, nor design, but operations. There, it will provide the operators with such information as which tapes to mount and which special forms to load.

11.6 Summary

Packaging is the successive refinement of the physical design of a computer system. Traditionally, the physical design was done all at once at the start of the design activity; the structured techniques, as they apply to analysis and design, permit us to do the physical design in successive steps working from job determination at the end of analysis down to final program determination at the conclusion of design. This technique allows us to make wiser physical decisions based on the known logical structure of the system to be built.

I summarize the decisions and activities of packaging below.

- At the end of analysis, the DFD is packaged into separate jobs based on business cycles, batch/on-line/real-time processing, and hardware configurations.

- Each job may have to be further divided into job steps based on limitations to resources, safety or audit requirements, or the use of special software packages. (For the sake of efficiency, as few job steps as possible should be created.) Each job step will become one structure chart.

- At the end of design, each structure chart is packaged into programs. In order to retain the full advantages of Structured Design, each module on the structure chart should ideally become a separate COBOL program. However, although this ideal is not attainable in practice — many modules will become SECTIONS or PARA-GRAPHS — each program should be made as "small" as possible.

- If reducing the overhead of dynamic calls is important, then frequently executed calls should be made into static calls by grouping the appropriate programs into a single load unit. Page faults can similarly be reduced by grouping the appropriate structure chart modules into one page.

- Jobs, job steps, load units, and programs should have high cohesion; have little coupling to other packages; be neither physically input-driven nor physically output-driven; and should preserve the logical structure of the system by superimposing only a minimal physical structure upon the logical design.

Exercises

1. Examine the fairly traditional systems flowchart shown below for the example considered in Section 11.5. What are its deficiencies as compared to the systems flowchart derived from the DFD and shown in Fig. 11.4?

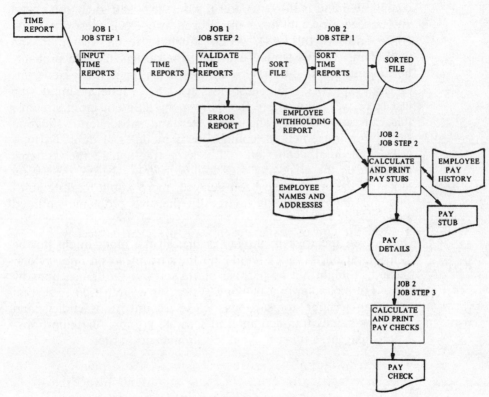

2. In Section 11.3, I mentioned that a good trick for improving the efficiency of a transaction-processing system is to sort the transactions by type before execution. Why might this trick not work?

238 PRACTICAL GUIDE TO STRUCTURED SYSTEMS DESIGN

Answers

1. First, there seems to be a mistake in the systems flowchart, in that it prints all of the pay stubs first and then it prints all of the pay checks. (Someone would have to go through the output after the run to collate pay stubs with pay checks.) Second, it's over-complicated and inefficient. JOB 1, JOB STEP 1, and JOB 2, JOB STEP 3 are unnecessary and have introduced two extra files (TIME RE-PORTS and PAY DETAILS), which will have to be written to and read from. In this simple example, the designer would probably not fall into the trap of having a superfluous input step. However, in larger systems, some designers tend to include an input step just to be safe. But where there are many different input streams, this can cause chaos. The input step and subsequent validation step, when implemented, contain many modules of dubious (typi-cally procedural) cohesion. If, as is traditional, the systems flowchart on the preceding page had been drawn before the logical model of the system had been derived, there would be little guid-ance for anyone wanting to rectify the two problems outlined above.

2. One reason the trick might fail is that all the input might not be available at once, which would be the case in an on-line system. Second, it might not be permissible to sort out the transactions by type. For example, in a banking system, it wouldn't do to sort all the open-account transactions, close-account transactions, and withdraw-money transactions into separate groups. Banking trans-actions like these must be kept in chronological order.

12

Implementation

What happens after the programmers in your shop have coded a module? Do they take the rest of the day off, or do they rush, adrenalin flowing, to code the next module? Or, do they do what your shop standards probably call for: unit-test the completed module before beginning to code the next one?

Although I know that the standards of many shops call for the testing of modules (or small groups of modules) as they're constructed, very few shops enforce such standards. A common excuse is, "We're behind schedule as it is; we just don't have time for testing now. We can do that at systems integration time."

The reality is that no one can be bothered to write the driver routines or the test data that are necessary to unit-test modules. But the bother of testing a module is small compared to the bother and cost of living with a badly tested system.

In Fig. 12.1 is a module called CALCULATE MONTHLY LOAN REPAYMENT being tested under a driver (otherwise known as a test harness). The driver obtains some test data, passes it to the module under test, accepts the module's output, and either reports the output for human scrutiny or checks it by another means (or both). As described, the test-harness process may seem simple. However, the arrangement isn't always so straightforward as the one shown, especially if more than one module is being driven. I once encountered a driver that was driving a task scheduler of an operating system and that had some subtle bugs in it. In exasperation, the developers were finally forced to test the driver under another driver!

Besides tedium, another reason that unit-testing has fallen into disrepute is that although it's a necessary part of testing, in itself, it is not sufficient. Unit-testing is the most effective way to test the logic within individual modules; but however thorough unit-testing has been, when all the modules are brought together, the result may still be a total shambles.

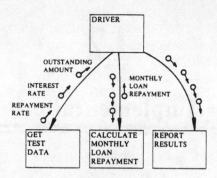

Figure 12.1

A strategy in addition to unit-testing is required to ensure the most effective testing of the complete system. The additional strategy consists of an incremental approach to implementation, by which unit-tested modules are brought together one by one, rather than all at once. But before we look at this in more detail, let's review the conventional implementation strategy.

12.1 Traditional approach to implementation

Traditionally, systems have been coded and tested in the following sequence:

- First, write, test, and debug each module (or small group of modules) separately. This is the *unit-test.*

- Then group all the units into subsystems and test and debug each subsystem. This is the *subsystem-test.*

- Next, combine the subsystems to form the whole system. This is *system integration.*

- Finally, test and debug the whole system. This is *system disintegration!* *

---

*These last three steps are also known by cynics as "shake and bake." You throw all the modules into a large "bag," shake it vigorously, and execute it until it bakes, in an attempt to get all the pieces to coalesce. (When they don't, *you* bake as you try to figure out why not.)

One of the most severe problems with the traditional approach is that the most crucial interfaces in the system — those between subsystems — are tested late in the project, when there is little time to spare to correct any bugs that may be found. Another problem with this approach is that it affords little opportunity for anyone to manage resources in an orderly way. It has no subtle variations: The only way you can throw something together all at once is to throw it together all at once.

The use of resources (human or machine) for testing and debugging in a traditional project typically looks as shown in Fig. 12.2.

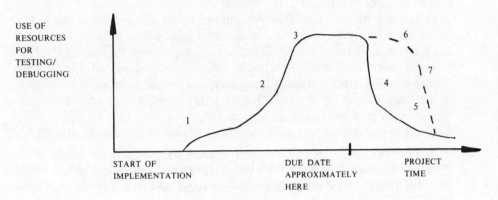

USE OF RESOURCES FOR TESTING/ DEBUGGING

START OF IMPLEMENTATION

DUE DATE APPROXIMATELY HERE

PROJECT TIME

Figure 12.2

In Fig. 12.2, seven key points are labeled: At point 1, the reluctance of the implementors to begin testing is evident; testing starts none too soon and is rather skimpy. By stage 2, the project team, aghast, sees the project deadline looming large and evil on the horizon, and quickly throws together whatever has been coded, and hurriedly "tests" it. (The mathematical term for the shape of this part of the curve is *panic.*) It's possible for a point to be reached (point 3 in the graph) at which there are no more available resources for testing: no more warm bodies, CPU cycles, or hours in a day. Everything has been thrown into a D-day style effort to "get the damn thing out the door." The problem is usually that when all the modules are fitted together, they don't. Optimism turns to frustration, then to exhaustion, and finally to anger. Bugs appear by the hundred in "successfully tested" modules. One group of implementors blames another group for its demonstrable incompetence in creating modules full of errors, which bring down *their* modules. The cold truth behind this hot political wrangle is that no single group of people or set of modules in isolation is to blame: The problem is in the interfaces between the modules.

(This problem, of course, is exacerbated by the high coupling that many traditional systems possess.)

By stage 4 — which is probably well past the date scheduled for delivery — most of the bugs have been exorcised. Rarely, however, are *all* the bugs removed before the system is cut over into production at stage 5; the remaining bugs are called "features" and their elimination is budgeted under maintenance, rather than under development. The system, barely working from its inception, may become a disaster when it's hit by a few user changes. The few poor souls who remained alive after stages 3 and 4 will become the maintenance programmers who have to deal with such traumas.

Point 6 marks an alternative curve, which occurs when the bugs are chased around the system in never-decreasing circles for months, until at point 7 they are all gone. . . . And so is the system! The manager has gotten sick of throwing good money after bad and watching most of his shop pursuing bugs as if they were hunting for the end of the rainbow. With his best-honed scimitar, he has axed the project — and possibly some of the people on it!

As Weinberg says, traditional implementation is "an old story":*

> The deadline is not met, and the workers continue to stumble through the testing phase until either they wear down the problems or the problems wear them down.

12.2 Incremental approaches to implementation

Incremental implementation is a more disciplined approach to systems implementation than is the traditional approach. It is carried out as follows:

```
repeat until the system is complete
      implement and unit-test a module
      add the module to the existing combination
      test and debug the new combination
endrepeat
deliver the system
```

Hence, implement the first module and then add modules to it, one by one, or in small groups. Throughout implementation, each time around the loop, the system is working — although perhaps it is not doing very much. The implemented portion of the system starts small but, with the gentle inevitability of gradualness, builds into the complete system.

---

*V. Weinberg, *Structured Analysis* (New York: YOURDON Press, 1978), p. 209.

Incremental implementation gives far more flexibility in the use of resources than phased implementation does, because it can be accomplished in a number of ways. For example, you can incrementally implement a bridge across a river from the left bank to the right bank, or from the right bank to the left bank, or from both banks toward the center. Similarly, you can incrementally implement a structure chart from the top to the bottom, or from the bottom to the top, or from the right to the left, or from the bottom left corner outwards, or in a hundred other ways. How you actually accomplish the implementation depends on the available resources and the nature of the system being implemented. But whichever approach you choose, you have to plan it in advance — good use of resources usually requires planning. The designer should derive the plan from the packaged structure chart, taking into consideration any priorities that may be assigned to certain functions of the system.

The typical use of resources for testing in an incremental implementation is shown in Fig. 12.3:

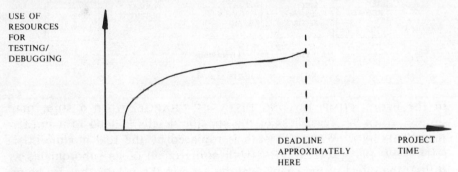

Figure 12.3

In the following sections, I elaborate on some of the most successful varieties of the incremental approach.

12.3 Top-down incremental implementation

The top-down approach involves implementing the top module of the structure chart* first, with each of its subordinates being simulated by a stub or dummy module. A *stub* is a module whose function is ru-

---

*In theory, top-down incremental implementation implies implementing and testing operations procedures first, followed by implementing and testing the job control statements. In practice, this is also a good idea, since both operations procedure and job control can be immediately determined from the packaged design.

dimentary; it is used simply as a place-holder for a real subordinate that hasn't yet been implemented. Each stub is then replaced by a real module (with its subordinates simulated by stubs) until the bottom of the structure chart is reached and the system is complete.

Figure 12.4 is a schematic example of top-down incremental implementation.

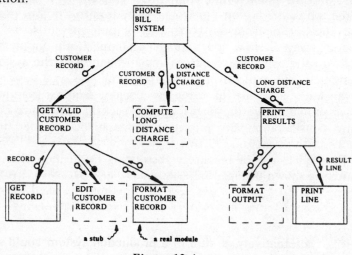

Figure 12.4

In the figure, COMPUTE LONG DISTANCE CHARGE, when a stub, may simply return $2, regardless of the specific details handed to it in CUSTOMER RECORD. When this stub is replaced by the real module COMPUTE LONG DISTANCE CHARGE (with some or all of its subordinates as stubs), the effect of the change can be seen in the results that are being printed.

If the results aren't in keeping with what you expected for the present level of sophistication of COMPUTE LONG DISTANCE CHARGE, then the first place to look for a bug is in COMPUTE LONG DISTANCE CHARGE. If COMPUTE LONG DISTANCE CHARGE is blighted by a bug, then that module can be removed for repair. The old stub can be put back, and implementation can continue without the faulty COMPUTE LONG DISTANCE CHARGE until it has been fixed.

Often no one module is to blame for a bug; the bug is caused by a disagreement between two modules. If you don't find the bug in COMPUTE LONG DISTANCE CHARGE, check the interface between COMPUTE LONG DISTANCE CHARGE and its boss. For instance, the two modules may be inconsistent in the type or order of their parameters. (Although

Structured Design should prevent this kind of inconsistency, mistakes can always happen.) With top-down incremental implementation, interface bugs can be corrected calmly and early.

The requirements of a stub depend on whether it's simulating an afferent, efferent, transform, or coordinate module. Afferent and transform stubs must return some data; efferent and transform stubs must accept some data. A coordinate stub (such as that at the top of a transaction-processing subsystem) needs to do nothing.

A stub can perform a variety of functions, and you can, of course, combine several functions into one stub. Following are some examples of possible functions of stubs (the letters in parentheses refer to the type of stub for which the function is applicable: A for afferent; E, efferent; C, coordinate; and T, transform). A stub may, for instance,

- do nothing — this isn't very useful, but it's simple to implement (E, C)

- display a trace message, such as "Hi, I'm module ARTHUR. I just got called." This may be used to trace the dynamic behavior of the system for debugging. (A, E, T, C)

  Alternatively, a stub in a production system could say, "Hi, I'm only a stub right now. The FORECAST ALL STOCK PRICES FOR 2 YEARS feature of the system, which you just invoked, won't be available until January 2001."

- converse with an interactive terminal. Now you too can be a stub! Typically, this is used with a stub that displays a trace message, indicating a module that can prompt for data to return to its boss. (A, T)

- return a constant value, for example, $100, or a random number, or a number from a table of test data (A, T)

- be a simpler version of the real module, such as a COMPUTE AIR FARE stub that can compute fares only for one-leg journeys; or be a rough approximation to the real module, for example, a COMPUTE BALLISTIC TRAJECTORY stub that simulates the trajectory by a simple parabola (A, E, T, C)

- test or display the data with which it's called, for example, a COMPUTE THRUST TO TURN SPACESHIP stub that checks whether it's always sent an angle between 0° and 360°. This is good defensive testing. It's a two-for-one deal in which the stub tests the rest of the system when it's a stub, and the rest of the system tests the real module when it's a real module. (E, T)

- be a NOTHING-TO-DO LOOP, which marks the passing of time. This kind of stub is useful in real-time or operating systems, in which you need to ensure that the system will function correctly given that a certain module will execute in less than, say, 19 milliseconds. The stub, when called, would merely wait 19 milliseconds before returning. (A, E, T, C)

  Alternatively, this type of stub could be used to simulate a piece of mechanical hardware that takes 19 milliseconds to operate.

Now, in what order should you replace stubs with the genuine articles? Some early advocates of top-down implementation stated that you should do it level by level: Replace all the stubs before you move down a level. The only benefit I can see in that scheme is that it looks pretty. In practice, that's probably the least likely way to fill the structure chart with completed modules. Below, I outline some more practical suggestions for the order of implementation of modules in a system.

For many systems, the "umbrella" variety of top-down incremental implementation is most applicable. With this approach, you implement part of the efferent side and somewhat more of the afferent side before beginning to implement any of the central transform. The reason for this is quite simple: You have to install part of the efferent side in order to see what results the system produces. Since the format of the output need not be very glossy, there's no need to implement many of the formatting modules. So long as the output doesn't appear in hexadecimal and so long as an occasional space appears between items of output data, all is well. Once you can enter data into the system and see some results, you can monitor the progress of the central transform as it is incrementally implemented.

There are good reasons for implementing more than just the bare bones of the afferent and efferent parts of the system before work begins on implementing the central transform. Although most of the major interfaces in the system occur at the top of the structure chart, there are also some crucial interfaces at the bottom — notably the user interface and the data-base interfaces. It's often beneficial to implement several of the formatting modules on the efferent side to ensure that the system's output fits onto the user's standard forms, or to fix the format of an output before ordering new forms from a manufacturer. With regard to input, there are user dialogues to be attended to, and screen formats and error messages to be determined. Usually, some experimentation is needed before these can be made satisfactory to the user. Additional benefits to implementation are that the system's editing modules are exercised early and often, and that the presence of at least some input formatting modules allows more painless entry of test data into the system.

A variation of umbrella incremental implementation is called "bottom-left umbrella incremental implementation." This type is most useful when performance requirements are stringent, for example, for systems with large volumes of input or with large data bases. This strategy involves starting at the bottom of the afferent leg and building clockwise until you reach (more or less) the bottom of the efferent leg, as shown in Fig. 12.5:

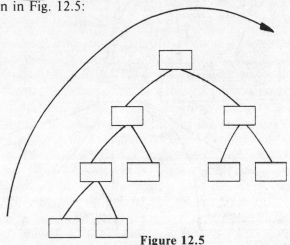

Figure 12.5

Bottom-left umbrella incremental implementation requires drivers and a few transform stubs for the afferent side, and stubs for the efferent side. (One advantage of this strategy is that afferent drivers and efferent stubs are both easy to create.) This strategy enables you to make some determination of the likely throughput of high volume data. Alternatively, particularly with data-base accesses, it affords a measure of the system's probable response-time curves. If you use this strategy, it's extremely valuable to have real input data available at the start of implementation.

The order in which the modules of the central transform are implemented depends on the nature of the system and the priorities to which you and the user have previously agreed. An indispensable tool for planning incremental system implementation is a log-book with one entry per module showing its projected progress from stub to full realization, together with its actual progress.

What might be the plan of attack for the small system for printing pay checks and pay stubs? The succession of versions might proceed as shown in Fig. 12.6.

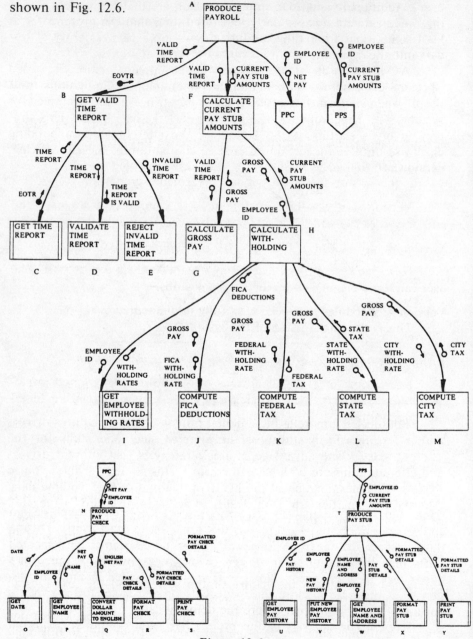

Figure 12.6

Version 1: Modules A, B, C, T, W, Y fully implemented
    D   a stub that reports every TIME REPORT as correct
    E   a stub that does nothing at all
    F   a stub that always returns the same amounts
    N   a stub that does nothing at all
    U   a stub that always returns the same amounts
    V   a stub that does nothing at all
    W   a stub that always returns "John Doe" and a fictitious address
    X   a stub that does nothing at all

Version 1 in Fig. 12.6 does nothing except produce pay stubs, bearing meaningless information in a reasonable format.

Version 2: Modules D, E, F, G, U, X fully implemented
    H   a stub that always deducts a constant proportion

Version 2 rejects invalid time reports, computes gross pay, and puts the gross pay and the actual employee pay history on the pay stub.

Version 3: Modules I, J, K, L, M, V, W fully implemented

Now, the system does everything except produce pay checks. The user can use Version 3 to produce his pay stubs.

Version 4: Modules N, O, P, Q, R, S fully implemented
This is the final version of the system.

12.3.1 The advantages of top-down, incremental implementation

I can think of eight advantages of top-down, incremental implementation. Some of them are top-down advantages; others are incremental advantages.

- *Important feedback to the user is provided when it's most needed, most useful, and most meaningful.*

During analysis, the project teams and the user were in close contact in their discussions of the user's requirements. The feedback loop was tight. But since the analysis stage, the project has been through design and programming, technical realms that are alien to most users. During those stages, the feedback loop was almost nonexistent. Unsuspected drifts may have occurred in design or in programming, or the user's needs may have changed. Now — as soon as possible in implementation — is the time to close the feedback loop and to let the user see a portion of the end product before the delivery date.

Even if the analysis of the project has been top-notch, using all the fabled philosophies and techniques of Structured Analysis, the specification may still contain errors. For example, the user himself may have been dead wrong, because perhaps he misinterpreted what a computer system could or couldn't do for him; or perhaps his requirements have subtly changed late in the course of the project. No specification is quite as real as a tangible, functioning system, which the user can see, touch, feel, and play with. Early in the implementation, it isn't too late for you to respond to remarks like: "Gee, I didn't realize that you'd have to re-enter the whole screen if one field was in error." Also, users can make errors in using the system, errors that you almost certainly haven't anticipated.

When I think of data processing, I sometimes think of that other service industry that has to cope with almost as many modifications to existing systems as we do: the garment industry. When I visit the tailor for a new suit, I choose my material and I am measured in every which way. But despite the apparently meticulous care taken in the specification, when I climb into the completed suit, it never seems quite to fit. Weathering such comments as, "My, Sir's left arm *has* grown this past month," or "Buttonless vests are all the rage this year," I quietly ask for the suit to be altered to my specifications.

But whether discrepancies are due to the tailor or due to my own expansion, it's almost impossible to derive a perfectly fitting garment directly from the measurements. The feedback loop has to be closed with the manufacture of an actual suit.

- *The user can use several skeleton system versions* to allow him to make a smooth transition from his old system to his new system.*

In the example of our pay check and pay stub system above, we would not have officially delivered Version 1 or Version 2 to the user, although we could have allowed him and his staff to experiment with these versions. However, although Version 4 was the final version of the system, the user actually could have used Version 3 to create pay stubs for hourly workers.

If, say, eight versions of a system are to be produced by top-down implementation, then quite often the user will receive, say, Versions 4 and 6 (and possibly 2) well before the deadline. He can use them to do some of his business, or to do some testing for the developers (but I don't guarantee that you'll always get your users to do your testing for you), or to help to train his staff. There's nothing worse for a computer-innocent staff than to have a new system dumped upon it like

---

*A skeleton system version is a partially implemented system that performs a small but useful subset of the functions of the complete system.

an abandoned baby one Monday morning, with a pile of unreadable documentation and a curt announcement stating, "That's what you asked for. Now get on with it." With incremental versions, people can get used to the system and its ever-increasing power gradually. The earliest version is likely to be so simple that not even the most timid individual could find it threatening.

Several years ago, I did some consulting for a shop that was about to espouse Structured Design for a financial management system. I preached to them about the fabulous rewards to be gained by delivering the system in versions. Eighteen months later, on another of my visits, the implementors complained bitterly to me that programming and testing were going so fast that as soon as one version was handed over to the user, the next version was ready for delivery.

Well, excuse me! But that does bring up an important point: Don't schedule myriad versions for production. The overhead of cutting a system over once is high enough (especially in the case of a user who wants to install the system in several remote offices). But even if only the final version actually gets into production, the other delivered versions should be seriously tried out by at least one user site.

- *The project is less likely to be axed if it falls behind schedule.*

A project, however structured, can always fall behind schedule. (If the whole development team contracts beri-beri, for instance, that will do it.) There's nothing more politically embarrassing in my experience than to have to face the user(s) in a meeting a few days before the due date to explain why the system will be six months late. It's no good coming armed with excuses ranging from "Systems integration proved more difficult than we thought" to "our best programmer got hit by a truck," or "our only data-base expert was kidnapped by urban guerillas and we're still trying to raise the ransom." Neither does it do any good to brandish a three-foot-thick listing of the COBOL code with the unconvincing accompaniment, "we're 95 percent complete." As far as the user knows, you rummaged through the waste-paper bins for those reams of gibberish and you may remain 95 percent complete for years.

A user will never be pleased with an overdue project. But if he can *see* a working version of the system, then he'll be more willing to believe that you haven't been totally idle for the last year or two. If he can actually do some work with the current version, so much the better, for he may be able to save face in his shop with *his* manager, who is probably mad at him. Also, it's better to be able to tell a user six months in advance that his system will be a month late than it is to tell him a month in advance that it will be six months late. Top-down incremental implementation tends to afford an earlier, more realistic measure of progress, since there'll be no mine field hidden close to the finishing line.

- *Major system interfaces are tested first and most often.*

If the system has been developed by Structured Design, then most of the important module interfaces should be at the top of the structure chart (or charts). These crucial interfaces will be tested in the first and in every subsequent version of the system.

- *Testing resources are distributed more evenly.*

As we already saw in Fig. 12.3, the graph of resource use for incremental testing/debugging has no nasty spikes, and represents a much more manageable use of resources than the graph in Fig. 12.2, which illustrates the traditional approach to implementation.

- *Implementors can see early results from a working system, so their morale is improved.*

The implementors as well as the user get a tremendous boost from seeing something working. Such positive feedback is a fundamental psychological incentive to working hard.

- *If time is short, coding and testing can begin before the design is finished.*

I don't recommend this practice (known as *radical* development) if you have any choice. However, I have seen it used successfully on the development of a taxation system, which was disastrously under-budgeted. Since it looked as if the project would still be in design when the deadline arrived, the implementors went right ahead with coding and testing even without a complete design. They left a firewall of at least four levels between the modules being coded and those being designed. At such a late stage, they could do without having to recode modules because of design perturbations at lower levels.

Managerially, that project was a catastrophe, although technically the outcome was quite happy. At the deadline, the implementors delivered a non-trivial version of the system to the user. The system was transaction-centered (always nice to build in versions); the delivered version handled some of the user's most often useful types of transactions.

- *Management has a better idea of the rate of progress by counting working modules, for example, instead of by "weighing" code.*

An unfortunate aspect of the introduction of both Structured Analysis and Structured Design into a DP shop is the psychological effect they produce on management. By this, I mean that a manager from the old sharpen-your-pencils-and-code school expects lines of code (regardless of quality) to begin appearing no later than two weeks into the project. If more than halfway through the project no code has emerged, then a nervous manager may be discovered standing on the Brooklyn Bridge contemplating eternity.

In talking your unhappy manager down from his windy ledge, you should emphasize that when code is at last written, it should be good, working code. He will be able to monitor the progress of the system as an actual working entity and not just as ink on line-printer listings. In fact, with top-down incremental implementation, *working* code will almost certainly be produced before it would have been produced using the traditional approach.

12.4 Bottom-up incremental implementation

Bottom-up incremental implementation is top-down incremental implementation turned upside down. You implement a module at the bottom of the structure chart and run it under a driver. Progressing upward in the structure chart, you replace the driver by the real superordinate module, putting under it all siblings of the original module.

Bottom-up incremental implementation can allow excellent parallel implementation at first (although it becomes more difficult to plan and manage as it proceeds). Since many structure charts are pyramid-shaped, the approach also solves the problem of what to do with the horde of programmers who may have been assigned to the project: Set them to work at the bottom. Another advantage is that it addresses the testing of a major interface of the system — the physical input and output — early.

However, the many other important interfaces at the top of the system are tackled last. The way in which they're integrated into the developing system depends critically on the relative speed of the teams working on each branch. Management can become so difficult at the top that the implementation degenerates into the chaos characteristic of traditional implementation. Other problems are that you cannot implement intermediate versions of the system, and that you're forced to complete the whole design before you begin implementation.

12.5 Sandwich incremental implementation

Sandwich incremental implementation combines the best of top-down and bottom-up implementation: You implement the top half of the system top-down and the bottom half of the system bottom-up and meet in the middle. Described as baldly as this, the strategy sounds like the plans for building an England-France channel tunnel mooted about twenty years ago. The French were to dig toward Dover and the English were to dig toward Calais, meeting roughly in the middle of the English Channel. Wags asked, "Do we really need two tunnels?"

Taken literally, this approach of just meeting in the middle — wherever that is — could cause severe interface problems. But surprisingly, used sensibly, the sandwich approach can combine the best of top-down and bottom-up implementation. It means implementing all of the utility modules at the bottom while implementing major functions at the top of the system top-down. Spotting a utility module is a subjective business, but high fan-in and a generally useful function are good indications. An example might be an EDIT STATE NAME module in a system that processes many types of transactions containing a state name. Other examples are a module that calculates the number of days between two dates or a module that validates the check digit of a credit-card account number.

Implementing real versions of utility modules is more productive than writing stubs, as a single utility module will be used by several bosses. Indeed, many utility modules can serve in several applications. Any module that you deem useful in one application deserves to be considered as a candidate for the shop's module library. Of course, like any module, a utility module should be well walked-through and tested before it's released to implementation.

The sandwich approach is one you might find yourself using automatically if you're implementing a transaction-centered system, transaction by transaction. Many of the low-level modules implemented for the first transaction can be used by subsequent transactions.

12.6 Testing techniques

The test plan is developed from the original specification of what the system is supposed to do.* Any special problems due to the imple-

---

*Specific methods of testing systems are beyond the scope of this book. However, a system developed by Structured Design offers some benefits for testing — in particular, the black-box, white-box methods of testing suggested by Myers [*The Art of Software Testing* (New York: Wiley Interscience, 1979)]. Myers' book is also invaluable for its comprehensive treatment of a disciplined approach to software testing.

mentation (for example, the packaging of the structure chart) should also be tested, using the packaged design as a guide. The test plan should contain test cases comprising test data deliberately and fiendishly crafted to expose as many bugs as possible, together with the predicted output for each test input, and a description of any additional tools (for example, a test-data generator), which will be used in testing.

12.7 Summary

Implementation is the coding and testing of a system. In the past, this phase of the project was performed in a quite undisciplined way. Usually the code for the system was completely written before any sub-systems had been integrated and tested together. The all-too-frequent result of this practice was that a system that seemed absolutely complete would disintegrate — in its final testing phase — to the horror of its implementors.

The incremental approach to implementation avoids the problem of eleventh-hour disasters in projects, since it allows crucial interfaces of a system to be tested early when very little code has been committed to paper. Additionally, its flexibility — we saw many variations on incremental implementation in this chapter — allows the implementors to tailor an implementation strategy to their resources. Finally, incremental implementation affords both real and psychological benefits to the implementors, their manager, and the user alike. They can all oversee the progress of a working system from its most rudimentary stage through eventual completion.

Exercises

1. In Section 12.3, I stated that if the bottom-left umbrella variation of incremental implementation is chosen as an implementation strategy, "it's extremely valuable to have real input data available at the start of implementation." Why might the use of real input data — as opposed to artificially crafted test data — actually be *harmful* to testing a system?

2. Does incremental implementation eliminate the need to unit-test modules?

Answers

1. The danger of testing with actual data is that most bugs in systems are exposed by input data that is beyond or just at the edge of its range of legal values. For example, an inventory system might happily accept an update of zero items to stock, whereas such an update is almost certain to be a data-entry error and should at least be questioned. Some file-summarizing programs I've seen would crash completely if they were ever given an empty file to summarize.

    A single sample of normal user data is likely to contain few, if any, boundary values. Therefore, it is unlikely to exercise those dark corners of systems where bugs often lurk. But remember: When a system is put into production it encounters improbable sets of data almost immediately; impossible sets take only a little longer to crop up! Therefore, the system must be tested with some artificial test cases that have been specially designed to include mid-range values, boundary values, "impossible" values, and also sheer garbage.

2. Definitely not! Unit-testing is a powerful technique for exercising individual paths through the logic of a single module. It's generally extremely difficult to execute specific paths through a module if you can access the module only via other modules, as is the case with incremental implementation. Incremental implementation is, however, a powerful technique for testing the interfaces between unit-tested modules.

13

Optimization

13.1 The qualities of a system

Throughout this book, I've proclaimed that the advantages of Structured Design are that it leads to systems that are correct, understandable, and maintainable. Nowhere have I said that Structured Design yields systems that run fast or consume a small amount of memory. That emphasis is deliberate, for the efficiency of a system has traditionally been greatly overrated. In certain situations, the execution time of a system or its use of memory may be important — but there are other more essential qualities: effectiveness, usability, reliability, and maintainability. Only after these qualities have been determined to be satisfactory can efficiency even be considered.

In this chapter, I demonstrate how the run time* of a system can be improved, if necessary, without endangering more important factors. But first, let me explain what I mean by effectiveness, usability, reliability, and maintainability.

- Effectiveness means doing the job correctly, and testably so. The job, like justice, should not only be done correctly, but should also be *seen* to be done correctly. It's not surprising that effectiveness comes at the top of my list. If I had to produce a transaction-processing system, one of whose specifications was that it didn't

---

*I won't dwell on the important aspect of people-efficiency in this chapter, because one of the tenets of Structured Design is to make the best use of human resources. Neither will I consider memory-efficiency, because sensible packaging (see Chapter 11) and modern virtual-memory systems will take care of memory constraints.

have to work, I could implement an incredibly efficient system within an hour. It would merely read each transaction and instantly throw it out.

- An unusable system acts as if you're bothering it whenever you try to use it. For example, if an on-line system requires 16 fields to be entered without any prompts and if the only error message is ERROR, then nobody is likely to use it. The system might as well not have been implemented. If anyone does try to use it, he is likely to waste a lot of human and machine time getting the fields in the right order.

- An unreliable system is one that often breaks down or produces inaccurate results. For example, an airline reservation system that crashes every 25 minutes and takes 15 minutes to fix, or a payroll system that prints a random number on the first check of every batch. An unreliable system is unusable in a very real sense: It's rarely available to be used!

- An unmaintainable system either contains unfixable bugs or cannot be adapted to keep up with the user's changing needs. A system that doesn't have this flexibility soon goes the way of the dodo.

- An efficient system makes good use of resources such as time and memory. Being reasonably efficient is an important quality of a system, but it's not so crucial as the four other qualities mentioned above. Aha, you say, what if an airline reservation system has a response time of 67 seconds or if a nightly order-entry system runs for 42 hours? Well, in such cases, efficiency *is* critical because it affects usability.

In the past, efficiency has been attained in a penny-wise, pound-foolish manner. There used to be a special breed of programmer who would remain at work long after his colleagues had gone home, browsing through obscure vendor manuals to find bizarre (or even undiscovered!) machine features that would allow him to save an instruction here or a memory cycle there. The only noticeable results of such tricky coding were damage to the maintainability, reliability, or effectiveness of the system. (Ironically, any improvement in *efficiency* was generally not detectable!) We have all heard statements like, "Gee, Louis, you've tightened this loop so much that I can't figure out what it does any more." Or, "Now that you've optimized our update system, Gonzo, it loses the first piece of activity against a new account."

There is no doubt that the road to hell is paved with tricky coding, or, as Wulf* puts it:

More computing sins have been committed in the name of efficiency (without necessarily achieving it) than for any other reason — including blind stupidity.

13.2 The structured approach to optimization

Structured Design has a four-part philosophy regarding the optimization of a system:

It's easier to get a working system efficient than it is to get an efficient system working.[†] You should first of all ensure that a system is well-designed, soundly implemented, and correct before you even consider optimizing it. Then you can tune it at leisure with full awareness of what you are doing to the system's effectiveness, usability, reliability, and maintainability.

Optimize a system only if it fails a performance test. It's futile to optimize a system just for the fun of it, if that optimization brings no practical benefit.

Jackson[‡] gives two rules for determining when to optimize:

1. Don't do it.
2. Don't do it yet.

Simplicity is a virtue that bears its own rewards. Not only is a simple system easy to understand, but it's also more likely to be efficient to operate than is a baroque, over-complicated system. For example, the low coupling of a well-structured system may of itself yield reasonable efficiency. Conversely, if the structure chart for a system looks like Custer's Last Stand, with flags and arrows everywhere, the resulting system will probably be inefficient. After all, flags have to be set and they have to be tested.

Optimize only the parts of a system worth optimizing. One of the old systems proverbs, the 90-10 rule, says: In a typical application, 90 per-

---

*W.A. Wulf, "A Case Against the GOTO," *Proceedings of the 25th National ACM Conference* (New York: Association for Computing Machinery, 1972), pp. 791-97; also, E.N. Yourdon, ed., *Classics in Software Engineering* (New York: YOURDON Press, 1979), p. 95.
[†]E. Yourdon, *Managing the Structured Techniques* (New York: YOURDON Press, 1979), p. 102.
[‡]M. Jackson, *Principles of Program Design* (New York: Academic Press, 1975), p. 232.

cent of the total run time is devoted to executing only 10 percent of the code.* (Real figures may be even more extreme: I once encountered a system where 99 percent of the run time was consumed by 5 percent of the code.) These lopsided percentages typically emerge because much of the code in a system handles exception, or other comparatively rare, conditions.

There are two implications of the 90-10 rule. First, the penalty that Structured Design might impose on the run time of a system will be small, for only a small percentage of module calls will have a noticeable effect on the system's efficiency. Second, it's important to find those parts of a system that burn up CPU cycles if you are to achieve successful optimization without damaging much of the system. The next section describes how you would discover these system hot spots.

13.3 Monitoring system performance

It's almost impossible to *guess* where hot spots in a system might be. Since such guesses have been notoriously unreliable in the past, hot spots can be located only by measuring the performance of the system. The result of measurement is an execution profile, an example of which is shown in Fig. 13.1.

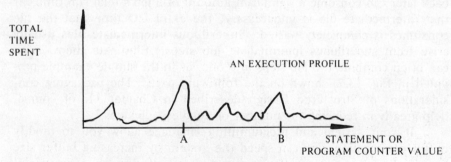

Figure 13.1

You should first optimize the code at the hot spot around point A. When you've done that, measure again. Point B may now be the highest peak — or it may still be at A. Solid measurement of the places

*This isn't the only 90-10 rule. Others are: 90 percent of the work is done by 10 percent of the people; 90 percent of all programs spend 90 percent of their time 90 percent complete; 90 percent of the project is done in 90 percent of the allotted time, and the remaining 10 percent is done in the remaining 90 percent of the time. (The original 90-10 rule was Vilfredo Pareto's Law: "90 percent of the wealth in Italy is in the hands of 10 percent of its citizens.")

at which optimization will be really effective prevents such lunacies as a zealous programmer wasting his time by tuning an ABORT routine.*

To arrive at an execution profile, you can use a facility of your operating system or a commercial package, to sample values of the program counter and to plot a histogram from these results.

Incidentally, in an unstructured system, it's not so easy to identify the hot code. The execution profile for such a system looks much flatter because, for instance, the instructions in a well-defined tight loop may be spread over a large area of code.

13.4 Tuning the system

Once you have determined where a system is behaving inefficiently, the next step is to decide what technique you should use to optimize it.

The physical interface between the executing code and the rest of the world often has a pronounced effect on the run time of a system. Input, output, and file accesses are worth investigating, in particular superfluous intermediate files, buffers, blocking factors, and access methods.

Writing out information to an intermediate file merely to read it back later can consume a significant amount of a job's total run time. If that intermediate file is unnecessary, the extra I/O time that the file consumes is completely wasted. Superfluous intermediate files usually arise from superfluous intermediate job steps. Eliminate them. You can often combine two job steps into one, as in the simple example provided in Fig. 13.2, shown on the following page. The packaging considerations of Structured Design described in Chapter 11, of course, help greatly in reducing the number of needless job steps.†

If your system and programming language allow you to modify buffer organization, you can speed the system by increasing buffer size or by changing single-buffering to double-buffering or even triple-buffering. An increase in block size will also decrease input-output overhead on sequential accesses. You can sometimes improve performance dramatically by changing the way in which you access your data base. The most extreme — and almost unbelievable — example I ever saw of this was in a nightly stock control system, which ran for 28

---

*Deriving a profile also gives you some free testing. By counting how often each statement is executed, you may find dead code or other errors of a more subtle nature in your system.

†Another way to cut out the overhead of intermediate files is to keep them in core. These "virtual intermediate files" don't suffer the I/O penalties of actual physical files.

hours! Upon discovery of this, the implementors of this system fled in horror to their data-base administrator to explain their predicament. Having elicited precisely what the data access requirements of the system were, the administrator was able to reorganize their data and to revise their access methods. The system's running time was reduced to less than one hour.

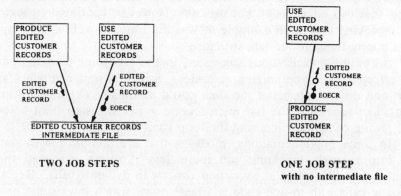

PRODUCE EDITED CUSTOMER RECORDS

USE EDITED CUSTOMER RECORDS

EDITED CUSTOMER RECORD

EDITED CUSTOMER RECORD

EOECR

EDITED CUSTOMER RECORDS INTERMEDIATE FILE

TWO JOB STEPS

USE EDITED CUSTOMER RECORDS

EDITED CUSTOMER RECORD

EOECR

PRODUCE EDITED CUSTOMER RECORD

ONE JOB STEP
with no intermediate file

Figure 13.2

If you see that a module (or a part of a module) is causing a peak on the execution profile, then you should check the module's algorithm. It may be inappropriate and inefficient. For instance, I remember giving the problem of drawing a line-printer histogram of student examination results to a group of freshman computer science students. The problem called for showing how many students had a grade of 0 percent, how many had 1 percent, . . . and how many had 100 percent. Most of my freshmen read in all the students' marks, counted how many students had 0 percent marks, then counted how many had 1 percent and so on up to 100 percent. This is roughly 101 times slower than the other way of doing it. In this case, the effect of the inefficiency on the overall program was noticeable. But, believe it or not, even two orders of magnitude of inefficiency may make little difference to an overall system if that inefficiency is in an unimportant area — and, as we saw, about 90 percent of the code *is* unimportant to efficiency!

If a hot module's algorithm is not at fault, then you should consider recoding the module in a more efficient language. Handwritten assembler is usually (but not always!) faster than code compiled from a high-level source. Note that I'm not saying that you should rewrite the *whole system* in an assembly language. Such systems are, in my experience, a nightmare to maintain.

There are other miscellaneous optimizations that can be used if all else fails. As we saw in Chapter 11, repackaging for the sake of virtual memory can reduce the time taken for swapping pages. Moving an invariant calculation from the inside to the outside of a loop keeps it from being recalculated on every iteration. I would like to advise you to avoid inefficient features of your language, but for every programming language there's so much tribal folklore about what is efficient and what is not, that this advice is all but useless. However, continually packing and unpacking data is an example of wasting time, as well as an example of poorly thought-out data structure.

All of the optimizations suggested in the preceding paragraph are best effected by an optimizing compiler. Some current compilers are smart and do a much better job than could a human. Others do dumb things, like squeezing the last microsecond out of the statement before a loop while completely ignoring the loop itself.

In some implementations, modules that are prelinked with static calls into a single load unit can incur less run-time overhead than modules that are linked at execution time with dynamic calls. Replacing static calls with in-line code is a last resort, which buys some extra speed only with that handful of frequently called modules that are typically found at the bottom of the structure chart. But the extra time taken by a call is very little: It's merely the time needed to execute at most a few dozen machine instructions. If you decide, despite my admonitions, to sacrifice maintainability and replace called modules by in-line code, don't just write the lines of code into another module. Use a PERFORM or a macro (for example, a COPY or an INCLUDE). A macro retains many of the advantages of Structured Design while saving some microseconds of execution time.

But don't forget what I stated before: Most of the code in a typical applications system deals with exceptional or unusual conditions. Since such code is executed comparatively rarely, it is pointless to optimize it, for the reduction in average run time will be so insignificant that you won't even be able to detect it. Also, the activities of the operating system are likely to affect run time or response time more than anything else within your system. To make your system run fast, restrict operating system intervention as much as you can. But don't optimize your system beyond all reason so that no other system on your time-shared machine will run.

13.5 An example of optimizing a module

A small example will illustrate some of the optimization techniques: Suppose that in a module called VALIDATE STATE NAME, there is a table of state names against which the STATE field is checked. The names are arranged in alphabetical order to allow a binary search to be made. As an experiment in optimization, we will make some modifications to it:

- Write it in assembler instead of in a high-level language.

- Make the search linear instead of binary. Theoretically, a binary search is faster than a linear one; but for small tables, the overhead of extra pointers and computations is not worthwhile. Additionally, having a linear search allows us to use the fast register auto-increment facility of our machine.

- Now that the search won't be binary, we are freed from the alphabetical arrangement of the state names. So, we can put the ones most likely to be used at the top of the list so that the linear search will find them quickly. This requires a little research, which yields NEW YORK at the top and NEVADA and ALASKA at the bottom.

When these three steps were actually carried out, they produced an average improvement of about 300 percent in the module's run time. Interestingly, most of that 300 percent was contributed by the last of the three steps.

13.6 The price of optimization

Nothing is free in this world — including optimization. You'll pay for optimization in degraded maintainability, especially flexibility and portability. This is an example of Fisher's* Fundamental Theorem, which states that the more highly adapted to its environment an organism is, the less adaptable it will be to another environment.

When you optimize, you must optimize to exploit some feature, for example, the most usual pattern of input data. If that pattern changes, the system may descend from being optimal to being almost pessimal.[†] So take care!

---

*R.A. Fisher, *The Genetical Theory of Natural Selection* (New York: Dover Publications, 1958).
[†]In systems parlance, "pessimal" is the opposite of "optimal."

Exercises

1. How is Fisher's philosophy borne out by the example of optimization in this chapter?

2. Optimization must be made with respect to some criterion, for example, to minimize memory usage. With respect to which criteria can you advocate *always* optimizing?

Answers

1. The use of an assembly, rather than a high-level, language — and the use of a specialized register instruction — commit the module to a particular family of machines. Ordering the state names in the way suggested in Section 13.5, for example, ties the module to a particular pattern of doing business or to a particular area of the country, and thus makes the system less portable.

2. The criteria are effectiveness, usability, reliability, maintainability, and, of course, cost.

SECTION VI
MANAGEMENT

There has been more resistance to the introduction of structured techniques from middle management than from either technicians or upper management. This is ironic, since middle-level managers have much to gain in terms of project control and quality assessment.

Chapter 14, entitled Management Aspects of Structured Design, discusses how to introduce Structured Design, how to organize its activities, and what benefits in smoother development progress can be expected.

14

Management Aspects
of Structured Design

Structured Design is a system-development technique that has an impact not only on those who use it but also on those who manage it. However, the topic of management is a monumental one, and certainly not a subject to be covered in one chapter. There are library shelves filled with fat volumes devoted to management problems, such as how to estimate this, coordinate that, and determine the critical path of the other. So, in this chapter, I will concentrate on how to manage Structured Design, and, more specifically, how Structured Design can help with the thankless task of managing a software project.

14.1 Introducing Structured Design

Structured Design makes its first impact on an organization simply by being introduced. It will require everyone to adapt to the structured approach and to abandon long-established habits. This change in design procedure tends to provoke one of three reactions in people:

- inertia, fear of inadequacy, and unthinking rejection of the new ideas (better the devil you know than the devil you don't know)

- wild and uncritical espousal of the new ideas (better the devil you don't know than the devil you do)

- a circumspect and cautious acceptance of the new ideas*

---

*Interestingly, all three of these reactions can be summarized as, "Well, you know, *I've* been using all these techniques for years; I just didn't have a name for them." This is never completely true and is usually almost totally false.

269

The third attitude, that of benign skepticism, is the one that all people — technical and managerial alike — should adopt. Innovations are not always good; and not all new techniques will be applicable to your shop. A good manager should encourage the third attitude in his technicians and he should offer them the chance to accept or reject Structured Design for themselves without heavy managerial pressure. People don't like to have anything foisted upon them, so if you provide an opportunity to review new ideas, you will increase the chances that the ideas will be palatable. There are two further tangible benefits: People learn better voluntarily, and they will probably weed out any truly inapplicable ideas during their review.

A managerial decision that is crucial to the acceptance of Structured Design is the choice of a good pilot project. Here, first of all, are some guidelines for a good pilot:

- Choose a small, fairly simple project. A good candidate for a pilot project is one that requires four person-years and lasts six months to one year. The project has to be long enough to be respectable, but short enough to provide reasonably early feedback.

- Choose a system that is not critical to the well-being of your organization. A sword of Damocles hanging over the designers' heads is likely to send them scurrying to the safety of their old habits if things go awry. Using a new technique is nerve-racking enough without the developers' knowing that if their project fails, so will their careers.

- Don't put your people on too many simultaneous learning curves. I remember a project to develop a property and machinery financial accounting system, which was to run on an IBM 370 using CICS, IMS, and COBOL. The development techniques were Structured Analysis, Structured Design, and Structured Programming. Not only was there almost no prior experience with using structured anything, but there was very little familiarity with IMS, CICS, or on-line systems in general. Many of the COBOL programmers were erstwhile assembler programmers who were hurriedly retrained. In addition, none of the analysts had much knowledge of taxation and depreciation.

You can guess the dénouement of that project. However, before it fell over the cliff, a panicked management doubled the development staff by hiring consultants specializing in each of the unfamiliar territories (they even hired a COBOL consultant!). However, adding too many diverse consultants to a project has the same effect as pressing down an automobile gas pedal. Whichever way the project is going, hiring the consultants will make it go faster in the same direction. So the project accelerated over the edge while everyone wondered who should be in the driver's seat.

A debacle is usually followed by a search for a scapegoat, which in this case was the newest technique, with the fewest consultants to defend it: the structured development techniques. The final report — the epitaph — on the project said, "Clearly the structured development methods are inapplicable to our environment. . . . We recommend that structured programming henceforth be banned [sic!] from the DP Applications Development Section."

- Choose normal people for the pilot project. If you pick a team comprising all the hottest designers and programmers in your shop, people will think that Structured Design is only for superstars. Also, when the project is over, Structured Design will receive little credit for any success.

- Choose committed people who won't throw up their hands at the first obstacle. The people on the team should be prepared to persevere with Structured Design even though, as is the case with most new techniques, its application might not always go perfectly smoothly.

14.2 Duration of structured activities

Although it's hard to generalize, these are the proportions of time that you can expect each major activity of development to take: Structured Analysis, 40 percent; Structured Design, 25 percent; with Structured Programming, Implementation, and Testing filling the remaining 35 percent of the development time.*

---

*Percentages obtained in studies conducted by two large utility companies and a major insurance company.

In a very complex project, analysis may take more than 40 percent; in a large but straightforward project, analysis and design *together* may take only 50 percent of the total time.

These figures indicate that structured development is a very front-loaded process, since more than half the time allotted to the project may have elapsed before one line of code has emerged. If this worries you, remember what I said in Chapter 12 about implementation: When code is at last written, it should be good, working code.

14.3 Activities of Structured Design

Although as a manager you may not be involved in the detailed techniques of Structured Design, it is important that you have a solid overview of the chief activities of this phase and what deliverables should be produced. The major activity of Structured Design is the derivation of the structure chart. The designers are unlikely to accept the first structure chart produced. The normal practice is to sketch out three or four skeleton structure charts for each job step in the system. The designers review them and determine which charts can be most easily refined into a good design, and then make some modifications and refinements based on Structured Design criteria such as coupling and cohesion.

If classical analysis rather than Structured Analysis has preceded Structured Design, then the designers will probably want to draw some fairly high-level DFDs before they approach development of the structure chart. First, it will give them a better grip on the problem. Second, it may bring to light errors, holes, or inconsistencies in the functional specification. Third, it will ease the technical transition from analysis to design.

By the end of design, the function of each module in the structure chart must be described. For a simple module, this description may be in the form of a specification of its inputs and outputs, with a brief statement of what it does to its inputs to obtain its outputs. If Structured Analysis has been performed, the mini-specifications of the DFD bubbles in most cases will be enough to tell the programmers what the modules do. Where that isn't so, the designers will have to provide further descriptions, probably in pseudocode.

The data dictionary developed during analysis must also be kept up to date with any new data introduced at design time.

An activity of all phases of a structured project that is crucial to the success of the project is the *walkthrough,* * which is a review by a small group of people of a product presented by its author(s). The product in a design walkthrough, in most cases, would be part of a structure chart. To the project technicians, the purpose of a design walkthrough is to anticipate as many problems in the design as possible while they are still only paper tigers. A problem discovered during design can be as much as ten to one hundred times cheaper to correct than the same design problem discovered during production. A walkthrough can be thought of as the practical implementation of "a stitch in time saves nine."

To the manager, the purpose of a walkthrough is to assess the project based on the reports generated. In the past, a manager has had to determine the progress of a project by measuring the quantity of documents produced. However, as I pointed out in Chapter 2, measurement of quantity is futile if quality is not ensured. The walkthrough is not only a tool to improve system quality, but also to communicate the current quality of every part of the system under development.

14.4 Activities parallel to Structured Design

A good manager, like a good cook, has to successfully coordinate many simultaneous activities. In this section, I will briefly describe the major development activities that go on at the same time as Structured Design, and illustrate how the activities relate to one another. The activities are: data-base design, implementation planning, implementation test preparation, system test preparation, acceptance test preparation, physical system interface specification, user documentation, and overall project planning. They are shown on the next page in Fig. 14.1.†

14.4.1 Physical data-base design

Physical data-base design is the determination of how the required access paths through data are to be implemented. For example, an access path may be implemented by chains, pointers, physical adjacency, or another mechanism. The physical paths are derived from the logical paths, which are discovered during analysis, and from physical constraints, such as volume, response time, and security, which are known by the end of analysis.

---

*The features of a successful walkthrough are covered in Appendix B. For further reading, see E. Yourdon's *Structured Walkthroughs* (New York: YOURDON Press, 1978).
†Activities that end before design or begin after design are not shown; neither are hardware activities.

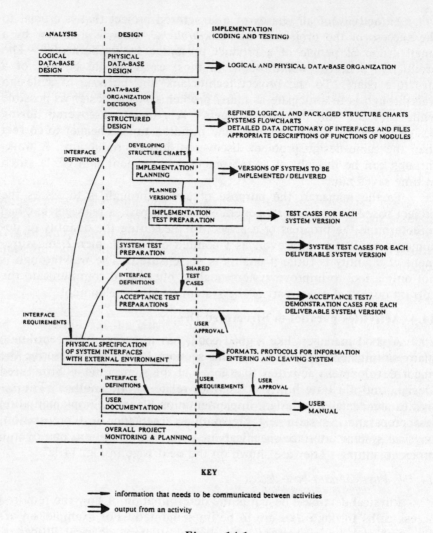

KEY

→ information that needs to be communicated between activities

⟹ output from an activity

Figure 14.1

The data-base designers cannot serve the interests of any one application, however. Their job is to satisfy the data-base needs of all applications in the organization. Therefore, the people designing an application will have to take advice from the data-base overlords on how best to access the data they want. Since data-base design for an application may go on in parallel with the Structured Design of an application, it's crucial that both sets of designers converse regularly about the area in which they meet — the interface to the data base.

14.4.2 Implementation planning

You can often glean some tentative ideas about how many and which versions of the systems should be implemented at the end of analysis. However, you will have to wait until at least the top levels of the structure chart emerge before you can confirm these notions. Then implementation planning has to proceed apace, because the plans and test cases for implementation will be required surprisingly soon after programming begins.

14.4.3 Implementation test preparation

For each version of the system that you implement, you should include specific tests for each function that version carries out. If possible, you should partition the package of test cases by function to give yourself flexibility in the order in which you implement and integrate modules.

14.4.4 System test preparation

There is a system test for each version of the system to be delivered. System testing is different from implementation testing in that you must do it *after* all the programming and implementation testing for the system version is completed. The test cases must cover every facet of a system in production: operations, user interface, internal functions, and so on. You can compose a test case as soon as the aspect of the system being exercised by that test case is known in sufficient detail. You don't have to wait until just before system testing to create all the test cases.

14.4.5 Acceptance test preparation

There is an acceptance test for each version of the system to be delivered. Acceptance testing involves putting the system through its paces so that the user can see that he hasn't been sold a shambling old nag when he paid for a sprightly young filly. Acceptance testing is technically similar to system testing. Politically, however, it's very different. System testing allows you to excise bugs in the system discreetly while no one is watching. But acceptance testing is carried out under a spotlight in the presence of the user, his audit representatives — wearing black suits, white ties, Fedoras, and shades — and possibly even his carnivorous contract lawyer. At acceptance time there is only one thought in your mind: "I wish I'd done more and better system testing!"

Acceptance test preparation may be completely in the user's hands. But more often the preparation is shared between the analyst and the user. The criteria for acceptance should be included in the structured specification before it is signed. If they are not, you should include a definite plan for agreeing on the criteria in the specification. In that case, you can do acceptance test preparation completely in parallel with system test preparation. Since you can probably share test cases between acceptance testing and system testing, you can make your system test a dress rehearsal for the acceptance test. The more problems you uncover during the dress rehearsal, the more likely it is that everything will go right on opening night.

14.4.6 Physical system interface specification

At the end of analysis, during the new physical stage, the analysts and the designers discuss with the user how information should enter and leave the system. The analysts offer the user a range of options: For $1.98, he can have the toggle-switch and magnetic-wire data-entry system, whose output will appear as a hexadecimal core dump; for $12,000,000, he can have the distributed multi-typeface optical-character-recognition direct-data-capture system, whose output will be delivered in spoken English (with a Finnish translation simultaneously relayed by satellite to the Helsinki branch office).

Thenceforth (not necessarily by the end of analysis but well before the end of design), physical decisions have to be made about the system's interfaces. Once the user has chosen his system, formats have to be agreed on, machine-machine protocol has to be defined, human-machine conversational protocol has to be worked out, . . . and so on. These physical details will affect the bottom-most levels of the structure chart.

14.4.7 User documentation

At the end of analysis, you can begin to write a brief description of the internal functions of the system. However, much more important to the user is the external view of the system, for he sees the system only through its interfaces. The documentation given to a user when he buys a system is similar to the operator's manual you'd give him if he bought a car. For a computer system, the documentation should provide instruction on how to install the system, how to operate it (start it, close it down, keep it running, check it periodically), how to prepare its input, how to use its output, and how to care for it generally. However, much of this documentation cannot be produced until the operations documentation is written, a task that follows design.

14.4.8 Overall project planning

It is a poor general who goes into battle without a plan. It is a worse general who won't change his battle plan in the light of events. I never fail to derive cheap amusement from the offices of some managers, where beautifully typeset, chronologically scaled PERT charts look down from the walls in mocking obsolescence at their conscientious young authors. Had Robert Burns been alive today, he would perhaps have said: "The most neatly drawn PERT charts of rodents and people frequently deviate from their initial layouts."

Managers and their planning tools should be flexible. During design, some parts of the structure chart are developed more quickly than expected — and other parts more slowly. User changes will arise, and possibly will require a whole new subsystem to be added. One should be able to adapt one's plan to new goals, new estimates, new schedules, and new budgets.

14.5 Estimating

Project estimating has two parts: the first is estimating the work to be done *(requirements estimating)*. The second is estimating the resources available *(constraints estimating)*.

A simple example of a requirements estimate is, "From the project survey, I estimate that the development of the system will require 16 ± 3 person-years with a minimum elapsed time of 20 months." A simple example of constraints estimating is, "We have up to 12 people of suitable skills available for this project. We have 30 months to get the system up; after that, the vendor of our current LEMMING system will withdraw his support."

Never allow the estimate of a constraint to influence the estimate of a requirement. In the small examples above, all is well: The requirements fit within the constraints. But what if you had only five people available for the project? Then clearly you couldn't implement the system, for there would have been only 12½ person years (5 people for 30 months) available for this 16 person-year project.

It's very tempting to say, "Well, Joe said that it *might* be possible in 13 person-years. That's pretty close to 12½ person-years, so I guess we're OK." And I guess they are not OK! Never alter an estimate to make it fit another estimate.

If the requirements for a project don't fit within its constraints, you have four options: Increase the available resources; decrease the amount of work to be done; do both of the above; or do neither and give up the whole idea.

Constraints are usually easier to estimate than are requirements. Why? First, they can be — and should be — estimated after requirements, so all that is needed is a lower bound on each constraint to see whether each requirement can be fulfilled. Second, constraints are usually more tangible than requirements. They are defined in terms of the number of programmers in your shop, the amount of money the user is willing to spend, and so on.

Estimating requirements is difficult because it means finding out *before* the work has been done how much work will be done, how long it will take, how many people it will need, and how much it will cost. As a species, we are blessed with 20-20 hindsight, but we are not so fortunate with regard to foresight.

Although you can never know precisely how much programming and integration effort will be required until it's actually completed, the structure chart provides a concrete basis for an estimate. It is a complete charter of everything to be implemented, conveniently split into small units that have minimal interactions with one another. Large problems are difficult to estimate because of their mind-boggling complexities. The structure chart presents a means of estimating the whole as the sum of its parts. It will never be exactly correct, but it will come tolerably close for a set of modules that are loosely coupled.

There are few factors more likely to make reality depart from an estimate than parts of a system obstinately refusing to work until the twentieth iteration of testing and debugging. Small, loosely coupled, well-walked-through modules are less likely to suffer from this complaint than are large, tightly coupled modules. Therefore, a system developed using Structured Design will be rather more likely to bear out that vision of Utopia that somehow always afflicts an estimator just before he makes his estimate.

Incremental top-down implementation enables management to spot slippages in a schedule earlier than if you had to wait for a momentous milestone to pass by before you can tell that anything is amiss. This inch-pebble approach* not only helps you to make an estimate, but also allows you to revise an estimate early. That information is necessary to the manager for monitoring and planning the project, and it's also valuable for keeping faith with the user. If you can see that you're going to slip the deadline, it's only fair to give the user as much advance notice as you can. He won't thank you for the warning,

---

*The inch-pebble concept is derived from the project milestone theory set forth in E. Yourdon and L. Constantine, *Structured Design: Fundamentals of a Discipline of Computer Program and Systems Design* (New York: YOURDON Press, 1978), p. 367.

but you'll be less likely to wind up in the ocean wearing cement shoes than if the user himself discovers the slippage at the eleventh hour.

At this point, you might complain that the end of the design phase is a little late to be making and revising estimates. I quite agree. Structured Design helps most with estimating the requirements for the activities following design. However, the DFD of Structured Analysis is a partitioning tool that will help in the estimation of design requirements. In fact, many shops use high-level DFDs in the project's survey to rough-estimate the work that the whole project will entail.

An inch-pebble approach is also likely to facilitate smoother progress. For instance, imagine that we have a project with only one checkpoint — the final deadline. It's likely that we can slip a long way behind schedule before we notice that anything is wrong, because the deadline is distant. Figure 14.2 illustrates the point:

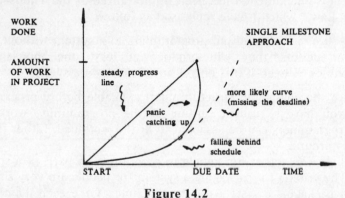

Figure 14.2

Inch-pebble monitoring is likely to allow steady progress. Slippages can be corrected more easily without undue panic (see Fig. 14.3).

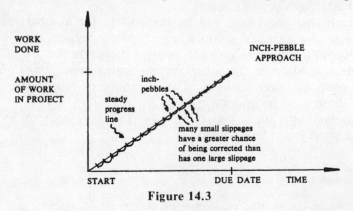

Figure 14.3

It's a very good idea to keep a comprehensive log of every project that you manage. The log should record at least who did what, and for how long, and how that tallied with your estimates for that task. The log won't help you tremendously on the project being logged, but it will be a great source of estimating wisdom for your next project.

14.6 Personnel allocation

In the past, there has been a notorious tendency on the part of management to let loose a horde of programmers on every medium-to-large-size project. Presumably, this was in the hope that, with more brute force than finesse, the masses would sweep all before them. Unfortunately, the system that such a mob produces is usually a piece of encapsulated chaos that bears little relationship to the problem to be solved. This phenomenon has been immortalized as the Thousand Programmer Law,* which I have rephrased as follows:

> If you assign a thousand programmers to a system without a prior design, they will produce at least one thousand modules — even if it is only a hundred-module system!

With the completed structure chart available before programming begins, you have a realistic outline of the programming work to be done. Programmers can be assigned to fit the workload, rather than the other way around.

But *how* do you assign people to program from parts of a structure chart? The criteria for packaging a system for people are very similar to those for packaging a system for the machine. Give each team of programmers a subsystem that is strongly cohesive and loosely coupled to other subsystems. Minimal interfaces between subsystems will ensure minimal interfaces between teams.

Given that each team will be responsible for a subsystem, how should you allocate roles within a team? Many organizations find the most successful way is to give the original designers the job of coding the topmost modules in the subsystem, assigning more junior programmers to code the lower modules. The designers, of course, oversee the work of these extra programmers.

Schematically, then, Fig. 14.4 on the following page shows how a structure chart might be assigned.

---

*For more on this concept, see Yourdon and Constantine, op. cit., p. 363.

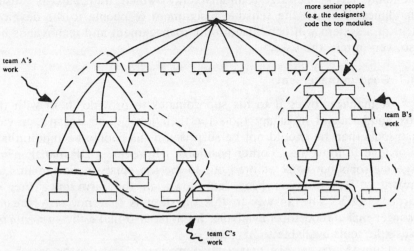

Figure 14.4

Notice that I've departed from vertical slices in one place: I've made a horizontal cut across the bottom and assigned most of the lowest modules to one team (team C). What's so special about the lowest modules? Typically, modules at the bottom will be utility modules and data-base accessing modules. It is often a good idea to allocate them to a team with special skills. But there's a more important reason: The modules at the bottom also represent the whole user interface. If too many people work on the user interface, fearsome inconsistencies might be introduced.

I remember fighting with an operating system, which had obviously been developed partly in Bhutan and partly in Bulgaria. For some job-control commands, the system parameters had to be entered in one order; whereas for other commands, they were required in a different order, probably because the two teams that developed the system had not talked to each other. For some commands, spaces were significant; for others, only commas were recognized. That system was an example of Conway's Law:*

The structure of a system reflects the structure of the organization that built it.

Allowing the user to perceive a homogenous system is also an example of what Brooks calls *conceptual integrity*[†] and what the Germans

---

*M.E. Conway, "How Do Committees Invent?" *Datamation,* April 1968, pp. 28-31.
[†]F.P. Brooks, *Mythical Man-Month* (Reading, Mass.: Addison-Wesley, 1975), p. 42.

splendidly term "benützefreundlichkeit," which translates as "user-friendliness." Thus, the sensible assignment of people to the development of a system will benefit not only management and technicians but also, very often, the user.

14.7 Good management

A manager owes it to his subordinates to provide them with the most modern and most apt tools for their job. If he doesn't provide such tools then he should not be surprised if his people become unhappy or tend to move on to other positions. However, a DP manager in a large metropolitan bank pointed out to me the opposite side of this argument: "How do you keep 'em down on the farm once they've learned S.D.?" The answer to this question is that not only must a manager make good tools available, he must also make the *opportunities* to use the tools available to his staff.

Philip Metzger says that a good manager "carries the water" to his subordinates, stating that:

> Whatever the product you are building, it's *your people* who put it together. Your job is to provide them with the environment and the tools they need to perform. . . . All a business *is* is its people. Take care of them.*

14.8 Summary

Through most of this book I've dwelt on the advantages of Structured Design to technicians: advantages such as tools to craft a design, criteria by which to evaluate and improve a design, strategies to create a reasonable design in a fairly straightforward way, and methods for packaging and implementing a design on an actual machine.

In *this* chapter, I've focussed on the advantages of Structured Design to managers — such as improved quality control, measurement of progress, ability to estimate requirements, personnel allocation, and overall project planning. Structured Design will never replace good old hard work, either for managers or for technicians. However, it should ensure that every effort that is expended contributes to the final success of the project rather than being wasted through lack of overall direction.

---

*P.W. Metzger, *Managing a Programming Project* (Englewood Cliffs, N.J.: Prentice-Hall, 1973), pp. 103, 144.

Exercises

1. Could a manager plan to introduce Structured Design at a shop where every minute of the day seems to be spent on fighting fires in a maintenance hell, and where no new systems are planned for the foreseeable future? If so, how?

2. Can you suggest any way in which incremental implementation might be exploited by a manager to derive good estimates of requirements.

Answers

1. Yes, the environment in which maintenance is a severe problem is exactly the one where Structured Design pays its greatest long-term dividends. However, that doesn't solve the short-term problem of how to find time even to introduce the discipline.

   There is certainly no magical way to convert a current unmaintainable system into a maintainable one. If it were possible, Structured Design would be pointless: You could develop a system in a quick-and-dirty way and then apply a mystical elixir to transform it into a clean, maintainable system.

   If you have no time or budget for the full redevelopment of a poor system, you should still be able to chip away at it piece by piece. This would be slow redevelopment under the guise (and budget) of maintenance. You would have to find a piece of the system that is minimally coupled to the rest of the system — check it out with a DFD — and redesign it as a little system in its own right. In this way you would progress through each system in your shop — slowly at first, but gradually picking up speed as maintenance pressures eased. The technique is analogous to removing a huge pile of garbage with a shovel when you asked for a bulldozer.

   The redesign of an existing, hard-to-maintain system is also an excellent candidate for a pilot project in Structured Design. There probably are several people in any shop who are extremely conversant with the current system. Therefore, the developers will have to learn Structured Analysis and Structured Design but at least the *system* won't also be new to them. And should —

heaven forfend — the project fail, there will still be the old system to fall back on as insurance.

2. The eternal problem with estimating is that an accurate estimate for the requirements of the whole project can only be made when the whole project is complete! However, the problem of needing an estimate for the whole without being able to study the whole is not new. In other disciplines, the problem has been solved by the technique of *sampling*.

    With incremental implementation it's possible to take a representative piece, a sample, of the design and monitor its progress through coding and testing. By determining how many person-months this sample consumed, and by determining what proportion of the system it comprised, you can make an estimate of the total requirements of the system.

    The two drawbacks to this technique are obvious: How do you choose a representative sample, and how do you determine what proportion of the system the sample represents? The structure chart provides the answer to both these questions — although, of course, neither answer will be *absolutely* accurate.

    Some shops adopt the incremental technique in the analysis phase, designing and implementing a part of the system before the analysis phase is complete. This method of project management is called *radical* development. (The more traditional phased approach is called *conservative* development.) The advantages of radical development are its ability to use the sampling technique and its ability to provide an early warning of implementation difficulties. Its primary disadvantage is the danger of having to discard written and tested code if flaws in early analysis are exposed by later analysis. I recommend for safety's sake that you don't get *too* radical in your first structured project.

Afterword

I wrote this book because of a tragic series of events, which took place many years ago, but which has haunted me ever since.

In a London shop, where I worked as a programmer/analyst, there was a very conscientious and industrious young maintenance programmer named Dorian. Not only was he bright and hard-working, but he was good-looking, too.

When Dorian joined the shop, he inherited the batch accounting system to maintain. Looking around him, he saw how other systems had deteriorated under maintenance, and he vowed that the accounting system would not go in the same way. Ready to go to such lengths to maintain the system's pristine condition, Dorian even made a pact with the Devil. He contracted that, in return for the system's being preserved as new, any changes that would have degraded the system would afflict his own person instead.

No one knew of Dorian's secret pact at the time. All that was known was that the accounting system never ABENDed: It ran to completion every night with perfect results. Every user change was implemented immediately without any problems in testing.

But as the months passed, and more and more user modifications were requested, people noticed changes in Dorian himself. His handsome, rather boyish countenance became wrinkled; his raven hair whitened at his temples; and his coding hand sometimes shook uncontrollably. After a year, boils broke out on his neck and four ugly warts appeared on his forehead.

Fifteen months later, a new version of the computer vendor's operating system was installed. All the systems in the shop underwent substantial revision, and all but one developed substantial problems. The exception was Dorian's accounting system, which ran as smoothly as ever. Dorian, however, developed a hunched back, and three of the fingers on his left hand grew twisted and useless.

Some two years later, when Dorian's sight had dimmed and his walk had deteriorated to a shuffling limp, it happened. At this time — so it was rumored — Dorian forsook his erstwhile good friends and fell

285

in with a bad crowd at a nether-world drinking establishment in East London. One morning, at 3 a.m., Dorian's heart stopped beating for no apparent medical reason, and he crashed into a stinking gutter in Whitechapel. Miraculously, cardiac massage revived him.

But, his collapses persisted and grew more frequent by the month. Sometimes, after lying motionless awhile, he would revive spontaneously; on other occasions, it would take great medical effort to bring him around.

Eventually, Dorian's once-proud body bowed to the inevitable. One morning, he didn't appear for work. Suspecting the worst, we went to his apartment. I still feel sick to my stomach when I recall what we saw. Dorian lay slumped on the floor with hundreds of large bugs crawling over his lifeless body.

I hope that never again will there be a system like the System of Dorian. Never again shall a maintenance programmer squander the gold of his youth on a system that is inherently unmaintainable. *The Practical Guide to Structured Systems Design* is dedicated to this hope, and to the memory of Dorian.

APPENDICES

A : The Structured Design Owner's Manual
B : Walkthroughs: Guidelines & Checklist
C : Structure Chart Symbols
D : Structured Design Activities
E : A Case Study in Structured Design

The appendices are chiefly devoted to providing reference material for the ideas and notations explained in the body of the book. However, Appendix E, the case study, is a little different from the other appendices: It shows how the techniques of Structured Analysis and Structured Design can be used in practice to design an automated system to replace an existing manual one. By showing their actual application, this case study is intended to make the ideas and techniques of Structured Design more concrete and to show in what sequence you would use the tools in a typical project.

APPENDIX A
The Structured Design Owner's Manual

Below I present a chart of the design weaknesses mentioned in Chapters 6, 7, and 8. If you discover one of them in your design, you should try to identify its cause and then apply the appropriate cure — so long as the cure isn't worse than the disease!

Problem	Cause	Cure	Possible Danger of Cure
communicational cohesion	combining functions that work on same data into one module	split module by function	increased fan-out of superordinate
procedural cohesion	flowchart-thinking	apply DFD/ transform analysis	—
	over-factoring or faulty factoring	unfactor and try again	—
temporal cohesion	flowchart-thinking	apply DFD/ transform analysis	—
	creating initialization or termination modules	split module by function and recombine each part with the rest of its function	—
logical cohesion	misguided attempts at efficiency	split module by function; fan-in to new modules at lower level, if necessary	—
	organizing modules based on similar functions, rather than on data flow	apply DFD/transform analysis	—

Problem	Cause	Cure	Possible Danger of Cure
coincidental cohesion	random design	see logical cohesion (above)	—
excessive data coupling	low cohesion of module(s)	see cohesion (above)	—
	failure to recognize a single problem-related data structure	create a good data structure	bundling
tramp data	poor module organization	apply DFD/transform analysis	
	decision-split	see decision-split (below)	—
	attempt to reduce data-base calls	use informational cluster/cache	—
	reporting an error far from where it is detected (a special case of a decision-split)	move error reporting nearer detection — typically, lower in the structure chart	error reporting moved too low in structure chart (see restrictive module)
unnecessary stamp coupling	failure to identify data substructures	couple only by necessary data	—
extremely complex stamp coupling	complex organiza-tion of data	use informational cluster	—
bundling	creating artificial, meaningless data structures	unbundle; see excessive data coupling (above)	—
control coupling	low cohesion of module(s)	apply DFD/transform analysis	—
hybrid coupling	misguided attempts to save memory (usually)	break hybrid data into separate pieces	—

Problem	Cause	Cure	Possible Danger of Cure
common coupling	laziness	apply DFD/transform analysis	—
	need to retain data for some time	use informational cluster	—
content coupling	totally unstructured design	read Chapters 1, 3, and 6 again	—
code for more than one function in the same module	underfactoring	factor	*slight* risk of factoring out a module of lower than communicational cohesion
module too large/complex	underfactoring	factor	
module dealing with too many data structures	underfactoring	factor; use Beneficial Wishful Thinking	creating a trivial module that serves little useful purpose in being a separate module
module "hiding" a potentially useful function inside it	underfactoring	factor	creating a module with poor coupling . . . but when in doubt, factor it out!
decision-split	having chosen the wrong boss	try another boss	—
	poor (typically procedural) cohesion	see cohesion (above)	—
	acting on a decision in the wrong place	move recognition and execution closer together	lowering cohesion; underfactoring; unbalancing the system

Problem	Cause	Cure	Possible Danger of Cure
physically input-driven or output-driven system	flowchart-thinking	use Beneficial Wishful Thinking; use DFD/ transform analysis	—
	disorganized editing	edit in layers	—
state memory	program inversion	check data structures to see if a program inversion exists (if there is one, there is no cure)	—
	factoring out an unnecessary transform module	unfactor the transform module	losing an advantage of factoring
multiple (inefficient) data-base accesses	requirement for information by same key in several places	informational cluster/cache	—
large initialization or termination modules	flowchart-thinking	see temporal cohesion (above)	—
restrictive module	failure to look ahead (or around) in choosing module's function	extend module's function	lowering module's cohesion
	tying a function to an afferent or efferent stream	factor function into a transform module	—
	physically input-driven or output-driven system (provides very restrictive input or output modules)	see physically input-driven or output-driven system (above)	—

Problem	Cause	Cure	Possible Danger of Cure
restrictive module (cont.)	error message issued from too low in the structure chart	move up the issuing of the error message	—
	assuming that a module will be used by a particular superordinate	make the module more free of its context of usage	creating an over-general module
	committing a value to a piece of data too early	defer commitment time	creating an over-general module; increasing coupling
	dealing with too few values or types of data	increase range of values or types of data that module can handle	creating an over-general module (slight risk)
over-general module	excessively imaginative choice of module's function	remove more bizarre features of module	creating a restrictive module (slight risk)
	committing a value to a piece of data too late	advance commitment time	creating a restrictive module
	dealing with too many values or types of data	decrease range of values or types of data that module can handle	creating a restrictive module
high fan-out	failing to recognize an intermediate level of a function	factor out intermediate-level modules	factoring out modules with less than communicational cohesion
	having a transaction center	no problem!	—

APPENDIX B

Walkthroughs: Guidelines & Checklist

B.1 Walkthrough guidelines

A walkthrough is a peer group review of a product for the purpose of finding any deficiencies in that product. Below is a list of suggestions for attitudes and techniques that you should adopt to achieve a successful walkthrough.

- *The product is guilty until proved innocent.* The walkthrough should be conducted like an ancient French court of law. If you assume there *are* bugs in the design, you're more likely to find them than if you assume there are none. But if you do find any flaws in the design, don't try to correct them during the walkthrough. Chances are that, if you do, the corrections will be hasty and ill-conceived. Have the producer himself fix the problems *after* the walkthrough.

- *The producer is always innocent because he's not on trial.* It's important to remember that the product and not the producer is being reviewed. It's difficult enough to preserve the producer's objectivity while his brain-child is being picked to pieces before his eyes. So don't make his role impossible by subjecting him to an explicit attack. The worst comment I ever heard in a design walkthrough was, "Where in hell did *you* learn to program!"

- *A walkthrough is not for the purpose of a salary review.* In the same vein, the project manager should be excluded from the walkthrough unless he is also an active technician. It is almost inevitable that he will use the walkthrough — perhaps subconsciously — to judge his staff members. Even if he doesn't, everyone will suspect that he does. In short, the presence of a supervisor or manager is likely to inhibit walkthroughs completely. Bugs will not be sought and will not be found. And soon walkthroughs will atrophy and die.

294

However, the project manager should receive a summary of what came to light during the walkthrough. This summary could be as simple as stating the product walked through, followed by whether the product was apparently flawless, had minor problems, or had major problems and would need large modifications and a further walkthrough.

- *A checklist of likely problems should be followed.* By systematically checking a list of popular faults, you will avoid wasting time. Of course, having such a list shouldn't prevent you from checking for something not on the list. (In the next section is a list of common design failings.)

- *There should be no less than three and no more than seven reviewers.* Having two reviewers is typically too few to afford a wide range of outlooks, which is the very rationale behind walkthroughs. At the other extreme, when you put eight or more people into a room, the gathering — whatever its stated purpose — always seems to degenerate into a committee meeting.

- *Choose walkthrough participants carefully.* Certainly, members of the team responsible for developing the part of the system under review should be present. In addition, someone from another part of the project should be included to lend a dispassionate objectivity to the proceedings, and possibly to serve as chairman or moderator of the walkthrough. If you can find someone from a different project, so much the better; but the chances of that person being familiar with your application and being willing to participate in your walkthrough are small. However, I have seen a shop organize a "Free Trade Agreement," whereby a designer from one group is loaned to another group's walkthrough; later, the favor can be returned.

New faces should be welcomed at a walkthrough. A walkthrough is a painless way to expose a new member of a project team to the current state of affairs. A reasonably competent newcomer can learn a great deal about the project — and about Structured Design — in this relatively informal manner. The training is not necessarily all one way either. A fresh mind may present a fresh outlook. Especially if he recently worked at another shop, the new recruit can sometimes diplomatically jolt a project team out of its rut. Far too often, a shop becomes stale and complacent for lack of outside ideas.

- *Keep the walkthrough short.* Limit each walkthrough to about an hour since few people have an attention span much longer than that. Occasionally, though, you'll reach a critical point in the project at which time you will need to review four or five hours' worth of material. In that case, break the walkthrough into forty-minute sessions with a ten-minute break between sessions. During the breaks, encourage the participants to walk around *within* the room, but don't allow them to wander away. Keep the temperature of the room about 2°F below a comfortable level and allow plenty of ventilation. That should prevent anyone from dozing!

- *Make it only as formal as necessary.* Walkthroughs range in formality from tuxedo-and-evening-gown affairs with gilt-edged invitations and RSVPs required to: "Hey, Bert and Ernie! Got a coupla minutes?" Most walkthroughs should be scheduled in advance for two reasons: It's polite and practical to give people notice of any meeting, and it saves time if you can distribute some of the materials to be reviewed before the walkthrough. The walkthrough will take too long if everyone comes to it unprepared and has to spend the first twenty minutes just reading the subject matter.

  However, if a designer is having some problems while developing a design, he can — and should — ask a colleague to help him informally. I don't know if you can call that impromptu gathering a "walkthrough": It's more like good neighborliness.

- *Make each walkthrough cost-effective.* A walkthrough can be costly in terms of salaries alone, but if you stick to the guidelines provided above, it is money well spent. If you depart from the guidelines too much, or waste walkthrough time on pointless wrangles and discussions, then the walkthrough becomes expensive. It no longer serves as a cheap tool to uncover design weaknesses at a stage when they can be corrected without major trauma.

A new design tool similar to the walkthrough is the *playthrough* (also known as a *dynamic design review* or *runthrough*).* In a

---

*See S. McMenamin's "The Playthrough: Walkthroughs and Theater," *The YOURDN Report,* Vol. 4, No. 2 (April-May-June 1979), pp. 3-5; as well as G.J. Myers' *Composite/Structured Design* (New York: Van Nostrand Reinhold, 1978), pp. 128-30.

playthrough, the product under review is mentally executed by the playthrough participants using a small set of test cases. This tool has been claimed to be effective by various proponents. I haven't found a detailed playthrough generally cost-effective, but it is certainly useful to illuminate areas a walkthrough *seems* to indicate are troublesome, such as problems in a complex algorithm. I have also found a less detailed playthrough useful to determine which functions are handled in which processes of a DFD and to ensure that no functions have been omitted.

B.2 Walkthrough checklist

In a design walkthrough, time will be saved if the designers have a list of points that they can use to check for potential design flaws. The list below is not exhaustive; however, these questions should expose the most common errors in a design.

1. Is there any module with less than communicational cohesion?

2. Is each interface between modules implemented cleanly? In particular, is there any control coupling, unnecessary use of a common area, unrequired data in an interface, tramp data, or complicated or unnecessary stamp coupling?

3. Can each module actually be implemented, with its given interfaces? In other words, are all the necessary calling parameters present?

4. Do all of the interfaces of a module with fan-in have the same number and types of parameters?

5. Is there any module that appears underfactored for any reason?

6. Is there a decision-split anywhere? Can the recognition and execution parts of the decision sensibly be moved closer together?

7. Is the system balanced — that is, do the modules at the top of the system deal with refined, unphysical data?

8. How is validation of input handled? Have all cases of invalid data been considered?

9. How is error reporting handled?

10. Does any module have unnecessary state memory?

11. Does the structure of the design conflict anywhere with the structure of the data being processed?

12. Are there any restrictive modules or modules performing overlapping functions? Are any modules over-general?

(13) Can any modules be replaced by library modules?

14. Does any module have too many immediate subordinates? If so, will that cause its logic to be horribly convoluted? Can strongly cohesive intermediate modules be introduced in order to reduce the fan-out?

15. Is the user interface simple and understandable, self-consistent, and consistent with the other interfaces of the system?

16. Will any modifications have to be made to the design for the sake of the programming language or operating environment?

17. Is there a specification of the function of each module?

18. Have the inputs and outputs of each module been specified as to type, value range, purpose, and composition?

19. Does the design fulfill the specification, the whole specification, and nothing but the specification? Can the design be related easily and obviously to the specification?

20. What are the twenty most-likely changes or extensions to the system that the user might reasonably request? How much impact would the user expect each change to make on the system? How much impact do *you* think it would make?

21. What assumptions does each module in the system implicitly or explicitly rely on to do its function? Is any assumption relied on by many modules? Is there *any* chance whatsoever that the assumption might have to be changed?*

22. Finally, a question to ask continually about the design: Will it work?

---

*This can be very subjective. Not only are some assumptions so obvious that they are not noticed, but it is often very difficult to assess whether an assumption might change. For example, we can safely assume there will be seven days in a week for a long time to come. But, what about the assumptions that zip codes will always be five digits long or that social security numbers will always be nine digits long? Remember that almost any decision you make at any time — whether conscious or subconscious — can have an effect on maintenance.

APPENDIX C
Structure Chart Symbols

The symbols below are most commonly used in structure charts.* Each symbol's explanation is italicized.

Modular symbols

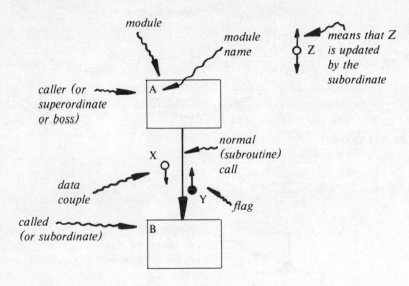

---

*Other symbols are described in Yourdon and Constantine's *Structured Design: Fundamentals of a Discipline of Computer Program and Systems Design* (New York: YOURDON Press, 1978), pp. 396-403; and in Myers' *Composite/Structured Design* (New York: Van Nostrand Reinhold, 1978), pp. 11-19.

Library module symbol

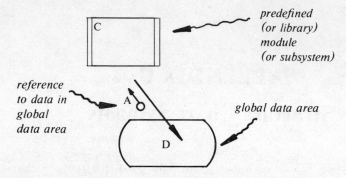

*predefined
(or library)
module
(or subsystem)*

*reference
to data in
global
data area*

global data area

Informational cluster

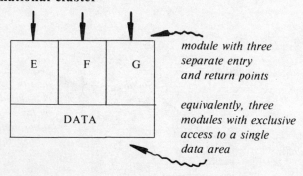

*module with three
separate entry
and return points*

*equivalently, three
modules with exclusive
access to a single
data area*

The hat symbol

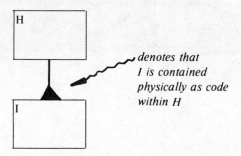

*denotes that
I is contained
physically as code
within H*

Connectors and page continuity

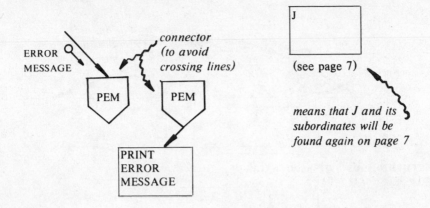

Interface table

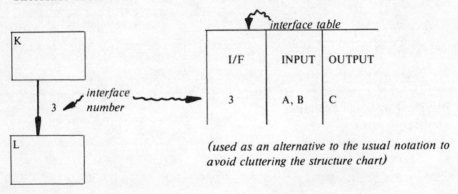

Iterative invocation symbol

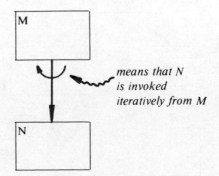

Transaction-center symbol

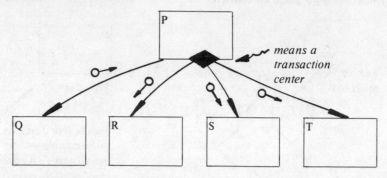

means a transaction center

Asynchronous activation symbol

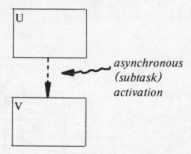

asynchronous (subtask) activation

Physical package depiction

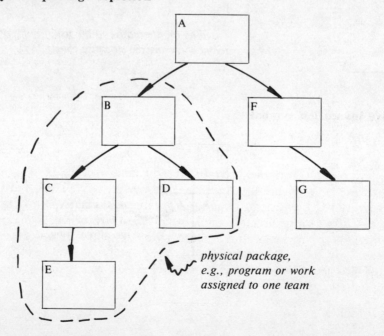

physical package, e.g., program or work assigned to one team

APPENDIX D
Structured Design Activities

In Chapter 2, we examined the early phases of a classical project. Figure D.1 shows how the early phases of a project might look after the introduction of Structured Analysis and Structured Design.

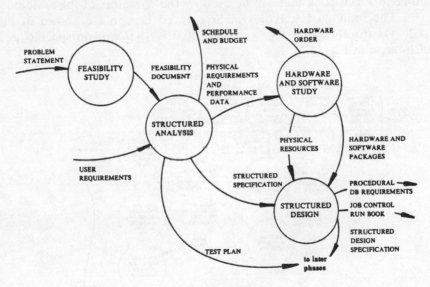

Figure D.1

As you can see, the preliminary and detailed phases of classical design have been consolidated into one design activity. The chief input to Structured Design is the structured specification containing data flow diagrams, the data dictionary, mini-specifications, data access diagrams, and physical data constraints. Other inputs include descriptions of hardware and software packages to be used, external data-base design, and the physical resources of the machine(s) on which the design will be implemented.

The chief output from Structured Design is the Structured Design specification (also known as the Structured Design blueprint). This comprises

- logical structure charts
- packaging considerations for programs and other implementation units
- a data dictionary definition (to the data element level) for each file and for each piece of data on a module interface
- a specification of (at least) the function of each module

Possible additional outputs from Structured Design are specific database organizational requirements that transpired during design and a job-control run book that will be used by the operators of the system.

The individual activities of Structured Design are shown in Fig. D.2. On the following page are notes that further explain specific areas of interest in Fig. D.2.

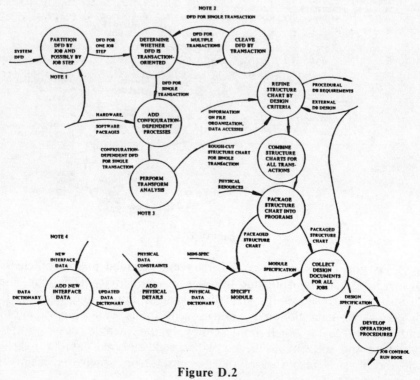

Figure D.2

Note 1   Partition the system DFD into jobs according to the criteria of packaging given in Chapter 11 — namely, by considering hardware boundaries, batch/on-line boundaries, and business cycle boundaries. Job steps are determined by the use of commercial packages, safety or defensive requirements, or limitations on resources.

Note 2   This loop is necessary because a transaction may be composed of a number of sub-transactions, each of which is composed of sub-sub-transactions, and so on.

Note 3   There is some disagreement about exactly when Structured Design begins: Some people claim that PERFORM TRANSFORM ANALYSIS is the first activity of Structured Design and that all preceding activities belong to Structured Analysis. Others claim that all of the activities shown on the diagram belong in Structured Design. This dispute can be resolved by saying that *technically* these early activities belong to design, but *managerially* they belong to analysis, since they must be carried out before the cost/benefits of the system can be determined.

Note 4   Any of the activities of Structured Design can potentially generate new interface data, which includes error codes, end-of-file indicators, and keys.

APPENDIX E
A Case Study in Structured Design

This case study demonstrates the application of Structured Design tools to develop a good design for a small order-entry system. I have assumed that Structured Analysis has been used to develop a structured specification before design begins. For the sake of continuity, I begin the case study with a brief résumé of the analysis.*

The system I've chosen is small, but it is recognizably a system, rather than a single program. There would be little point in attempting a case study of a large system: Its complexity would obscure the illustration of the design process. But virtually all of the characteristics of large transaction-processing systems appear in this example.

I'm sure you will find many points at which the case study deviates somewhat from a typical order-entry system. But this case study is intended to illustrate Structured Design, not order-entry systems. In order to cover all aspects of order-entry systems, I'd have to add a whole throng of details, which would be irrelevant to the course of Structured Design. Neither have I tried to implement a sophisticated data-base mechanism for this system. Instead, I've opted for simplicity even at the expense of some redundancy in data stores.

You may find the following case study to be a helpful model for developing a system of your own, but please don't take it to be gospel. Feel free to modify and to enhance the model to suit the needs of your organization or application. After all, nothing is quite typical.

E.1 Analysis of the system

Eric J. Lurch Wheeling and Dealing, Inc., is a distribution company for automobile parts, such as wheels, cylinder heads, and spark plugs. It retains stock for parts that customers most frequently order; it orders more exotic parts from wholesale vendors only as needed.

---

*As you go through the Structured Design portion of the case study, you might like to refer to the activities of Structured Design in Appendix D.

306

To give you the background to the analysis, I'll show you how the company's order-handling is currently — manually — organized. We will study three departments: Sales, Receiving, and Accounting, which for the purposes of the analysis are defined by the DFD in Fig. E.1:

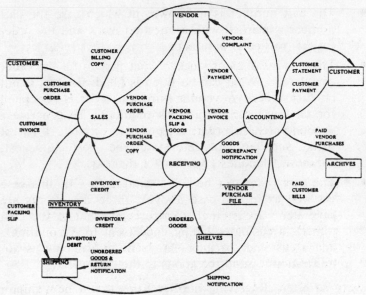

Figure E.1

Figure E.2 shows the details of the operations of Sales:

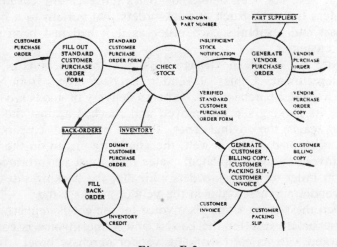

Figure E.2

When a customer's purchase order is received (either through the mail or over the telephone), its details are copied onto an order form with a unique order number. The order for each part is then checked against the inventory of parts available. One of three things may happen:

- The part number is unknown, in which case the part number is marked with a question mark and the order for that particular part stops.

- There is insufficient stock of that part to fill the order completely. What can be filled is filled; the rest is put on back-order. A vendor purchase order is generated for (at least) the extra stock required. To generate a vendor purchase order, a purchaser consults a list of parts' suppliers to determine the best (quickest, cheapest, friendliest) vendor for that part.

- The part order can be filled completely. In this case (as well as in the case above), three documents are generated: a customer invoice copy (sent to the customer); a customer billing copy (sent to Accounting); and a customer packing slip (sent to Shipping as authorization to send the goods to the customer).

Every so often, Receiving notifies Sales that a new shipment of goods has arrived from a vendor, by means of an inventory credit. When that happens, Sales attempts to fill back-orders for any of the goods that have not been delivered. Sales retrieves any customer purchase orders from the batch of back-orders that pertain to a newly received part and resubmits each order as if it had just been received from the customer.

Figure E.3 on the next page illustrates the functions of the Receiving department. Copies of vendor purchase orders from Sales are stored in a vendor purchase file. When a delivery of goods arrives from a vendor, its packing slip is removed and checked against the physical goods and against the original order. If there are any discrepancies, Accounting is notified. If all is well, the goods are placed on the shelves, and the inventory file is updated. Sales then must be informed of the delivery in order to fill back-orders. Finally, the packing slip is stored with its vendor purchase order in the vendor purchase file.

When the vendor sends his invoice for the goods delivered (which may arrive before or after the goods) and if the invoice is correct, it, too, is stored with its corresponding vendor purchase order. If it isn't correct, it is marked and rejected as a goods discrepancy notification. When both the vendor's packing slip and invoice have arrived, that vendor purchase order is marked with a blue tag, signaling it to be paid.

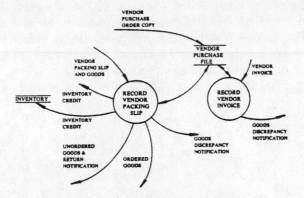

Figure E.3

Accounting has three independent functions, as shown in the three parts of Fig. E.4.

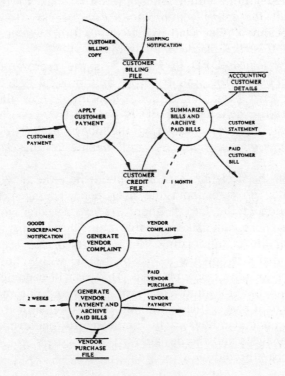

Figure E.4

I use dotted lines on a DFD to indicate control. In the case of Fig. E.4, the open-ended dotted lines marked with specific time periods show triggers to processes that operate periodically without any stimulus from another process. Structured Analysis purists object to this notation — they record the trigger in a mini-spec — but I find my dotted lines to be a more immediate way to show periodicity.

In Fig. E.4, the customer billing copy from Sales is stored in the customer billing file, along with the shipping notification from Shipping. Each customer payment is added to any credit that a customer may have from a previous overpayment. The total amount is then applied to the customer's bills, in sequence by date of invoice. Any excess that is insufficient to pay an invoice completely is returned to the customer credit file.

Every month, the customer billing file is scanned, and a statement is prepared listing each customer's bills on file, his credit (if any), and the total sum owed. As the file is scanned, any paid invoices are removed and archived. When Receiving sends a goods discrepancy notification, Accounting either sends a letter or makes a telephone call of complaint to the erring vendor. Every two weeks, the vendor purchase file is scanned. Each bill that is due within two weeks is pulled out and paid. It is then placed in an archive.

The new logical DFD in Fig. E.5 is the representation of the essential functions of the system before any physical details of the implementation have been determined. Explaining how the structured analyst derives the new logical DFD is beyond the scope of this book; but, broadly, it involves discovering the policy underlying the user's current methods of doing business and making any necessary changes to that policy.

Although the designers care little about how the new logical DFD is derived, they do care about the user policy changes affecting the further evolution of the DFD. There are two reasons why they care: First, the designers can make valuable contributions in assessing the cost and feasibility of automating various parts of the DFD. Second, once it is decided just how the new logical DFD will be automated, the DFD — now known as a new physical DFD — will become the property of the designers. It's important that analysts and designers work together in this final part of the analysis in order to ensure continuity and to avoid misunderstandings. (In practice, to achieve this liaison between the analysts and the designers, the designers would attend the later analysis walkthroughs.)

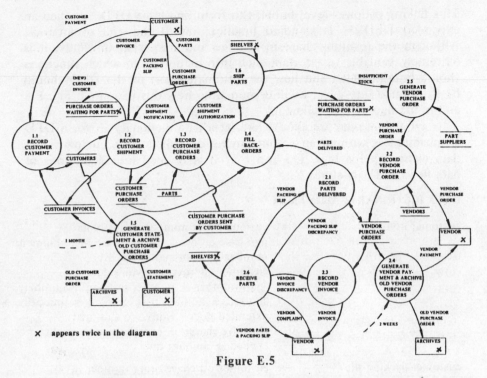

X appears twice in the diagram

Figure E.5

Figure E.5 contains 12 bubbles, which is rather too many for one diagram. In fact, this diagram is the fusion of the child bubbles of the two processes shown in Fig. E.6.

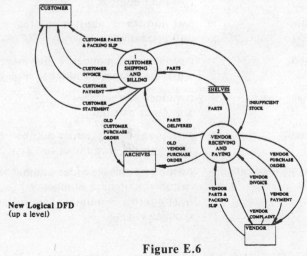

New Logical DFD
(up a level)

Figure E.6

This linking of lower-level bubbles to form one large DFD — called an expanded DFD — is standard practice toward the end of analysis. Although the resulting diagram is large and somewhat unwieldy, it is extremely valuable to ascertain such information as to which functions should be automated and how the automated part of the DFD should be partitioned into jobs. I will demonstrate how this is done in Fig. E.8 and in the figures that follow it.

First, however, we should look at a data dictionary — for a DFD is meaningless without an accompanying data dictionary. Below is the data dictionary for Figs. E.5 and E.6; it is divided into definitions of data flows and data stores.*

DATA DICTIONARY: Data Flows

customer invoice	=	customer acct number + customer purchase order number + customer shipment number + customer name + customer address + invoice date + {part number + number ordered + number shipped + number back-ordered + unit price + extended price} + invoice sub-total + shipping charge + invoice total + credit applied + amount due
customer packing slip	=	customer purchase order number + customer shipment number + {part number + number shipped + number back-ordered} + customer name + customer address
customer part line	=	part number + number ordered + unit price quoted
customer payment	=	customer acct number + [payment amount + {customer shipment number + payment amount}]
customer purchase order	=	customer acct number + {customer part line}
customer shipment authorization	=	customer purchase order number + {part number + number ordered}
customer shipment notification	=	customer purchase order number + customer shipment number + {part number + number shipped} + shipping charge

---

*For a description of the symbols used in a data dictionary, see Section 4.2.2.

customer shipment number = customer invoice number

parts delivered = {part number}

vendor invoice = acct number + vendor purchase order
number + vendor shipment number + name +
address + invoice date + {part number +
number ordered + number shipped +
unit price quoted + extended price} +
invoice sub-total + shipping charge +
invoice total

vendor packing slip = vendor shipment number +
vendor purchase order number +
{vendor part line} + name + address

vendor part line = part number + number shipped

vendor purchase order = name + address + vendor purchase
order number + {part number +
number ordered + unit price quoted}

DATA DICTIONARY: **Data Stores**

customer invoices = {customer shipment number +
customer purchase order number +
customer acct number + invoice date +
{part number + number ordered +
number shipped + number back-ordered +
unit price quoted + extended price} +
invoice sub-total + shipping charge +
invoice total + credit applied +
amount due}

customer purchase orders = {customer purchase order number +
customer acct number + order date +
{part number + number ordered +
total number shipped + number back-ordered +
unit price quoted}}

customer purchase orders
sent by customer
= {customer acct number +
{customer purchase order number}}

customers = {customer acct number +
customer name + customer address +
customer credit balance}

part suppliers = {part number + {vendor number}}

partial customer
back-orders
= {customer purchase order number +
{part number}}

parts	=	{part number + part name + standard part price}
purchase orders waiting for parts	=	{part number + {customer purchase order number}}
shelves	=	{part number + physical part}
vendor purchase orders	=	{vendor purchase order number + date sent + vendor number + {vendor invoice number} + {vendor shipment number} + {part number + number ordered + unit price quoted}}
vendors	=	{vendor number + vendor name + vendor address}

You may have noticed that most data stores hold information about an object. For example, CUSTOMERS, which is keyed by customer account number, provides customer name, customer address, and customer credit balance. Some data stores, however, serve solely to relate other data stores. An example is CUSTOMER PURCHASE ORDERS SENT BY CUSTOMER. Given a customer account number, this file provides a list of the customer purchase order numbers sent by the customer.

Figure E.7 is a data access diagram* that graphically depicts informational data stores and their correlations. The informational data stores appear as boxes; the correlative data stores as arrows.

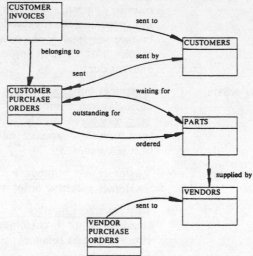

Figure E.7

---

*See Section 4.2.4 for a full description of this tool.

Two other files do not appear in Fig. E.7: SHELVES, which is where the physical parts reside, will not be part of the data base. Neither will PARTIAL CUSTOMER BACK-ORDERS, which constitutes a temporary storage area used in the implementation of the system (Fig. E.19).

The next step in the analysis process is to draw the manual/automated boundary on the new logical DFD by dividing activities into those done by humans and those done by machines.

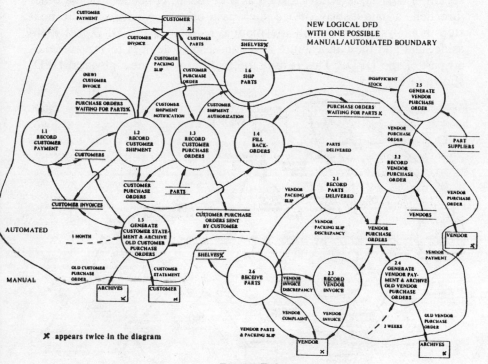

Figure E.8

As shown in Fig. E.8, almost every bubble on the DFD has been marked for automation. The three exceptions are

- SHIP PARTS (Bubble 1.6), which would require a robot to take the parts from the shelves. (Such robots do exist, but they are very expensive!)

- GENERATE VENDOR PURCHASE ORDER (Bubble 2.5), which would not be easy to automate because choosing a vendor to supply a part involves subjective discretion. Some vendors have low prices but are slow to deliver; others are more expensive but are quick to deliver and slow to bill, . . . and so on. However, if the user had a consistent policy for selecting a vendor, then this process would be a candidate for automation.

● RECEIVE PARTS (Bubble 2.6) is again an inherently manual process that could only be automated with a robot.

Wherever data crosses from the manual region to the automated region, a data-capture device such as a keyboard is needed; in the other direction, a data-display device such as a printer is needed. The next step in analysis is to cut off the manual regions of the DFD, set them aside, and add the data-capture and data-display devices to the automated part of the DFD.* This results in creation of the new physical DFD, shown in Fig. E.9.

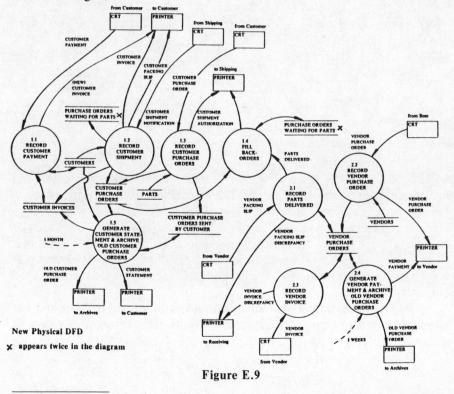

New Physical DFD

X appears twice in the diagram

Figure E.9

---

*Using the manual pieces of the DFD that were set aside, the analyst must determine the impact of the new automated part of the system on the manual part. For example, it's obvious that the people doing the SHIP PARTS job will have to be trained to use the data-display device, since they will be using it to enter information into the automated part of the system.

Figure E.9 (like Fig. E.5) is an expanded version of two higher level bubbles. These bubbles are shown in Fig. E.10.

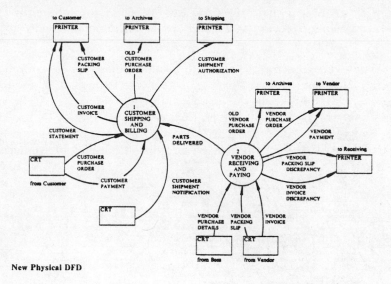

New Physical DFD

Figure E.10

Sometimes, the manual/automated boundary goes through the middle of a bubble. All that means is that you must show more detail by splitting the bubble into two or three smaller bubbles. This leads to formulation of a more general rule: The level of detail shown in a DFD depends on its use. Try to show just enough detail in each area of the DFD so that you deal with whole bubbles — never half a bubble. That is why we had to form the expanded DFD of Fig. E.5: There just wasn't enough detail in Fig. E.6 to discriminate the manual/automated boundary.

The next boundaries to draw on the new physical DFD are the job boundaries. In the case of our order-entry system, most of the system will be on-line (labeled JOB 3 in Fig. E.11), with two smaller parts — the periodic reporting and summarizing parts — being batch (JOB 1 and JOB 2). The boundary around JOB 3 was drawn somewhat arbitrarily. For example, you can argue the case that the bubble RECORD VENDOR PURCHASE ORDER in JOB 3 should need a separate batch job. But this illustrates exactly the kind of flexibility of choice that drawing a logical DFD gives.

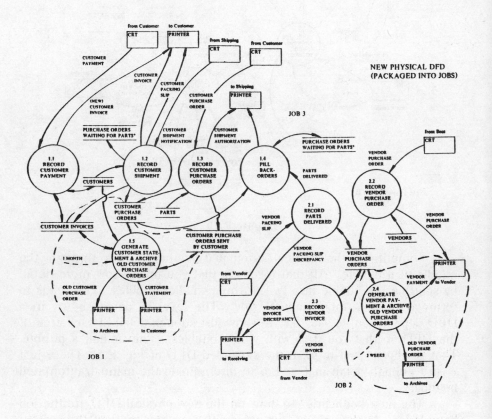

Figure E.11

Now we take the scissors again to cut out the separate jobs. JOB 1 and JOB 2 are small and straightforward.* JOB 3, however, is more complicated because it contains most of the system.

---

*But it's pointless to try to combine them into a single job, since one is monthly and the other is biweekly; besides, each job uses a different file.

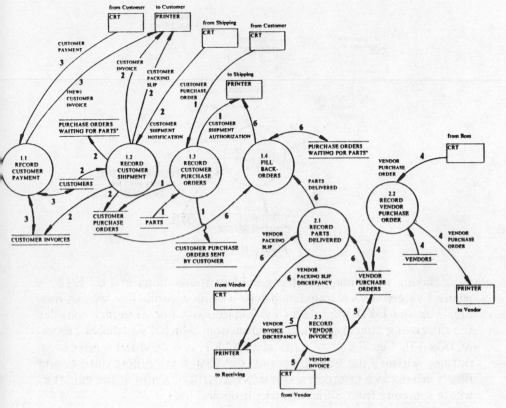

Figure E.12

E.2 Deriving a structure chart

How can we convert the DFD for JOB 3 into a structure chart? Applying transform analysis doesn't look very hopeful. It's very difficult to say where the central transform of the DFD is: Virtually the whole diagram looks like the central transform! Neither does it seem profitable to pick a boss bubble and suspend the DFD from that bubble, as many of the bubbles in the DFD are not even connected.

The solution to this problem is to use transaction analysis — specifically, a technique I call "route-mapping." Route-mapping means charting the path of each transaction type as if it were a train running through the system. The only difference is that a train can run along only a single line, whereas a transaction can cascade out to run along several data flows at once.

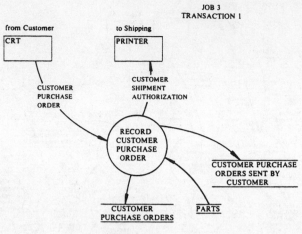

Figure E.13

Having route-mapped the individual transactions in Fig. E.12 — where I've given each transaction type a unique number — we can now break up the DFD transaction by transaction.* For example, consider the CUSTOMER PURCHASE ORDER transaction, which I've labeled TRANSACTION 1 in Fig. E.13. It starts at the CRT as a CUSTOMER PURCHASE ORDER, activates the bubble RECORD CUSTOMER PURCHASE ORDER, and finally arrives as a CUSTOMER SHIPMENT AUTHORIZATION at the PRINTER, where someone from Shipping picks it up and uses it.

The single bubble RECORD CUSTOMER PURCHASE ORDER would be the only process in TRANSACTION 1 if we lived in an ideal world. However, data entered into the system needs to be validated, and data output from the system needs to be formatted. When we add processes (so-called configuration-dependent processes, meaning processes required to accomplish an actual implementation of the system) to carry out validating and formatting, we get the revised diagram shown in Fig. E.14 on the facing page.†

---

*If you use a vendor-supplied transaction-processing package, this also will be the time to address its idiosyncracies (such as message queues and control blocks).
†The parentheses in, for example, (VALID) CUSTOMER PART LINE means that this data name would be found in the data dictionary under CUSTOMER PART LINE and not under VALID CUSTOMER PART LINE.

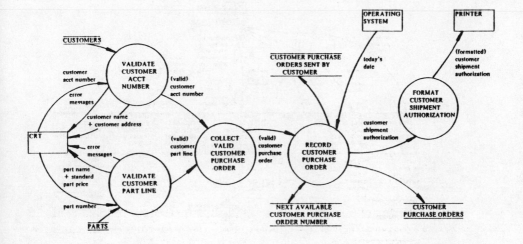

Figure E.14

The central transform for the DFD for TRANSACTION 1 is very small: It comprises only the bubble RECORD CUSTOMER PURCHASE ORDER. This, of course, was the only bubble in the transaction in Fig. E.13 before we added the configuration-dependent bubbles. In general, the central transform of a DFD almost always coincides with, or is a part of, the configuration-*independent* part of the DFD.

When we pick up the bubble RECORD CUSTOMER PURCHASE ORDER, dangle the rest of the DFD, and add READ and WRITE modules, to follow the rules of transform analysis from Chapter 10, we obtain the first-cut structure chart shown in Fig. E.15 on the next page.

JOB 3
TRANSACTION 1

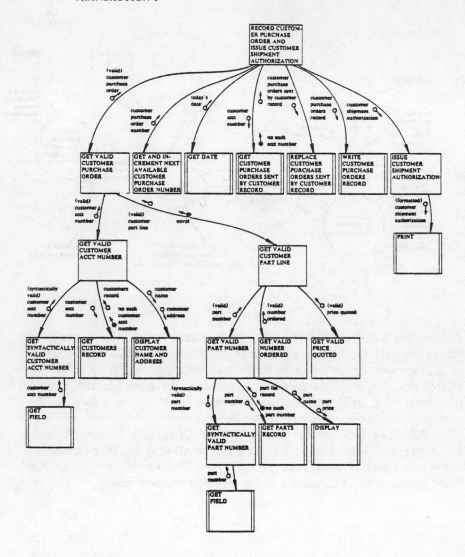

Figure E.15

Further factoring yields Fig. E.16:

JOB 3
TRANSACTION 1

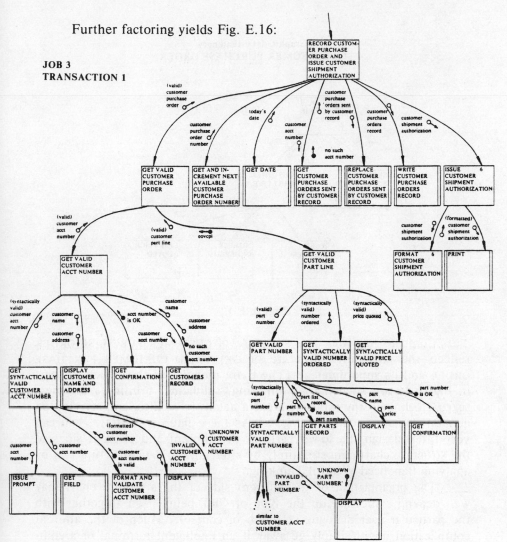

Figure E.16

The factoring of the structure chart in Fig. E.16 (especially at the bottom) was guided by the structure of the data being processed. To illustrate, consider the structure of a CUSTOMER PURCHASE ORDER (see Fig. E.17).

Graphic data dictionary
for CUSTOMER PURCHASE ORDER

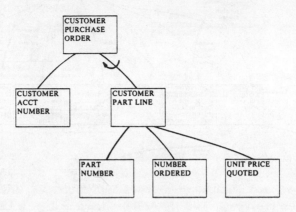

Figure E.17

Compare how the data structure of CUSTOMER PURCHASE ORDER reflects the procedural structure of GET VALID CUSTOMER PURCHASE ORDER and its subordinates. (The extra modules in the structure chart in Fig. E.16 are needed for prompting, validating, printing error messages, "echoing" the input with extra details from files, and carrying on general human/machine dialogue.) As these figures illustrate, you can very often design the lower parts of the afferent and efferent sides of the structure chart almost entirely by studying the data structure and by applying Beneficial Wishful Thinking.

The organization of the afferent side of the structure chart may well depend somewhat on the type of CRT being used (together with the particular user dialogue selected, of course). Much of the afferent complication might simply go away if an intelligent terminal or a commercial transaction-entry package were used to subsume many of the editing and conversational activities. Similarly, some of the efferent activities could be taken over by hardware or by specialized report-generating software.

TRANSACTION 6 is a little more complex than TRANSACTION 1. Figure E.18 is its DFD:

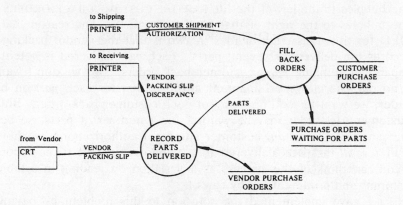

Figure E.18

Next, we add configuration-dependent processes, the validating and formatting processes, with the result shown in Fig. E.19. For simplicity, fewer details have been shown in Fig. E.19 than were shown in Fig. E.14 for TRANSACTION 1.

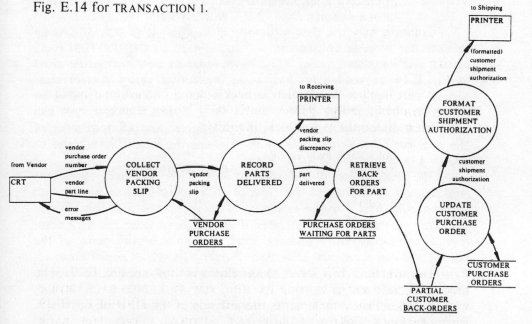

Figure E.19

The most interesting characteristic of TRANSACTION 6 is that it falls into two pieces — but those two pieces are *not* the two bubbles RECORD PARTS DELIVERED and FILL BACK-ORDERS. The two parts are the bubbles to the left of the file PARTIAL CUSTOMER BACK-ORDERS and the bubbles to the right of that file, in Fig. E.19. The reason that the DFD for this transaction divides in two is that the vendor packing slip records the delivery of several parts. Each part delivered is potentially capable of fulfilling *many* customer back-orders. But we don't want to send out one customer shipment authorization for each *part* on back-order; we want to send one out for each customer back-order. But the customer back-order may be waiting for a number of parts; so before we can start issuing *any* customer shipment authorizations, we have to wait for *all* the parts delivered in a vendor shipment to be recorded. (You can think of this process as a variation on reading in a table by columns and printing it out by rows.)

I have implemented the solution to this problem by having an area of storage called PARTIAL CUSTOMER BACK-ORDERS, which is gradually built up by ADD PART NUMBER TO PARTIAL CUSTOMER BACK-ORDER (see Fig. E.20). PARTIAL CUSTOMER BACK-ORDERS at a certain time might look like this:

CUSTOMER PURCHASE ORDER NUMBER	PART NUMBER
27931	27, 492, 83
29144	27
12911	492, 83

If part number 929 (which is back-ordered on customer purchase orders numbered 29144, 93217, and 10037) is now recorded, PARTIAL CUSTOMER BACK-ORDERS will look like this:

CUSTOMER PURCHASE NUMBER	PART NUMBER
27931	27, 492, 83
29144	27, 929
12911	492, 83
93217	929
10037	929

The structure chart for TRANSACTION 6 is shown in Fig. E.20. The module RECORD VALID VENDOR PACKING SLIP AND BUILD BACK-ORDERS with its subordinates implements the left side of the DFD of Fig. E.19, while PRODUCE CUSTOMER SHIPMENT AUTHORIZATIONS FOR BACK-ORDERS with its subordinates implements the right side. I could have arranged the left side and the right side as separate job steps with PARTIAL CUSTOMER BACK-ORDERS as an intermediate file, except that in some on-line operating systems, that arrangement might be awkward to implement or might be very slow to execute.

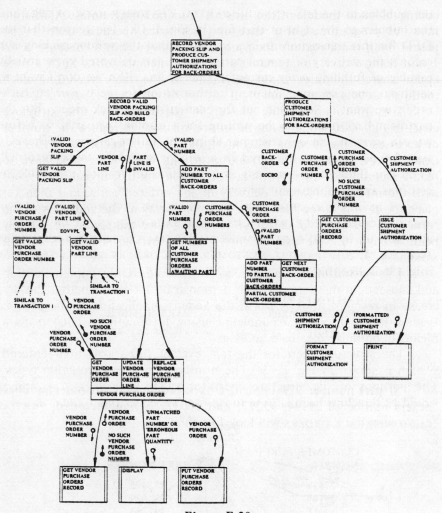

Figure E.20

Notice that I've annotated two modules in Fig. E.20 with the number 1, because these same modules are also used in TRANSACTION 1. If I drew TRANSACTIONS 1 and 6 on the same page, the fact that the module ISSUE CUSTOMER SHIPMENT AUTHORIZATION has two bosses would be readily apparent. Transaction-centered systems typically have several modules that are shared by many transactions.* It's important that such modules be carefully noted, so that problems in assigning the

_____

*This is true so long as modules are not made too restrictive, of course.

coding of such modules don't arise at programming time. A module must be programmed only once and not twice (because team 1 and team 6 both think that it's their job), and not zero times (because team 1 and team 6 each think that it's the other team's job). Such a note about shared modules could be made in the table recording each module's development status.

The information-hiding cluster in the middle of the structure chart in Fig. E.20 is the result of an optimization to reduce the number of accesses to the VENDOR PURCHASE ORDER file. RECORD VALID VENDOR PACKING SLIP AND BUILD BACK-ORDERS would otherwise have to read a record from the VENDOR PURCHASE ORDER file, update the record with the information about delivery of the ordered parts, and then replace the record in the file. With this optimization, the additions to the record can be made "in core," so to speak, since the record has already been brought in for use by GET VALID VENDOR PURCHASE ORDER NUMBER.

This optimization may not be worthwhile. Only implementation and subsequent measurement can demonstrate for sure whether the decrease in response time is worth the added complication to the design. I show it simply as an example of using informational clusters as a means to optimize data-base accesses.

The structure chart for the top level of this transaction-centered system is shown in Fig. E.21. The numbers indicate transaction types. The portions of the structure chart for TRANSACTIONS 2, 3, 4, and 5 would be developed similarly to those for TRANSACTIONS 1 and 6.

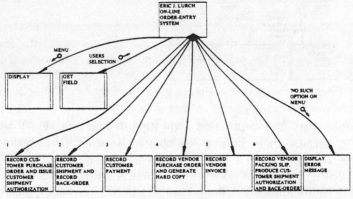

Figure E.21

The structure chart in Fig. E.21 is very simple: The boss module determines which type of transaction the user wants and then invokes the appropriate module to deal with it. Larger systems may have more complex arrangements of transactions than that shown in Fig. E.22; for example, one transaction may invoke a second, which may in turn invoke a third, which may then return to the first transaction. Commercial transaction-processing packages cater directly to this kind of flexibility. If you use one of these packages, then you would not need the structure chart of Fig. E.21; you would merely allow your package to invoke the appropriate transaction module 1 through 6.

E.3 Preparing for implementation

The remaining steps of Structured Design to be carried out before programming begins are listed below.

- Refine the structure chart in keeping with the Structured Design criteria and possibly data-base usage.
- Perform any further packaging that may be necessary or desirable for implementation.
- Add any new information to the data dictionary.
- Specify modules.
- Plan the implementation.
- Organize people.

E.3.1 Refine the structure chart

A structure chart derived from a DFD by transform analysis tends to have highly cohesive modules that are loosely coupled. However, the structure chart may well need further factoring. In doing the necessary factoring in the case study example, I applied the Structured Design criteria — especially cohesion — as I went. Consequently, no further refinement is required in that area.

To know how efficient any data-base accesses might be, we need to know how the data base is organized. That is the domain of the data-base gurus, whom you should always consult if you think there might be data-base access problems. However, as I pointed out in Section 8.8 and illustrated in Fig. E.20, you can use the information-cluster idea to reduce the total number of data-base accesses. Other data-base issues that you should consider include password and security requirements (such as the use of file interlocks in multi-user systems).

E.3.2 Perform any further packaging

In a transaction-processing system, the transactions themselves are natural breaking points for packaging. So, if we were packaging the system in, say, COBOL programs, we would initially package each transaction into a separate program. Then almost certainly we could further package each transaction into smaller programs in order to partition work among programmers and to reduce the amount of procedural code to which each item of data is exposed. For example, JOB 3, TRANSACTION 6 (see Fig. E.20) could be packaged into programs as shown in Fig. E.22:

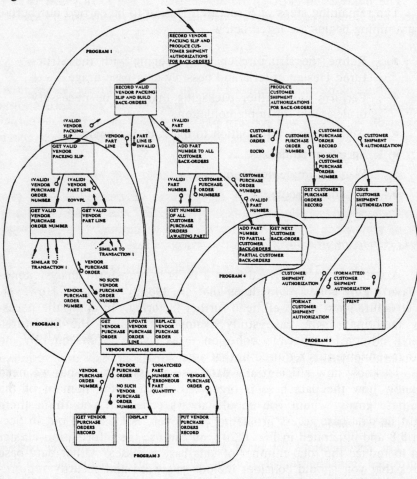

Figure E.22

Notice that PROGRAM 3 is necessary to communicate VENDOR PURCHASE ORDER between PROGRAM 1 and PROGRAM 2. If PROGRAMS 1 and 2 had been combined, PROGRAM 3 could have been absorbed into PROGRAM 1 (with VENDOR PURCHASE ORDER simply becoming an item in PROGRAM 1's WORKING-STORAGE SECTION).

PROGRAM 4 is not necessary, but it is desirable in order to hide the details of how the PARTIAL CUSTOMER BACK-ORDERS are organized and accessed. It would have two entry (and exit) points: one for ADD PART NUMBER TO PARTIAL CUSTOMER BACK-ORDER and one for GET NEXT CUSTOMER BACK-ORDER.

The modules in PROGRAM 5 also appear in JOB 3, TRANSACTION 1. Hence, the same program serves in both TRANSACTION 1 and TRANSACTION 6.

E.3.3 Add any new information to the data dictionary

Any items of data introduced for the first time during design must be added to the data dictionary. But, most of the new information gleaned during design will concern physical details about data — particularly about the format of data elements. For example, CUSTOMER ACCT NUMBER might be defined as

customer acct number = 5 digits in range 00001 — 99999

Other more mundane data elements to be defined in our case study include end-of-file indicators, error codes, and so on. The formats of some data composites also need to be defined. For example, (FORMATTED) CUSTOMER SHIPMENT AUTHORIZATION might be

(FORMATTED) CUSTOMER SHIPMENT AUTHORIZATION

CUSTOMER PURCHASE ORDER NUMBER
  2 blank lines
    PART NUMBER   NUMBER ORDERED   } repeat for
  1 blank line   each part

Other physical details — such as volumes of data and required response times — are normally added to the data dictionary during the analysis.

E.3.4 Specify modules

The specifications for many afferent and efferent modules can be determined from the data dictionary (which is an unlikely place to find *module* definitions!). For example, the module FORMAT AND VALIDATE CUSTOMER ACCT NUMBER (see Fig. E.16) is specified by the format and valid range defined for that data element in the data dictionary. Similarly, the module FORMAT CUSTOMER SHIPMENT AUTHORIZATION is

specified by the format of a (FORMATTED) CUSTOMER SHIPMENT AU-
THORIZATION.

Other modules are specified by the data structures around them.
For example, the code for the module GET VALID CUSTOMER PART LINE
in Fig. E.16 would practically fall out of the structure of a CUSTOMER
PART LINE (see Fig. E.17) — it would simply be a series of invocations
of the modules that get each component of a CUSTOMER PART LINE.

More complicated modules, however, need some additional
specification. For example, the module ADD PART NUMBER TO PARTIAL
CUSTOMER BACK-ORDERS (Fig. E.20) might be specified in pseudocode
like this:

```
module add part number to partial customer back-orders
    uses (valid) part number,
        customer purchase order numbers /* a list of orders —
            in ascending sequence — that are awaiting the part */

    for each customer purchase order
        scan partial customer back-orders until you find
        customer purchase order number
        if you don't find it
        then append it to the foot of partial customer back-orders
        endif
        append (valid) part number alongside
        customer purchase order number in partial customer back-orders
        if that part number is not already there
    endfor
endmodule
```

Modules that are still more complicated than the one above probably concern user policy and have therefore already been specified by
mini-specs during analysis. For example, the policy for RECORD CUS-
TOMER PURCHASE ORDERS (see Fig. E.5) might be defined as follows:

RECORD CUSTOMER PURCHASE ORDERS

1. **for each** part ordered **do the following**:

    1.1 **enter** part number + number ordered **on** customer shipment authorization.
    1.2 **set** total number shipped **to** 0.
    1.3 **set** number back-ordered **to** 0.
    1.4 **enter** part number + total number ordered + number shipped +
        number back-ordered + unit price quoted **on** customer purchase orders record.
2. **set** customer purchase order number **to** next available customer purchase order number.
3. **set** order date **to** today's date.
4. **enter** customer purchase order number **on** customer shipment authorization.
5. **enter** customer purchase order + order date
    on customer purchase orders record.
6. **put** customer purchase orders record **in file**
    using customer purchase order number **as key**.
7. **append** customer purchase order number **to** customer record
    using customer account number **as key**.

This mini-spec serves as the specification for the module RECORD CUSTOMER PURCHASE ORDER AND ISSUE CUSTOMER SHIPMENT AUTHORIZATION (the top module on Fig. E.16). Although the code for this module won't be identical to the structured English in the mini-spec, the differences will be clear to the programmer when he looks at the structure chart. (If you, the designer, think that the differences might *not* be clear, then attach notes to the mini-spec to complete the module specification.)

Technical details that should be explicitly stated before programming begins include precise descriptions of access methods for files and data bases, and various initialization and termination requirements. An often-overlooked instance of initialization is clearing state memory in modules. For example, in JOB 3, TRANSACTION 6, the area PARTIAL CUSTOMER BACK-ORDERS (see Figs. E.19 and E.20) has to be cleared each time the transaction is invoked. More obvious cases of initialization and termination are the opening and closing of files.

In general, there are many ways to specify a module (see Chapter 5). Whatever method you select, you should obey the following guidelines:

- Choose the most appropriate specification method for each module.
- Try not to duplicate anything already documented, unless doing so significantly improves readability.
- Be brief.
- Be clear.
- Be informative and programmer-friendly.

E.3.5 *Plan the implementation*

In a transaction-oriented system like this order-entry system, the most obvious implementation plan is an incremental, transaction-by-transaction plan. The order in which the transactions are implemented often depends on the proximity of the deadline, the needs of the user, and so on. But, putting those considerations aside, you should implement a small-to-medium-sized transaction first. This transaction will be a "pioneer" transaction, used to discover bugs and problems — in the specification, in the software, in the hardware, in anything — which can then be avoided in future transactions.

The pioneer transaction should be large enough to be non-trivial and fairly representative of other transactions, but small enough to give feedback in reasonable time. This latter point is important if you want to use the pioneer transaction to help you to estimate how long it will take to implement the other transactions.

If the pioneer implementation is successful, then you can proceed to implementing a more ambitious transaction. For example, JOB 3, TRANSACTION 1 would be a good pioneer transaction and JOB 3, TRAN-SACTION 6 would be a good follow-up. If the pioneer implementation is not successful because of numerous bugs and problems, then you must resolve the problems and choose a transaction of similar (or lesser) complexity for the next implementation.

It's usual, especially in a transaction-processing system, to overlap the design and programming activities.* For example, you could begin programming and testing the "customer" side of our system even while the "vendor" side of it is still being designed. Coding and testing should be overlapped in the implementation of any system, for they are really inseparable.

E.3.6 Organize people

Designers should join a project before the end of analysis (the new logical stage, shown in Fig. E.5, is about the right time).† Similarly, programmers should be introduced to the project just after transform analysis (at Fig. E.15 for JOB 3, TRANSACTION 1). The programmers will take an active part in the further factoring and refinement of the struc-ture charts — each programmer taking a special interest in the part of the system he will be programming. Bringing programmers in early also helps to ensure that they will understand the module specifications more clearly.

A simple piece of folklore for assigning work is: Two teams won't fit into one transaction and two programmers won't fit into one pro-gram. But, of course, this generalization won't always hold, as for ex-ample, when the transactions or programs are large. And, equally obvi-ously, teams should communicate and review one another's work — as should individual programmers within teams.

When a team has finished implementing one transaction, it should move to a transaction of a similar type to, or having a large interface with, the transaction it has just completed. In our case study, the same team would probably implement both TRANSACTION 1 and TRANSACTION 6 in JOB 3.

---

*If you are on your first structured project, you may not feel confident enough to begin programming before you complete your design. But you should try it next time around.
†Most shops do not have the job title "designer." For example, your analysts may also do design; or design may be the realm of your programmers. Some shops make their analysts senior designers, and their programmers junior designers. So, you must tailor my advice to your particular organization.

E.4 Future considerations

Clearly, the system as I've described it would not meet the complete needs of most users, who would certainly require some enhancements. For example, there are very few facilities for updating files. At present, the user is unable to add a new customer, delete a customer, change or correct an existing customer's record, or generate reports about customers. Similar difficulties also occur with the other files, of course. However, I think it should be clear by now that such features and any necessary audit and order-tracing capabilities could be quite easily added to the system with minimum disturbance to the parts already in place. If I may indulge in an immortal cliché, "I leave such enhancements as an exercise for the reader."

E.5 Summary

In this case study of the Eric J. Lurch Wheeling and Dealing order-entry system, we've traced the development of a system from its original manual implementation to the point at which the programming of an automated replacement for the system is about to begin. In Section E.1, I rapidly covered the analysis of the project in order to provide some background to the system and to show briefly what a structured analyst does and what he provides to you, the designer.

The first three phases of Structured Analysis belong to the analyst and to the user: They are the old physical phase, in which the current system is studied; the old logical phase, an important phase of analysis, but one that this case study glossed over, in which the fundamental functions of the current system are elicited; and the new logical phase, in which the current functions are augmented with new requirements. The final phase of Structured Analysis is the new physical phase, in which the new implementation of the system is determined. It is at the new physical phase that the designer first becomes heavily involved in the project. Technically, the new physical phase can be considered to be the first phase of design.

In the new physical phase of the case study, we partitioned the DFD into a manual part and an automated part. Once we had added the physical devices for capturing and displaying data to the automated sections of the DFD, we had begun Structured Design proper. We cleft the DFD by job — we needed no job steps in this system — and then by transaction using the transaction analysis technique of route-mapping. Next, we added the configuration-dependent processes necessary for editing and formatting data and we were ready for transform analysis.

The outputs from transform analysis were structure charts for each type of transaction that we had identified during transaction analysis. The structure charts, as usual, needed factoring. Most of the factoring on the afferent and efferent sides of the structure charts was accomplished by inspecting the data structures being processed and by making the module structures match the data structures wherever possible. Very little further modification of the structure charts was necessary to make them conform to the design guidelines of Chapters 6, 7, and 8. That again is usual after transform analysis. However, as an optimization to reduce physical data-base accesses, we introduced one informational cluster.

Next, we completed transaction analysis by combining all the structure charts for individual transactions into a single transaction-centered structure chart, and made notes of any modules that could be shared among different transactions.

The final stages of the Structured Design of the order-entry system were packaging it into programs, updating the data dictionary with design information, specifying modules, formulating an implementation plan, and assigning the programmers to specific parts of the structure chart.

E.6 Postscript to Appendix E

My journey through this case study was not a smooth one. For every diagram or data dictionary entry shown, I threw away at least two others. That's the way it should be when you develop your systems: If you don't throw away at least one rough attempt, you are probably not being critical enough of your products.

Even now, I have failed to achieve perfection. If you find any bugs in this case study, then the tools of Structured Design are doing their principal job — to communicate a model of a system to another human being.

Glossary

abstraction
: the consideration or representation of a general quality or characteristic above and apart from any actual instance or specific object that possesses that quality or characteristic

afferent module
: a module that obtains its input from its subordinate(s) and delivers it upward to its superordinate(s)

afferent stream
: a hierarchy of afferent modules on a structure chart; or on a data flow diagram, a string of processes whose chief function is to collect or transport data from its physical source, or to refine input data from the form provided by its source to a form suitable for the major functions of the system

algorithm
: a deterministic procedure that, when followed, yields a solution to a problem

anticipatory retrieval
: (alias input buffering) a technique for optimizing the reading of data from a slow storage device by fetching more data than is immediately required and by retaining it in a faster medium until it is actually needed

balanced system
: a system that is neither physically input- nor physically output-driven (q.v.); a system in which the top modules deal with logical rather than physical data

balancing
: the correct correspondence in leveled data flow diagrams between a process and its decomposition in a lower-level diagram, particularly with regard to its input and output data flows

Baskin-Robbins effect

the effect of "31 flavors of code," occurring when a system has been subjected to the stylistic idiosyncrasies of many generations of maintenance programmers

Beneficial Wishful Thinking

an informal problem-solving strategy by which one identifies the particular details of a problem that hamper its solution and then, by imagining a more perfect world, one ignores as many details or constraints as necessary in order to arrive at a broad first-cut solution

benützefreundlichkeit

(literally "user-friendliness") the philosophy that a system should be constructed with the interests of the user as the chief concern

black box

a process with known inputs, known outputs, and a known function but with an unknown (or irrelevant) internal mechanism

bottom up

proceeding from the particular to the general or from the detailed to the broad

bottom-up implementation

(equivalent to bottom-up testing) a special case of incremental implementation (q.v.), in which modules at a lower level on the structure chart are implemented and tested before those at a higher level

bug

a euphemism for a defect (q.v.)

bundling

the collection of unrelated items of data to form an artificial and meaningless composite data structure

cache

a method for reducing the access time to data that is stored in a large, slow medium by retaining the most often accessed data in a smaller, faster medium

central transform

the portion(s) of a data flow diagram or structure chart that remains when the afferent and efferent streams have been removed; the major data-transforming functions of a system

cohesion

(alias strength) a measure of the strength of functional association of processing activities (normally within a single module)

coincidental cohesion	a random grouping of activities
commitment time	(alias binding time) the time during the life cycle of a system at which a value is assigned to an item of data
common coupling	a type of coupling characterized by two modules referring to the same global data (area)
communicational cohesion	a grouping of activities such that each activity uses the same input data and/or contributes to producing the same output data (without regard to order of execution)
composite data	(alias data structure) data that can be decomposed into other meaningful items of data
computer system	part of a system (q.v.) that is implemented on an electronic automaton
computer systems design	the activity of transforming a statement of what is required to be accomplished into a plan for implementing that requirement on an electronic automaton
constraints estimating	the determination of resources available to carry out a project
content coupling	(alias pathological coupling) a type of coupling in which one module affects or depends upon the internal implementation of another
context diagram	the top-level diagram of a leveled set of data flow diagrams
control coupling	a type of coupling in which one module communicates information to another module for the explicit purpose of influencing the execution of the latter
Conway's Law	an observation by Mel Conway that the structure of a system reflects the structure of the organization that built it
coordinate module	a module concerned with coordinating the activities and information of subordinates
coupling	the degree of dependence of one module upon another; specifically, a measure of the chance that a defect in one module will appear as a defect in the other, or the chance that a change to one module will necessitate a change to the other

data access diagram	(alias data structure diagram) a graphic tool for depicting the ways by which a data store can be referred to by means of the information contained in another data store
data base	a collection of interrelated data stored together with controlled redundancy to serve one or more applications, so that the data stored are independent of the programs that use them and so that a common, controlled approach can be used for adding, modifying, and retrieving data
data coupling	a form of coupling in which one module communicates information to another in the form of parameters, each parameter being either a single field, or a table, each of whose entries holds the same type of information
data dictionary	a repository of definitions of all data flows and data stores in a data flow diagram, in a process specification, or in the data dictionary itself; defines composite data (q.v.) in terms of its components, and elementary data (q.v.) in terms of the meaning of each value that it can assume
data flow	a pipeline along which information of known composition is passed
data flow diagram	(alias bubble chart) a graphic tool for depicting the partitioning of a system into a network of activities and their interfaces, together with the origins, destinations, and stores of data
data store	a reservoir in which data can be held for an indefinite period
data structure	synonym for composite data
debugging	the process of removing defects from a computer system
decision-split	the existence of the data for a decision's recognition part and that for its execution part in different modules
decision table	a normalized (i.e., non-hierarchical) tabular form of a decision tree (q.v.)

decision tree	a graphic tool for portraying a hierarchy of independent conditions and the activities resulting from each valid combination of conditions
defect	(euphemistically, bug) a discrepancy between an actual system and its specification
deferred storage	(alias output buffering) a technique for optimizing the writing of data to a slow storage device by retaining the data in a faster medium until enough has been collected to be written out in a large group
device cluster	a set of modules that have exclusive right of access to a particular device (normally used to localize the physical characteristics of the device to a small part of the system)
driver	(alias test harness, test monitor) a primitive implementation of a superordinate module, which is normally used in the bottom-up testing of subordinate modules
dynamic call	an invocation of one module by another, each being in a different load unit (q.v.) (see also static call)
effective system	a system that demonstrably works according to its specification
efferent module	a module that obtains its input from its superordinate(s) and delivers it downward to its subordinate(s)
efferent stream	a hierarchy of efferent modules on a structure chart; or on a data flow diagram, a string of processes whose chief function is to transport or dispatch data to its physical sink, or to format output data from the form produced by the major functions of the system to a form suitable for its sink
efficient system	a system that uses few resources
elementary data	data that is not decomposed into other items of data
factoring	the separation of a function contained as code in one module into a new module of its own

fan-in	the number of immediate superordinates of a module
fan-out	(alias span of control) the number of immediate subordinates of a module
Fisher's Fundamental Theorem	the law first stated by the biologist Ronald A. Fisher that the better adapted a system is to a particular environment, the less adaptable it is to a new environment
flag	a piece of information that either describes other data (a descriptive flag), or is used to explicitly influence the future execution of the system (a control flag)
flowchart	a graphic tool for depicting the sequence of activities in a system
functional cohesion	a grouping of activities such that each and every activity contributes to the execution of the same single problem-related function
functional primitive	a process on a data flow diagram that is not further decomposed on a lower level; a bottom-level bubble
graphic data dictionary	a depiction of a data dictionary (q.v.) as a diagram in a form first proposed by Jackson
gray box	a process whose function cannot be fully determined without studying the mechanism that accomplishes that function
hat	a symbol on a module signifying its compression into the module's superordinate; the unfactoring symbol
heuristic	a partly deterministic procedure that, when followed, is likely to yield a result that is close to a desirable solution to a problem
hrair limit	(alias conceptual counting limit) an informal term for the limit to the number of problems, activities, or items of information that can easily, correctly, and simultaneously be dealt with by the brain
hybrid coupling	the use of different parts of a range of values that a data item can assume for different and unrelated purposes
implementation	the activity of a project during which the design of a system is tested, debugged, and made operational

incremental implementation	(equivalent to incremental testing) an implementation/testing strategy whereby one part of a system is implemented and tested, and then other implemented and tested parts are added, one by one, until the system is complete
informational cluster	a set of modules that have exclusive right of access to a particular item or items of data (normally used when the data has a complex structure or has sensitive security)
intermediate file	a temporary file used to communicate data between job steps or, sometimes, jobs
inversion of authority	a special case of control coupling (q.v.) in which a subordinate module communicates information to a superordinate module for the explicit purpose of influencing the execution of that superordinate
job	a sequence of one or more job steps that is activated by a human operator (or another agent outside of the executing computer); the smallest unit that can be activated in this way (see also job step)
job step	one main program that has (optionally) a hierarchy of one or more subprograms and that is activated by an operating system; the smallest unit that can be activated in this way (see also program)
literal	a raw constant that does not have a name
load unit	a hierarchy of one or more programs whose calls are linked before execution time (see also program)
logical	free of the characteristics or constraints of any particular implementation; opposite of physical (q.v.)
logical cohesion	a grouping of activities based on a real or imagined similarity of implementation (without regard to data flow, order, or time of execution)
main program	a program that is called by the operating system

maintainable system — a system whose defects are easy to remove; a system that can be easily adapted to meet the changing requirements of its users or the changing environment in which it operates

Mealy's Law — an observation by George Mealy that there is an incremental person, who, when added to a project, consumes more resources than he adds

mini-specification — (alias process specification) a statement of the policy that governs the transformation of input data flow(s) into output data flow(s) for a given functional primitive (q.v.)

model — an intentional arrangement of a portion of reality (the medium) to represent another portion of reality (the subject) such that in certain ways the model behaves like the subject; the part(s), the set(s) of details, and the abstraction(s) of the subject that the model represents are called the *viewpoint* of the model; the set of ways in which the model is intended to behave like the subject is called the *purpose* of the model

module — a collection of program statements with four basic attributes: input and output, function, mechanics, and internal data

nag flag — a colloquial term for a control flag (see flag)

new logical data flow diagram — an old logical data flow diagram (q.v.) modified by the addition of any new, required functions and by the deletion of any old, unrequired functions

new physical data flow diagram — a data flow diagram that portrays the projected future (often, largely automated) implementation of a system

old logical data flow diagram — a data flow diagram that portrays the essential functions underlying a policy without committing to any particular means of implementing that policy

old physical data flow diagram — a data flow diagram that portrays the current (often, largely manual) implementation of a system

optimization	the modification of a system with respect to a criterion to approach the stated criterion as closely as possible, while changing other qualities of the system as little as possible; often used with respect to system run time
orthogonal set	(in the context of system development) a set of tools or programming constructs that do not overlap in function or purpose and, hence, can be used independently
over-general module	a module that has an unnecessarily broad function or that can handle data of a greater range of values, types, or structures than is ever likely to be needed
packaging	the set of decisions and activities that subdivide a system into implementation units; or the result of those activities
physical	having some characteristics of a particular implementation, by (a) being dependent on a particular medium for bearing information; (b) being dependent on a particular agent for executing an activity; (c) being partitioned or organized in a way that has been constrained by (a) or (b) or by the requirements of time, space, cost, or politics; or (d) containing activities or data only necessary to satisfy the constraints of (a), (b), or (c); opposite of logical (q.v.)
physically input-driven system	a system that does too little processing on its afferent side, so that the top modules have to deal with raw, physical, unedited input data
physically output-driven system	a system that does too little processing on its efferent side so that the top modules have to deal with the particular physical formats of the output data
playthrough	(alias dynamic design review, runthrough) the mental execution of a product by a small group of people using a set of test cases to discover defects in the product
procedural cohesion	a grouping of activities based on order of execution in a particular implementation (without regard to data flow)

process
an activity on a data flow diagram that transforms input data flow(s) into output data flow(s)

program
the smallest set of computer instructions that can be executed as a stand-alone unit; in COBOL, the set of computer intructions that comprises four divisions (IDENTIFICATION, ENVIRONMENT, DATA, and PROCEDURE) and that can be either a main program (q.v.) or a subprogram (q.v.)

program inversion
an arrangement of the procedural components (e.g., modules) of a system that is inverted with respect to the structure of the data being processed

pseudocode
a language tool used chiefly for module programming, but also for module specification and for module maintenance; normally, pseudocode is at a higher level than any existing compilable language

recursion
the act of invoking (or the ability to invoke) a module as a subordinate of itself

reliable system
a system that is consistently available and consistent in its results

requirements estimating
the determination of the resources needed to carry out a project

restrictive module
a module whose function is needlessly specific or is confined to handling data of a smaller range of values, types, or structures than is likely to be needed

ripple effect
the manifestation of a defect in one part of a system as a defect in other parts of the system; the effect of a change in one part of a system causing defects in other parts of the system and/or necessitating further changes to other parts of the system

route-mapping
an informal term for the decomposition of a data flow diagram into simpler diagrams, each of which depicts the flow of a single transaction

sandwich implementation	(equivalent to sandwich testing) a special case of incremental implementation whereby selected modules at the bottom levels of the structure chart are implemented and tested bottom-up, whereas modules at higher levels of the structure chart are implemented and tested top-down (or by the umbrella method, q.v.)
schema	a chart of the overall logical structure of a data base
sequential cohesion	a grouping of activities such that output data produced by one activity serves as input data to another activity
sink	a receiver of data flows from a system
skeleton system version	a partially implemented system that performs a small but useful subset of the functions of the complete system
source	a provider of data flows for a system
stamp coupling	a type of coupling characterized by two modules referring to the same composite data structure
state memory	data internal to a module that survives unchanged from invocation to invocation of that module
static call	an invocation by one module of another module such that both modules are in the same load unit (see also dynamic call)
stepwise refinement	an alias for top-down design (q.v.) that is used in Structured Programming
structure chart	a graphic tool for depicting the partitioning of a system into modules, the hierarchy and organization of those modules, and the communication interfaces between the modules
structure clash	a term coined by Jackson to describe the situation in which N items of data A are required to produce M items of data B (N and M being relatively prime)

structured	bounded in content; limited for the sake of orthogonality; arranged in a top-down way in both level of detail and degree of abstraction; partitioned to achieve minimal interfaces between parts; concerned with both data and activities; as simple as possible
Structured Analysis	the activity of deriving a structured model of the requirements for a system; specifically, the activity of deriving a structured specification (q.v.)
Structured Design	the development of a blueprint of a computer system solution to a problem, having the same components and interrelationships among the components as the original problem has
Structured Design specification	(alias Structured Design blueprint) a structured plan of the parts of a system that are to be implemented on a computer; specifically the target document of Structured Design comprising structure charts, a data dictionary, module specifications, systems flowcharts, and a minimal amount of additional information
structured English	a tool that is used for describing policy, and that is a subset of the English language (with a restricted syntax and vocabulary), imbedded in the procedural constructs of Structured Programming
structured information modeling	the activity of identifying and representing informational objects, references, properties, relations, and time dependencies in a way that is independent of any particular computer implementation
Structured Programming	a programming technique for developing source code logic that is understandably and verifiably correct; specifically, a technique that employs a top-down refinement strategy to produce code built from a small set of logical constructs (chiefly, the sequence construct, the decision construct, and the loop construct)
structured specification	a structured model of the manual and automated procedures of a system; specifically, the target document of Structured Analysis (q.v.) comprising data flow diagrams, a data dictionary, mini-specifications, data access diagrams, and a minimal amount of additional information

stub	(alias dummy module) a primitive implementation of a subordinate module, which is normally used in the top-down testing of superordinate modules
subprogram	a program that is called by another program
subschema	a chart of one user's or one application's view of the data stored in a data base
system	a set of manual and automated activities that is organized in such a way to reproducibly accomplish a set of stated purposes; (on a computer) a set of application-related jobs (q.v.)
system integration	an implementation/testing strategy in which all the subsystems of a system are brought together at once to be tested and debugged
systems flowchart	a graphic tool for depicting a computer system in terms of its inputs, outputs, jobs, job steps, intermediate files, and physical devices
tag	(alias transaction code) an item of information associated with a transaction (q.v.) for the purpose of identifying the type of that transaction
temporal cohesion	a grouping of activities based on time of execution in a particular implementation (without regard to data flow or to order of execution)
testing	the fiendish and relentless process of executing all or part of a system with the intent of causing it to exhibit a defect
top down	proceeding from the general to the particular or from the broad to the detailed
top-down design	an informal design strategy in which a problem is arbitrarily decomposed into yet simpler problems; each simpler problem then is successively decomposed into yet simpler problems until the problems are simple enough to be solved by means of available program statements; top-down design is a subset of structured design
top-down implementation	(equivalent to top-down testing) a special case of incremental implementation (q.v.) in which modules at a higher level on the structure chart are implemented and tested before those at a lower level

tramp data   an item of data that, although irrelevant to the function of a given module, has to pass through that module in order to reach another module

transaction   any element of data, control, signal, event, or change of state that causes, triggers, or initiates some action or sequence of actions; a (usually composite) item of data that can be any one of a number of types, each type having a specific set of processing that must be performed on it

transaction analysis   (alias transaction-centered design) a design strategy by which the structure of a system is derived from a study of the transactions that the system must process

transaction center   a portion of a system that can obtain a transaction, analyze it to determine its type, dispatch it in the way appropriate to its type, and complete the processing of the transaction

transform analysis   (alias transform-centered design) a design strategy in which the structure of a system is derived from a study of the flow of data through a system and of the transformations to that data

transform module   a module that obtains its input from its superordinate and returns its output to the same superordinate

umbrella implementation   (equivalent to umbrella testing) a special case of incremental implementation (q.v.) in which modules on the afferent and efferent branches of the structure chart are implemented and tested (usually in a top-down manner) before those in the central transform of the structure chart

walkthrough   (alias static review, peer-group review) the review of a product by a group of people to discover the flaws in the product

white box   a process whose function can be determined only by studying the mechanism that accomplishes that function

Index